T3-BUL-879

U.S. Government Leaders

MAGILL'S CHOICE

U.S. Government Leaders

Volume 3

Richard M. Nixon–John Winthrop

623–934

edited by

Frank N. Magill

consulting editor

John Powell

SALEM PRESS, INC.
Pasadena, California Englewood Cliffs, New Jersey

Original essays which appeared in *Great Lives from History: American Series*, 1987, and *Great Lives from History: American Women Series*, 1995, have been updated and reformatted; new material has been added.

∞ The paper used in these volumes conforms to the American National Standard for Permanence of Paper for Printed Library Materials, Z39.48-1984.

Library of Congress Cataloging-in-Publication Data

U.S. government leaders / edited by Frank N. Magill; consulting editor, John Powell.
p. cm. — (Magill's choice)
Includes bibliographical references and index
ISBN 0-89356-954-2 (set : alk. paper). — ISBN 0-89356-955-0 (v. 1 : alk. paper). — ISBN 0-89356-956-9 (v. 2 : alk. paper). — ISBN 0-89356-957-7 (v. 3 : alk. paper)
1. Statesmen—United States—Biography—Dictionaries. 2. Politicians—United States—Biography—Dictionaries. 3. United States—Biography—Dictionaries. I. Magill, Frank Northen, 1907-1997. II. Powell, John (John Douglas). III. Series.
E176.U23 1997
920.073—dc21 97-22519
CIP

First Printing

PRINTED IN THE UNITED STATES OF AMERICA

Table of Contents

Volume 3

U.S. GOVERNMENT LEADERS

Richard M. Nixon

Born: January 9, 1913; Yorba Linda, California
Died: April 22, 1994; New York, New York

A realist in foreign policy, Nixon renewed American relations with the People's Republic of China, achieved détente with the Soviet Union, and ended the United States' involvement in Vietnam. Ironically, because of his "Watergate coverup," he aroused public and congressional opposition to the "imperial presidency."

Early Life

Richard Milhous Nixon was born in Yorba Linda, in Southern California, on January 9, 1913, the son of Francis A. Nixon and Hannah Milhous Nixon. "Frank" Nixon was a small businessman, and Richard as a boy worked in the family store, driving into Los Angeles early each morning to buy fruits and vegetables and then going on to school. He attended public schools, was graduated from Whittier College in 1934, and from Duke University's law school in 1937. As a young man Nixon was above average in height, strong, but slender, weighing a little more than 150 pounds. His most prominent physical characteristics were a "ski-slide" nose, a dark beard despite frequent shaving, and a rather stiff manner. Despite a good record in law school, he found no job in New York City or even with the Federal Bureau of Investigation, which may have made him wary of the "Eastern Establishment." He practiced law in California from 1937 to 1942, in 1940 marrying Thelma Catherine "Pat" Ryan. They had two daughters, Patricia and Julie. Soon after the United States entered World War II, Nixon, a Quaker, became a lawyer with the Office of Price Administration but in the summer of 1942 joined the United States Navy and served as a transportation officer in the South Pacific. He was released from active duty as a lieutenant commander.

Life's Work

In 1946 Nixon ran as a Republican for United States representative from the Twelfth District of California, winning after a harsh campaign. Reelected in 1948, in 1950 he sought a senate seat from California, defeating the popular Helen Gahagan Douglas after another controversial campaign. In both house and senate, Nixon's record was one of moderate conservatism but also one of strident anticommunism, which fitted America's mood in the early Cold War. He helped secure the conviction of Alger Hiss for perjury in a case which made Nixon famous. He won the Republican nomination for vice president in 1952 largely because his youth, his "hard line" position, and his being from the West balanced the presidential candidate, General Dwight D. Eis-

Richard M. Nixon *(Library of Congress)*

enhower. Nixon found himself to be vice president in charge of the Republican Party because of Eisenhower's wish to remain above partisan politics. He relished his trips abroad for Eisenhower, to Asia, Latin America, and the Soviet Union. He was again a controversial campaigner in 1956 because of his harsh attacks on opponents. Admired by party regulars because of his faithful partisan services, Nixon easily secured the Republican nomination for president in 1960. Nixon lost to Senator John F. Kennedy, probably because of televised debates in which Nixon showed his exhaustion from campaigning while Kennedy gained an image of vigor and competence. The margin of defeat was extremely narrow in the popular vote—119,000 out of 68,838,000 cast—but 303 to 219 electoral votes.

Nixon then practiced law in California, seeking the governorship in 1962 but losing to Edmund G. Brown. He again became controversial by bitterly attacking the press after the election, in effect accusing its people of deliberately defeating him. Moving to New York, he joined a Wall Street law firm, becoming a partner in 1964. With the overwhelming defeat that year of Senator Barry Goldwater, Nixon again became a major contender for the presidential nomination. He continued to travel widely abroad, meeting important leaders, and maintained his political contacts, campaigning for many Republican candidates in 1966. In 1968 he again won the presidential nomination and defeated Vice President Hubert Humphrey by 510,000 popular votes out of 63,160,000 cast for the two men, and by 301 to 191 electoral votes, probably because of public disillusionment with the Democrats' handling of the Vietnam War and their catastrophically divided presidential convention.

As president, Nixon was most interested in foreign policy, commenting that a competent cabinet could look after the country. Reflecting his moderate conservatism, his administration did nothing about civil rights except to oppose some laws already enacted, sought to win Southern segregationists into the Republican Party, stressed "law and order" issues, tried to shift some emphasis to state and local government through revenue sharing, sought reform of the welfare system, and took some steps toward environmental protection. Strangely, it did not cut down "big government" much or reduce tax burdens. Vice President Spiro T. Agnew and Attorney General John Mitchell became especially controversial because of Agnew's attacks on the "media" and Mitchell's recommending one questionable nominee for the Supreme Court and then one unsuitable one. The Senate rejected both. The administration was also hurt by its changing responses to "stagflation," a new term for a slowing economy with continued inflation, a situation created by the Vietnam War and then by a sudden oil price rise because Arab states were angry at the American-aided Israeli victory in the Yom Kippur War of 1973. Nixon's task was made no easier by his facing a Congress controlled by Democrats.

Nixon revealed his foreign policy position by appointing as his chief adviser Dr. Henry A. Kissinger of Harvard University. Kissinger, a student of *Realpolitik*, fitted Nixon's own wish for realism. Nixon had shed his earlier bitter anticommunism and also recognized the fact that because of the Vietnam War Americans would no longer support endless intervention abroad. Seeking to end United States involvement in Vietnam without South Vietnam's collapsing, he bombed and invaded Cambodia, helped a South Vietnamese invasion of Laos, and tried "Vietnamization," a massive buildup of South Vietnam's armed forces accompanied by the withdrawal of many thousands of United States troops. He later intensified United States bombing of North Vietnam and ordered the mining of its major harbors, all this to apply sufficient pressure for a peace settlement. His reelection in 1972 left North Vietnam only Nixon to deal with, and in January, 1973, the United States and North Vietnam signed an agreement which ended the United States' involvement in Vietnam but which was so loosely worded that the war never really ended and South Vietnam fell in 1975.

With the Soviet Union Nixon concluded agreements for grain sales and, most important, arms limitation. A 1972 agreement, called the "strategic arms limitation treaty" (SALT I), limited antiballistic missiles and, in effect, granted to two superpowers equality in nuclear weapons. By warning the Soviet government and ordering a middle-level alert of United States armed forces, Nixon may also have kept the Soviet Union from intervening in the Middle East during the Yom Kippur War. Nixon's major foreign policy triumph was his 1972 trip to Beijing, China, and meetings with Mao Tse-tung and Chou En-lai. While Nixon and Kissinger could not solve all the problems between the two countries, the renewal of contact led ultimately to the renewal of Chinese-American diplomatic relations, which had ended in 1949. Nixon also paved the way for a renewal of American trade with China, which aided China in its modernization. Chinese-American relations may also have restrained some Soviet actions. The only exceptions to a record of sound diplomacy were Nixon's aiding the overthrow and murder of Chilean President Salvador Allende in 1973 and his support for Pakistan despite its murderous behavior toward its own people in East Pakistan as the latter broke away to become Bangladesh.

Nixon was overwhelmingly reelected in 1972, defeating Senator George McGovern by 520 to 17 electoral votes and by 47,170,000 to 29,170,000 popular votes. Public opinion polls revealed massive approval of Nixon's foreign policy, especially detente and relations with China, but fairly strong disapproval of his handling of domestic matters. Unfortunately, high officials in the Nixon campaign sponsored or allowed a burglary of the national Democratic headquarters in the Watergate building. This was probably a symptom of the Administration's atmosphere, one of near siege, of feeling surrounded by enemies and of sharing Nixon's demand for overwhelming reelection as a vindication of himself. There was also a rejection by "Middle America" of everything that McGovern allegedly stood for: left-wing liberalism and the "counterculture" of the 1960's. When others tried to cover up their roles in "Watergate," Nixon himself became involved in the "cover-up." Tape recordings made of conversations in the president's office, intended to be the basis of a historical record, proved Nixon's role in attempted deception. About to be impeached by the House of Representatives, Nixon resigned the presidency on August 9, 1974; he was the first president in the United States' history to do so. Earlier, Vice President Agnew, himself under indictment, had resigned, and under the new Twenty-fifth Amendment, Nixon had appointed Representative Gerald R. Ford, who thus became president after Nixon.

In retirement, first at San Clemente, California, and later at Saddle River, New Jersey, Nixon was quiet for a time and then began to travel again, to Europe and twice to China. With the help of able assistants, he produced four books in addition to his memoirs: *The Real War* (1980), *Leaders* (1982), *Real Peace* (1984), and *No More Vietnams* (1985). He also took part in a number of televised interviews, entertained members of the press, and with other former presidents represented the United States at the funeral of assassinated Egyptian President Anwar el-Sadat in 1981. He was in general silent on President Gerald Ford, critical of President Jimmy Carter, and supportive of President

Ronald Reagan. His books reveal a mixture of a wish for lasting world peace and a hard-line approach toward the Soviet Union.

Summary

In some ways, Nixon represented millions of post-World War II Americans: Well educated, he was a professional man and also a veteran who wanted to succeed in life and also build a better world for his family. He was highly ambitious, driven by the example of his father, who never really succeeded, but also controlled by his mother's example of piety and manipulativeness. He thus created the public image of a patriotic young man of ambition but decency. As such, he was repeatedly elected to public office but was sometimes defeated and was always suspect to millions of voters. Behind the public image remained the real man who revealed himself occasionally: remote, lonely, under tremendous stress in his drive to succeed, and angry at those who opposed him. When, during the Watergate crisis, this inner person was revealed, there was public shock and his defenders melted away. He had built up presidential power and prestige, and there arose opposition to what was named the "imperial presidency." His legacy, aside from foreign policy successes, was one of increased public distrust of government.

Bibliography

Aitken, Jonathan. *Nixon, A Life*. Washington, D.C.: Regnery Publications, 1993.

Brodie, Fawn M. *Richard Nixon: The Shaping of His Character*. New York: W. W. Norton and Co., 1981. The best attempt at a "psychobiography," based on exhaustive interviews with relatives, classmates, and others; connects Nixon's character with his behavior in office.

Evans, Rowland, Jr., and Robert D. Novak. *Nixon in the White House: The Frustration of Power*. New York: Random House, 1971. A critical but penetrating analysis of the Nixon Administration's early successes and errors, on a case-by-case basis, ranging from appointments to legislative strategy.

Hoff, Joan. *Nixon Reconsidered*. New York: Basic Books, 1994.

Kissinger, Henry A. *White House Years*. Boston: Little, Brown and Co., 1979.

__________. *Years of Upheaval*. Boston: Little, Brown and Co., 1982.

These two volumes form a highly personal account of Nixon's foreign policy by his chief adviser and secretary of state. Egocentric, reluctant to admit errors or even his ignorance of parts of the globe, Kissinger subtly places himself ahead of the president.

Morris, Roger. *Richard Milhous Nixon: The Rise of an American Politician*. New York: Holt, 1990.

Nixon, Richard M. *Leaders*. New York: Warner Books, 1982. A superb example of Nixon's later writings, highly egocentric and revealing Nixon's wish to be seen as a pragmatist with ideals, who knew and dealt with so many great men. Especially revealing is Nixon's treatment of Winston Churchill and Charles de Gaulle.

__________. *RN: The Memoirs of Richard Nixon*. New York: Grosset and Dunlap, 1978. Revealing even when they try to conceal, as in refusing to admit guilt for Watergate or the cover-up, these offer Nixon's version of what he wants as his public image. Emphasizes his parents' positive qualities, his own struggles, but above all the presidency, Nixon overstating his administration's achievements.

__________. *Six Crises*. Garden City, N.Y.: Doubleday and Co., 1962. Memoirs of Nixon in the Congress and the vice presidency, including the Checkers speech, trips abroad, and defeat for the governorship of California.

Safire, William. *Before the Fall*. Garden City, N.Y.: Doubleday and Co., 1975. An "insider's account" which covers such conversations as Nixon's comments on trips to China and Russia, and internal struggles within the Administration.

White, Theodore H. *Breach of Faith: The Fall of Richard Nixon*. New York: Atheneum Publishers, 1975. The best account of Watergate, the cover-up, and Nixon's resignation, based on interviews as well as the presidential tape recordings, and revealing of who in the Administration was how deeply involved.

Wicker, Tom. *One of Us: Richard Nixon and the American Dream*. New York: Random House, 1991.

Wills, Garry. *Nixon Agonistes: The Crisis of the Self-Made Man*. Boston: Houghton Mifflin Co., 1970. Nixon as the self-made man who built flaws in himself, the classical liberal believing in competition, a representative of America itself, placed in the setting of the disorderly decades of the 1950's and 1960's.

Robert W. Sellen

THOMAS PHILIP O'NEILL, JR.

Born: December 9, 1912; Cambridge, Massachusetts
Died: January 5, 1994; Boston, Massachusetts

Tip O'Neill was a lifelong defender of social legislation and an energetic leader of the House of Representatives whose ten years as Speaker saw a resurgence of congressional authority.

Early Life

Thomas Philip (Tip) O'Neill, Jr., was born on December 9, 1912, in Cambridge, Massachusetts, the son of Thomas Philip and Rose Ann (Tolan) O'Neill. O'Neill was nicknamed "Tip" after baseball player James Edward O'Neill of the St. Louis Browns, who was famous for hitting foul tip after foul tip until he was finally walked to first base. His father, Thomas, Sr., was the son of an immigrant bricklayer from County Cork, Ireland, and a dedicated member of the Democratic Party. Beginning in 1900, Thomas, Sr., served six years as an elected member of the Cambridge City Council. As a result of his upbringing, Thomas, Jr., remained close to his Irish-immigrant, working-class, and Democratic roots throughout his public career.

Educated exclusively in Catholic schools, O'Neill began his education at St. John's Grammar School and continued at St. John's Parochial School, where he was considered an average student at best. Equally unimpressive in athletics, he nevertheless was elected captain of both the football and basketball teams. At the age of fifteen, O'Neill experienced his first taste of politics when he campaigned for the Catholic Democratic candidate Al Smith in his unsuccessful bid for the presidency in 1928.

After his graduation from secondary school in 1931, O'Neill enrolled at Boston College. During his senior year, he ran for city council and lost; this would prove to be the only electoral defeat of his entire career. He lost by only 160 votes, largely because he had taken his own neighborhood for granted and had failed to solicit votes there. This loss, accompanied by his father's advice that "all politics is local," formed a lesson O'Neill would never forget.

After graduating from Boston College in 1936, O'Neill was elected

Thomas P. "Tip" O'Neill *(Ricardo Watson/Pictorial Parade/Archive Photos)*

to the Massachusetts state legislature. While serving there, he married his sweetheart of many years, Mildred Miller, in June, 1941. As a legislator during President Franklin D. Roosevelt's New Deal, O'Neill formed his liberal democratic principles. By such acts as arranging jobs for out-of-work constituents and advocating quality education for the working class, O'Neill earned a reputation as a friend of the people. As a result, in 1948 he was made the youngest majority leader in Massachusetts history. As leader, he pushed through a broad program of social legislation popularly known as the "Little New Deal."

When then Congressman John Fitzgerald Kennedy launched his senatorial campaign in 1952, O'Neill decided to run for the vacant position. Enjoying strong support from the heavily Democratic Irish and Italian working-class wards of the Eleventh Congressional District, O'Neill was easily elected to the U.S. Congress.

Life's Work

O'Neill's ascension to the U.S. House of Representatives marked the start of over three decades of service in Washington. As the protégé of House Democratic Whip John W. McCormick, a fellow Bostonian, O'Neill was quickly introduced to the House power structure. Soon, O'Neill was invited to Speaker of the House Sam Rayburn's informal "board of education" meetings, held after-hours for congressional leaders and friends. At these meetings, congressional business was discussed in casual detail, allowing O'Neill an inside track in the rough-and-tumble world of Washington politics.

These contacts would gain him a coveted position on the House Rules Committee in only his second term, a rare appointment for a freshman congressman. The committee regulated the flow of legislation to the House floor, exposing O'Neill to all facets of the legislative process and helping to make him a more well-rounded, less parochial congressman. Following Sam Rayburn's advice—"If you want to get along, go along"—O'Neill proved himself an adept compromiser, able to steer his bills around the deadlocks resulting from the 1950's split between liberals and conservatives.

In keeping with his roots, Congressman O'Neill routinely voted along liberal Democratic lines, casting votes in favor of housing redevelopment, expansion and improvement of mass-transit facilities, the Economic Opportunity Act, and the Civil Rights Acts of 1956, 1957, and 1964. His advocacy of adequate health care, education, and increased worker opportunities all reflected his New Deal roots. Later, O'Neill supported strict gun-control laws, busing to achieve racial equality in schools, and strong environmental legislation.

By the mid-1960's, the Vietnam War had come to dominate the national consciousness. Initially, O'Neill backed President Lyndon B. Johnson's Southeast Asia policies, as did most of O'Neill's blue-collar constituents. Eventually, however, O'Neill reconsidered his position at the urging of both his own children (Thomas III, Christopher, Michael, Susan, and Rosemary) and the intellectual communities of Harvard University and the Massachusetts Institute of Technology, both of which were in his district. After much soul-searching, O'Neill concluded that Vietnam was a civil conflict from which the United States needed to withdraw. He made his opinion known to President Johnson in 1967, long before "dovish" (antiwar) positions were popular, and he backed the Democratic peace candidate Eugene McCarthy in the 1968 presidential primaries.

Thereafter, O'Neill worked to withdraw American troops from Southeast Asia. In March, 1971, he cosponsored a bill setting a date for U.S. withdrawal contingent upon the release of American prisoners of war. He also supported legislation in August, 1973, that would have cut off funds for the continuation of air raids against North Vietnam. In November, O'Neill voted to override President Richard Nixon's veto of the War Powers Bill, which effectively limited the executive's war-making powers.

O'Neill's opposition to the Vietnam War eventually gained him the respect and support of many younger members of Congress, who would be largely responsible for his rise to the Speakership. O'Neill's rise began in 1971, when he was appointed majority whip. When majority leader Hale Boggs died in a plane crash the following year, O'Neill assumed his position.

O'Neill was pivotal in leading the charge for House reform. He lessened the autocratic power of committee chairpersons, pushed for the publication of committee votes, and advocated limiting the number of chairs a representative could hold. O'Neill also urged Congress to embrace its responsibility to oversee the actions of the other branches of the federal government, a desire reflected in his calls for the investigation and impeachment of President Nixon when the Watergate scandal broke in 1973.

O'Neill's ability to compromise, along with his affability and overwhelming popularity, led in December, 1976, to his election by acclamation as Speaker of the House. In 1977, in the shadow of Watergate,

O'Neill helped to pass a far-reaching government ethics bill as his first official act as Speaker.

Jimmy Carter entered the White House at about the same time that O'Neill became Speaker. During Carter's four years as president, it seemed that the two men shared only their party affiliation. As politicians, they were direct opposites: Carter a Washington outsider elected to office on his anti-politician credentials, O'Neill a politician who had raised himself through the party ranks. Yet despite their differing views, O'Neill as a loyal Democrat felt bound to support Carter. This he did by backing the president's foreign-policy initiatives (such as the Camp David Peace Accords between Israel and Egypt) and by pushing for passage of Carter's energy legislation.

Carter's defeat in the 1980 presidential election brought to Washington the former governor of California, Ronald Reagan. On the surface, O'Neill and Reagan had many similarities. Both were from blue-collar, Irish backgrounds and had outgoing personalities; they also shared an interest in sports and were the same age. The similarities ended there, however; according to O'Neill, Reagan had forgotten his roots. From 1981 to 1987, O'Neill led congressional opposition to the Republican president.

The remainder of O'Neill's career as Speaker was largely spent performing damage control, as the Reagan Administration worked to slash spending on government social programs—including Social Security, Medicare, employment-training programs, and college-aid programs—and increase defense spending. O'Neill constantly reminded members of Congress and the public that it was these programs that had enabled many people to rise to their current status, and he implored them not to deny these same benefits to others. By stressing the theme of fairness, he resisted Reagan's efforts to slash social programs and helped to preserve New Deal legislation, much of which O'Neill himself had originally helped to implement.

On October 18, 1986, O'Neill retired from the House of Representatives, bringing his fifty-year career in politics to a close. Thirty-four of those years were served as a member of Congress, and ten as Speaker of the House of Representatives—the longest continuous term of any Speaker in history. Throughout, O'Neill made certain he never lost touch with his roots. On January 5, 1994, he died in his hometown of Boston at the age of eighty-one.

Impact

A liberal New Deal reformer in the Roosevelt mold, O'Neill never forgot his origins. Having grown up in a working-class community, he worked tirelessly to raise men and women out of poverty by way of social legislation. Believing the federal government to be the only body capable of creating a solid middle class, O'Neill stuck by these principles even when they were unpopular. Above all, O'Neill stressed fairness. His generation had been saved from the depths of the Depression by government intervention, and a solid middle class had been created. To O'Neill, it was unfair for these very people to kick out from behind them the ladder that had allowed their ascent, denying others the same opportunity for upward mobility. As Speaker, he headed a resurgent Congress no longer willing to concede all initiative and authority to the president. Tip O'Neill fought his entire life to assure people their government's help in achieving the American Dream.

Bibliography

Clancy, Paul R., and Shirley Elder. *Tip: A Biography of Thomas P. O'Neill, Speaker of the House*. New York: Macmillan, 1980. A comprehensive and readable biography that follows O'Neill's development as a politician from childhood to the Speakership. Provides a solid bibliography to aid further research on O'Neill's life, career, and influence on American politics.

Kennon, Donald R., ed. *The Speakers of the U.S. House of Representatives: A Bibliography*. Baltimore: The John Hopkins University Press, 1986. Provides a brief synopsis of O'Neill's career up until 1984, followed by a comprehensive bibliography. Organized by topic; easy to follow.

O'Neill, Tip, with Gary Hymel. *All Politics Is Local: And Other Rules of the Game*. New York: Random House, 1994. A guide to politics as envisioned by O'Neill. Provides insight into his life, political tactics, and relationships; also useful as a guide to modern U.S. politics.

O'Neill, Tip, with William Novak. *Man of the House: The Life and Political Memoirs of Speaker O'Neill*. New York: Random House, 1987. A valuable primary source that provides a careful and detailed personal recollection of O'Neill's life from his boyhood to his retirement.

Peters, Ronald M., ed. *The Speaker: Leadership in the United States House of Representatives*. Washington D.C.: Congressional Quarterly, 1994.

Describes and reviews the Speaker's role in the House. Specific contributions are also made by former Speakers such as O'Neill, his predecessor Carl Albert, and his successor Jim Wright. Delineates these men's various views on politics and on how power should be used in the House.

Vogler, David J. *The Politics of Congress*. 5th ed. Newton, Mass.: Allyn and Bacon, 1988. Provides a good overview of the workings of Congress. More specifically, however, it shows the tremendous influence O'Neill had on Congress, especially during his years as Speaker.

James Edward Zacchini

William Penn

Born: October 14, 1644; London, England
Died: July 30, 1718; Ruscombe, England

A leading Quaker, Penn contributed to the early development of the sect through his traveling ministry, his numerous religious tracts, intervention with English authorities for toleration, and establishment of Pennsylvania as a refuge for dissenters.

Early Life

William Penn was born October 14, 1644, on Tower Hill in London, England. His mother was the widow Margaret Vanderschuren, the daughter of John Jasper, a Rotterdam merchant. His father, Sir William Penn, was an admiral in the British navy who first achieved prominence under Oliver Cromwell and, after the Restoration of the monarchy in 1660, went on to further success under the Stuarts. Despite some ups and downs in his career, the elder Penn accumulated estates in Ireland, rewards for his services, providing sufficient income so that the younger Penn was reared as a gentleman and exposed to the upper echelons of English society.

Penn received his early education at the Chigwell School, followed by a stint at home with a tutor who prepared him for entrance into college. In 1660, he was enrolled at Christ Church, Oxford University, where he remained until March, 1662, when he was expelled for infraction of the rules enforcing religious conformity. He then went on a grand tour of the Continent and spent a year or two at Saumur, France, studying languages and theology at a Huguenot school. After returning to England, he spent a year as a law student at Lincoln's Inn. His legal studies were somewhat sporadic and were never completed, a pattern that was typical for gentlemen of the day. They did, however, influence his subsequent writings and his ability to argue his own cause as well as those of others.

In Ireland, first as a child and later while acting as an agent for his father, Penn was exposed to Quakerism. It was in 1666, while managing the family estates, that he was converted by Thomas Loe, a Quaker preacher. Much to the horror of his father, young Penn took to preaching at Quaker meetings, quickly achieving prominence among the members of the still relatively new nonconforming sect. Parental disapproval continued until a reputedly dramatic reconciliation at the admiral's deathbed.

Life's Work

It was as a Quaker that Penn found his true calling. In 1668, he was in London preaching at meetings, and he produced his first religious tract, *Truth Exalted*. From that time onward, he spent a good portion of his life traveling, preaching, and writing religious tracts. He made several extended trips to the Continent, speaking at Quaker meetings as well as trying to convert others to the faith. By the end of his life, he had written some 150 works, most of them on religion. Some were descriptions of Quaker doctrines, such as *No Cross, No Crown* (1669); others were defenses of Quaker principles and actions—for example, *Quakerism: A New Nick-Name for Old Christianity* (1672).

There was no toleration in England in the 1660's for those who dissented from the Anglican Church. As a result, Penn, like numerous other Quakers, was arrested for attending Quaker meetings, for preaching, and for publishing a religious tract without a license. Indeed, several of his works were written while he was in prison. As a result of his experiences, as well as of observation of his coreligionists and friends, Penn became an advocate of religious toleration. He wrote several tracts, including *England's Present Interest Discovered* (1675), which pleaded with the government to recognize liberty of conscience for all, not only for Quakers. Penn used his position and friendship with the Stuart kings, Charles II and James II, to aid others.

Support for civil rights also came out of Penn's advocacy of religious toleration. His arrest for preaching at a Friends' meeting in 1670, a violation of England's stringent religious laws, led to two trials that ultimately contributed to the independence of juries. In the first case, Penn and his fellow Quaker William Mead were found not guilty of unlawful assembly by a jury which refused to alter its verdict after being ordered to do so or else "go without food or drink." Members of the jury were then fined; they appealed their case and ultimately were vindicated in their right to establish a verdict free from coercion.

Politically, Penn was caught, both in his beliefs and friendships, between the liberal dissenting Whig politicians and the conservative followers of the Stuart court. In 1678, he gave his support to Algernon Sidney's bid for a seat in Parliament, while maintaining his friendship with the Duke of York. Penn's attempt to keep his balance in the volatile English political scene of that period failed with the Glorious Revolution, when England exchanged the Catholic Duke of York, James II, for Mary, his Protestant daughter, and her husband, William of Orange. Accused of treason and at one point placed under arrest, Penn fled and for several years after 1691 went into hiding. It was not until after the turn of the century, under the rule of Queen Anne, that he again safely participated in the English political scene. Penn's position between the two major camps of the period is also evident in his writings and in the constitutional provisions he made for his colony, Pennsylvania, since they exhibit both liberal and conservative features.

For Americans, Penn is best known for his colonization efforts. His interest in the New World stemmed from his association with the great Quaker leader and preacher George Fox, who traveled through the Colonies. Penn's first involvement was in West Jersey, where he acted as an arbitrator in a complex dispute between two Quakers with claims to that colony. He ultimately became one of the proprietors of West Jersey, as well as, after 1682, of East Jersey. Yet because Quaker claims to the government of the Jerseys were under question, he sought a colony of his own, and it was on Pennsylvania that he expended most of his efforts. In 1681, he obtained a charter from Charles II for extensive territories in America, ostensibly as payment owed to his father; the grant gave him rights to the government as well as the land of the colony.

In establishing Pennsylvania, Penn wanted both to create a refuge for Quakers where they would be free to worship without fear of imprisonment and a government with laws based upon their principles. At the same time, as proprietor of the colony, he hoped that the venture would be profitable. He started by preparing a constitution and laws for the colony, consulting numerous friends for their suggestions and comments. The resulting first Frame of Government proved too complex for the colony and was followed by other modified versions. Penn also worked to obtain both settlers and investors for his project and advertised it in pamphlets such as *A Brief Account of the Province of Pennsylvania* (1681) and *A Further Account of the Province of Pennsylvania and Its Improvements* (1685), which were published in several languages and distributed in both England and on the Continent. Expecting to be the resident proprietor and governor of the new colony, Penn made plans to move there. He journeyed to America twice, first in 1682 and again fifteen years later, in 1699, each time remaining for about two years. Both times he scurried back to England to protect his proprietorship, the first time from a controversy with Lord Baltimore, the proprietor of neighboring Maryland, over boundaries, and the second, to respond to a challenge from English authorities to all proprietary governments.

In the long run, Penn's colony was a success for everyone but him. His anticipated profits never materialized—a serious disappointment because, with advancing age, he was increasingly in financial difficulty. The Quaker settlers also proved to be a disappointment in their failure to get along with one another as well as with Penn. Indeed, they proved to be an exceedingly contentious lot, and the boundary controversy with Maryland was not solved in Penn's lifetime. After 1703, Penn negotiated with English authorities to sell his province back to the Crown, a deal which fell through because he suffered an incapacitating stroke in 1712. Pennsylvania, however, grew rapidly, and Philadelphia, the capital city that he had carefully planned, was an impressive success.

Penn is remembered for more than simply his religious writings and the establishment of Pennsylvania. In 1693, he wrote *An Essay Towards the Present and Future Peace of Europe*, which offered proposals for the establishment of peace between nations. In 1697, he proposed a plan of union for the Colonies, suggesting the creation of a congress of representatives from each colony which would meet once a year.

Penn was also a warm, affectionate, and concerned family man. In 1668, he married Gulielma Maria Springett; they had eight children, only three of whom survived childhood. In 1696, two years after his first wife's death, he married Hannah Callowhill, fathering another five children. Unfortunately, his children, like his colony, were a source of disappointment. His oldest son, and favorite, Springett, died at the age of twenty-one. His second son, William Penn, Jr., renounced Quakerism and was something of a rake. The surviving children of his second marriage were, at the time of his death, still young; it was to them that he left his colony of Pennsylvania.

Also contributing to Penn's woes in his later years was a festering problem with his financial agent, Philip Ford. Both were at fault, Ford for making inappropriate charges and Penn for a laxity in supervising his personal affairs. The result was that Ford's wife and children (after his death) pushed for payment—including Pennsylvania—for what they claimed were debts; they had Penn arrested and put in prison. When the dust settled, the Ford claims were taken care of and Pennsylvania had been mortgaged to a group of Penn's Quaker friends.

Summary

Although Penn was never more than a brief resident in the Colonies, his contributions to American history were substantial. He played a prominent role in the proprietorships of both East and West Jersey and was the founder of Pennsylvania. Penn was one of a handful of influential Quaker preachers and authors, and although his ideas were not original, he powerfully expressed and defended the sect's beliefs in numerous pamphlets, as well as in the laws and Frames of Government of Pennsylvania. As a colonizer, his efforts ensured a Quaker presence in America and the sect's role in the political and religious life of the middle colonies.

Penn's advocacy of religious toleration, of protection of the right to trial by jury, and of constitutional government carried across the Atlantic; as a result, provisions for all three were made in the colonies with which his name was associated. Penn thought that settlers would be attracted to America not only for its land but also for the freedoms it could offer, maintaining that Englishmen would only leave home if they could get more, rather than less, of both. He worked to make this happen. Thus, Penn used his connections among Whig and court groups on the English political scene to protect his fellow Quakers, his colony, and his proprietorship.

As the founder of Pennsylvania, he was the most successful of English proprietors and yet personally was a financial failure. He was a gentleman and a Quaker who could be contentious, particularly in religious debates, stubborn in maintaining his position against all opposition, and anything but humble in his life-style. In many ways, he was an uncommon and contradictory individual.

Penn's place in American history rests on his success in helping establish one colony and in founding another. The name Pennsylvania, standing for "Penn's woods," continues as a reminder of his significance. Sometimes overlooked, but also important, are his contributions to the fundamental political traditions which Americans have come to take for granted.

Bibliography

Beatty, Edward C. O. *William Penn as Social Philosopher*. New York: Columbia University Press, 1939. Reprint. New York: Octagon Books, 1975. Beatty examines Penn's philosophical and social ideas, viewing him as a political theorist, statesman, pacifist, humanitarian, and family man.

Bronner, Edwin B. *William Penn's Holy Experiment: The Founding of Pennsylvania, 1681-1701*. New York: Columbia University Press, 1962. Concerned with Penn's vision in establishing Pennsylvania and how it worked out. Contrasts plans and reality.

Dunn, Mary Maples. "The Personality of William Penn." *American Philosophical Society Proceedings* 127 (October, 1983): 316-321. Dunn portrays Penn as a restless rebel, a poor judge of people, and always the aristocrat.

__________. *William Penn: Politics and Conscience*. Princeton, N.J.: Princeton University Press, 1967. Argues that Penn was a creative thinker who, along with others of his age, wrestled with the question of what was constitutional government. The key to Penn's political ideas was liberty of conscience; a key to his behavior was the desire to protect his title to Pennsylvania.

Dunn, Richard S. "William Penn and the Selling of Pennsylvania, 1681-1685." *American Philosophical Society Proceedings* 127 (October, 1983): 322-329. Discusses Penn as a salesman and businessman.

Endy, Melvin B., Jr. *William Penn and Early Quakerism*. Princeton, N.J.: Princeton University Press, 1973. Concentrates on Penn's religious thought and its relationship to his political and social life. Also evaluates his significance for early Quakerism.

Illick, Joseph E. *William Penn the Politician: His Relations with the English Government*. Ithaca, N.Y.: Cornell University Press, 1965. Illick is primarily concerned with Penn as a practical politician who threaded his way through the perilous waters of English politics. Penn, as proprietor, is viewed as more successful, despite some ups and downs, in his dealings with the English government than with his own colonists.

Lurie, Maxine N. "William Penn: How Does He Rate as a Proprietor?" *Pennsylvania Magazine of History and Biography* (October, 1981): 393-417. Compares and contrasts Penn as proprietor with those who established other proprietary colonies.

Morgan, Edmund S. "The World and William Penn." *American Philosophical Society Proceedings* 127 (October, 1983): 291-315. A good, brief discussion of Penn's life which tries to put his experiences in the context of English society. Emphasis is on Penn as a Protestant, a gentleman, and an Englishman.

Morris, Kenneth R. "Theological Sources of William Penn's Concept of Religious Toleration." *Journal of Church and State* 35, no. 1 (Winter, 1993): 83-111.

Nash, Gary B. *Quakers and Politics: Pennsylvania, 1681-1726*. Princeton, N.J.: Princeton University Press, 1968. Concentrates on Penn's conflicts with the settlers in Pennsylvania, as well as their problems with one another. Nash emphasizes the religious and economic background of the disagreements. Good source for information on the dynamics of early Pennsylvania politics as well as on Penn.

Peare, Catherine Owens. *William Penn: A Biography*. Philadelphia: J. P. Lippincott Co., 1956. The standard modern work on Penn. A readable account with a sometimes excessively flowery style. There are numerous other, older, biographies, but this one is the best.

Penn, William. *The Papers of William Penn*. Edited by Mary Maples Dunn, Richard S. Dunn, et al. Philadelphia: University of Pennsylvania Press, 1981- . This is the result of a project to collect and make available the widely scattered papers of Penn. Volumes are well annotated and a pleasure to use. In addition to the printed volumes, there is also a more complete microfilm series.

Maxine N. Lurie

FRANCES PERKINS

Born: April 10, 1880; Boston, Massachusetts
Died: May 14, 1965; New York, New York

Perkins, as secretary of labor for twelve years under President Franklin Delano Roosevelt, was the first woman to serve in a president's cabinet. As secretary of labor, she was instrumental in developing legislation to improve labor conditions for workers. Her most notable achievement was to chair the committee responsible for developing the social security system.

Early Life

Frances Perkins was born on April 10, 1880, in Boston, Massachusetts. In 1882, her family moved to Worcester, Massachusetts, where her father prospered in the stationery business. Known as Fannie Coralie Perkins until her twenty-fifth year, she was raised in the fashion typical of middle-class girls of her generation. Her conservative, New England family upbringing influenced her early life. She was taught to behave like a lady, to be seen but not heard, and to accept her father's authority on all matters. Her childhood was comfortable and sheltered. She learned to read at a young age and was encouraged to do so by her father. Although she was extremely shy as a young girl, at school she discovered her ability to express herself through words.

School broadened her range of experiences, and she was very involved in a variety of activities. Her ability to debate enabled her to pass her courses with ease, and she was graduated from high school in 1898. Not sure what she wanted to do with her life, Perkins decided that she would pursue teaching because that was an acceptable occupation for a woman of her time. She convinced her father that attending college would help her find a good teaching position, so he agreed to let her attend Mount Holyoke College in western Massachusetts.

Perkins entered Mount Holyoke with no particular direction for her studies. After taking a required chemistry course, however, she discovered her skills and interest in the sciences. She pursued chemistry as her major, but in her last year at Mount Holyoke she took a course that changed her life. It was an economics course, but unlike other courses, it involved the direct observation of factories and industry. Perkins was deeply affected by the working conditions of women and children in the factories. This experience gave Perkins an awareness of social conditions that affected her the rest of her life.

After she was graduated in 1902, Perkins taught briefly at several girls' schools until finding a permanent job teaching chemistry at Ferry Hall School in Lake Forest, Illinois, outside of Chicago. Although it was far from her family, her father agreed to let her go, and in 1904 she left for Chicago.

Perkins taught for two years, spending her free time in Chicago working with many of the social reformers there. She was greatly inspired by the efforts of settlement workers, and in 1906 she left teaching to live at Hull House, the settlement house founded by Jane Addams. Although she was there for only six months, the experience greatly influenced her, and Perkins was convinced that her calling was to strive to change working conditions for laborers, particularly women and children.

Life's Work

Frances Perkins' first paid employment in reforming labor conditions came in 1907, when she left Chicago to become the secretary of the Philadelphia Research and Protection Association. The organization helped immigrant girls from Europe and African American girls from southern states who came to Philadelphia looking for work. The young girls were often preyed upon by unscrupulous employers or forced into prostitution. As secretary, Perkins was responsible for gathering facts and using them to pressure city officials to legislate changes in employment practices. In this first job, Perkins developed skills she used throughout her professional life. She learned to gather data on working conditions and use it to influence policymakers to develop laws to protect workers. Perkins felt that the best way to help workers and the poor was through government action.

Perkins left in 1909 and went to study at the New York School of Philanthropy. In 1910, she graduated with a master's degree in political science from Columbia University. With her social work and political science training, she was well prepared to follow her chosen path of working for labor reform and rights. Perkins became the executive secretary of the New York City Consumers' League in 1910. In this position, she was responsible for investigating the conditions that existed in industries employing primarily women workers. Living in Greenwich Village near many of the factories, Perkins witnessed the Triangle Shirtwaist Factory fire of 1911, the worst factory fire in New York history. The sight of young women jumping out of windows because there were no fire escapes reinforced Perkins' commitment to social and labor reform. After witnessing that event, she realized that organizing and union efforts, while important, were not enough. She became convinced that only through the power of legislation could there be real change.

The aftermath of the Triangle Shirtwaist Factory fire did bring legislative action. The New York State assembly founded the New York State Factory Commission in 1911. Perkins was director of investigation for the commission until 1913.

In 1912, while serving on the State Factory Commission, Perkins took the position of executive secretary of the New York Committee on Safety. Already experienced in lobbying, from her work with the Consumers' League, she was active in influencing the passage of numerous regulations protecting workers and improving labor conditions. Included in her legislative efforts were reorganizing the state labor department and limiting the workweek for women to fifty-four hours. These were the first legislative efforts at labor reform by any state.

In 1913, Perkins married Paul Wilson, an economist and budget expert with the Bureau of Municipal Research. As intensely private people who were committed to their work, they kept their personal lives separate from their public lives. Perkins chose to keep her birth name, for she felt she had made much progress and saw no reason to take her husband's name. Over the next few years, she maintained her work with the Committee on Safety. In 1916, after experiencing two unsuccessful pregnancies, she gave birth to a daughter Susanne, her only child. Perkins limited her travels and lobbying, but stayed with the Committee on Safety until 1917.

Perkins' years with the Consumers' League and work on state commissions brought her close to a number of New York politicians. In 1918, she campaigned for Al Smith, a legislator who had supported her early labor reform efforts. Smith was elected governor of New York, and after he took office in 1919, he appointed Perkins to her first public position, as a member of the New York State Industrial Commission. Perkins served in Smith's administrations until 1929. During those years, she mediated strikes between workers and management, improved factory inspections, regulated working conditions, and administered workers' compensation. When Smith, who ran unsuccessfully for president, was replaced as governor by Franklin D. Roosevelt, Perkins was appointed industrial commissioner of the State of New York. Perkins thus became the first woman to serve on a governor's cabinet.

With the full support of Roosevelt, Perkins was able to make significant reforms in working conditions in New York. She expanded employment services, increased factory investigations, and created data-gathering systems to provide information necessary to support legislative change. Among her legislative initiatives were reducing the work week for women to forty-eight hours, creating a minimum wage, and developing unemployment insurance. These efforts proved to be the blueprint for the work she did with Roosevelt years later in Washington, D.C.

Perkins served under Governor Roosevelt until his election as president of the United States. Without hesitation, President Roosevelt asked Perkins to serve as his secretary of labor. In 1933, Frances Perkins became the first woman ever to be appointed to a cabinet-level position. She accepted the position with the understanding that she was free to pursue the social reforms she had begun in New York and had advocated throughout her professional career.

Initially, labor and business leaders were critical of the idea of a female secretary of labor. Fully aware of that fact, Perkins developed a leadership style that brought together labor and management through cooperation and conciliation. As secretary of labor, Perkins also tried to bring together different factions of the labor movement. With the Great Depression looming, Perkins viewed reforming labor conditions as a way to improve economic conditions.

Over time, Perkins was successful in facilitating legislative reforms. Major relief legislation passed during Perkins' first years included the establishment of the Federal Emergency Relief Administration, the Civilian Conservation Corps, and the Public Works Administration. These programs represented the first major employment efforts by the federal government. Additional legislation was passed to regulate minimum wages, child labor, and work hours.

Perkins' major contributions as secretary of labor were the development of a data system to track statistics on employment and unemployment, standardization of state industrial legislation, and the development of the social security system. Perkins chaired the Committee on Economic Security, which crafted the Social Security Act of 1935. For both Perkins and Roosevelt, the Social Security Act represented a major accomplishment because it established minimum securities for workers through national insurance. In 1938, Perkins realized another major labor reform through the Fair Labor Standards Act, which set minimum wages, maximum work hours, and child labor prohibitions.

Perkins remained secretary of labor throughout Roosevelt's years as president. She resigned in 1945 and served on the U.S. Civil Service Commission until 1953. Her last years were spent writing and teaching at Cornell University. Frances Perkins died on May 14, 1965, in New York City.

Summary

Frances Perkins' work demonstrated a rare blend of social concern and political action. Her early years in settlement houses and investigating working conditions propelled her to work toward changing the American labor system and improving the lives of working women and men. Perkins was convinced that what the labor system needed was legislative reform, not a complete overhaul. She devoted her professional career to influencing legislation that supported the needs of workers, particularly women and their families.

Perkins' role as a member of the presidential cabinet paved the way for future women to be directly involved in government action. She held public office before women could even vote. As a lobbyist and public official, she was instrumental in establishing government as a developer and regulator of legislation to protect workers. Under her influence, programs such as workers' compensation, unemployment insurance, minimum wages, and social security were formed. Such social legislation changed the face of organized labor forever and formed the foundation of modern workers' rights.

Bibliography

Colman, Penny. *A Woman Unafraid: The Achievements of Frances Perkins.* New York: Maxwell Macmillan International, 1993.

Martin, George W. *Madam Secretary*. Boston: Houghton Mifflin, 1976. A comprehensive and extensive biography based on Perkins' oral history, this book provides a very personal view of Perkins' life.

Mohr, Lillian Holmen. *Frances Perkins: That Woman in FDR's Cabinet!* Croton-on-Hudson, N.Y.: North River Press, 1979. A biography of Perkins with some emphasis on the role of Perkins as a woman in government.

Severn, Bill. *Frances Perkins: A Member of the Cabinet*. New York: Hawthorn Books, 1976. Chronicles Perkins' life from her youth throughout her years in government.

Sternsher, Bernard, and Judith Sealander, eds. *Women of Valor: The Struggle Against the Great Depression as Told in Their Own Life Stories*. Chicago: Ivan R. Dee, 1990. This collection of essays by various women includes a piece by Perkins, excerpted from her book *The Roosevelt I Knew*. It gives insight into the kind of government official she was.

Wandersee, Winifred D. "I'd Rather Pass a Law than Organize a Union: Frances Perkins and the Reformist Approach to Organized Labor." *Labor History* 34, no. 1 (Winter, 1993): 5-32. Describes Perkins' approach to working with organized labor during her cabinet years.

Elizabeth A. Segal

H. Ross Perot

Born: June 27, 1930; Texarkana, Texas

An immensely successful entrepreneur, Perot spent his first sixty years dedicated to improving American business. Thereafter he would devote his life to political reform and making government responsible to the people.

Early Life

Henry Ross Perot was born on June 27, 1930, in Texarkana, Texas, a quiet cotton-dependent town that lay on the state line between Texas and Arkansas. His father Gabriel earned his living as a cotton broker in Texarkana, where he met and married Lulu May Ray, a secretary for a local lumber company. Because of Gabriel's skills as a merchant, the Perot family lived comfortably despite the Great Depression. He and Lulu also provided hot meals to the poor from their back door.

Gabriel Perot taught his son the importance of relationships in business, stressing that a businessman's good word allowed him to continue to do business. From his father, Ross learned to love the art of buying and selling. An equal influence on Ross was his mother, Lulu May, a strong and spiritual woman who demanded honesty, uprightness, and perfect manners from her children. Instead of whipping her children when they misbehaved, she chose to lecture them for their punishment. She taught him the importance of setting high standards for himself and of judging himself rather than waiting for others to judge him.

When he turned eighteen, Perot began sending letters to congressmen, seeking an appointment to the U.S. Naval Academy. After several rejections, Perot received an appointment and was sworn in on June 27, 1949. He was graduated only 454th in a class of 925 graduates, but his leadership record was impeccable; he served as class president and as head of the school's honor committee. While at the academy, he met Margot Birmingham, a student at Goucher College, on a blind date, and they were married in 1956 in Greensburg, Pennsylvania.

Upon his graduation in June, 1953, Perot was assigned to the destroyer USS *Sigourney* as an assistant fire-control officer, and the ship headed across the Pacific to take part in the Korean War. On the way, however, a truce was signed between Allied and Communist forces, and the ship headed home by continuing west through the Suez Canal and into the Mediterranean Sea. For his second assignment, Perot served as assistant navigator aboard the aircraft carrier USS *Leyte*. While escorting visitors aboard ship, Perot met an International Business Machines (IBM) executive who suggested that Perot interview with the company. Following his discharge in 1957, Perot and Margot left for Dallas, Texas, where IBM accepted Perot as a trainee.

In November, 1995, Ross Perot (far right) visited high school newspaper editors in North Dakota as part of his bid for the presidency. *(AP/Wide World Photos)*

Life's Work

Perot proved extremely successful selling computer systems for IBM. He consistently achieved 100 percent of his yearly sales quota and persuaded difficult accounts to sign with IBM; however, he became irritated that his supervisors would not listen to his suggestions. In 1962, therefore, Perot formed Electronic Data Systems Corporation (EDS) with only $1,000 in initial capital. His sales pitch was simple but effective: Rather than selling customers computer systems that they would not know how to operate, he proposed to do the computing and data processing for them.

In February, 1963, Perot landed his first contract, with Frito-Lay; other contracts soon followed. EDS's profits remained modest until 1965, when the passage of Medicare legislation suddenly increased the demand for computers, programmers, and storage—all of which Perot and EDS provided. Demand for the company's services was extremely high, and there was little competition. Because of the tremendous growth, Perot began selling stock to the public in September, 1968. The shares sold quickly, giving EDS $5 million in capital and Perot $5 million in cash; he became a millionaire nearly overnight. Only two years later, Perot's portion of the stock had risen in value to $1.4 billion.

In 1969, Perot received a call from Secretary of State Henry Kissinger asking for his assistance in getting the North Vietnamese to improve the conditions for U.S. prisoners of war. In response, Perot formed the United We Stand committee to collect money and buy advertising to pressure North Vietnam into improving prison conditions. A week before Christmas in 1969, Perot announced that United We Stand would deliver Christmas dinners to the POWs. Suspicious, the North Vietnamese refused to admit the United We Stand representatives, however, and the mission failed. Perot, nevertheless, remained deeply committed to the effort to locate POWs.

EDS broke into the international market with a $41 million contract with the Iranian social security system in November, 1976. An exciting situation turned critical in December, 1978, when revolutionary officials began jailing many Iranian officials with whom EDS had dealt. Partly in reaction, EDS notified the government that it was suspending operations. Soon afterward, Perot ordered all EDS workers and dependents out of Iran, except for the company's top officials. Without warning, Iranian revolutionaries arrested the EDS manager in Iran, Paul Chiapparone, and his assistant Bill Gaylord on charges that EDS had diverted millions from the Iranian treasury, a claim that was never proven. When diplomacy failed to get the two released, Perot sent ex-Green Beret colonel Arthur D. Simons and a team of EDS executives to try to free them from an Iranian prison. The executives were released by mistake before the team could implement its plan, but Perot's agents did succeed in getting them safely out of the country. Novelist Ken Follett later chronicled the effort in his 1983 nonfiction account *On Wings of Eagles*.

In June, 1984, Perot agreed to a merger between EDS and General

Motors (GM). He was given a position on the GM board of directors and was allowed to run EDS as a separate organization within GM. Soon, however, differences emerged between Perot and Roger Smith, GM's chairman and chief executive. Perot disagreed with the way GM was being run, and Smith disliked the amount of independence Perot demanded. Finally, after Perot publicly criticized GM in November, 1986, the board of directors agreed to buy out Perot's interest for $742.8 million.

In the years following his ouster, Perot began to receive pressure from various sources to run for president. On February 20, 1992, he appeared on the *Larry King Live* television show on the Cable News Network (CNN) to state how he thought America could be "fixed." Throughout the interview, Perot claimed that the American people needed to take back control of their government, and he hinted that if the public gave him sufficient encouragement, he would run as an independent candidate. Although he never declared himself as an official candidate, Perot funded a campaign to get himself on the ballot in all fifty states. By late June, many polls showed that Perot would win a substantial number of votes. On July 17, however, he withdrew his name from candidacy, stating that the Democrats had begun to address his concerns. Following his withdrawal, his supporters formed an organization called United We Stand America, which continued to work to get Perot's name on the ballot in every state, and he continued to fund these efforts.

Stating that he wanted the campaign to focus on economic issues, Perot reentered the race on October 1. He appeared on television in paid commercial spots in which he presented his plan for saving the American economy and reforming the government.

Ultimately, though, Perot was unable to regain the political strength that he had shown in the summer. Nevertheless, he finished with 19 percent of the popular vote, the strongest showing by a third-party candidate since 1912, and many political analysts claimed that Perot's candidacy contributed to Bill Clinton's victory.

In January, 1993, Perot announced that United We Stand America would continue to receive new members and would become a non-profit citizens' action group. Perot planned for the organization to pressure lawmakers for political reform and debt reduction. The group, however, failed to work together as he had hoped. Members of

United We Stand America's volunteer staff complained that the Dallas headquarters acted in a dictatorial fashion, and the movement weakened.

Over the next three years, Perot continued his watchdog tactics. In June, 1995, he invited President Clinton and the principal contenders for the Republican nomination to a conference in Dallas. The convention met in August with political leaders such as Jesse Jackson, House Speaker Newt Gingrich, and Senator Bob Dole in attendance. The Republicans were particularly interested in pleasing Perot in order to keep him from running for president in 1996. Perot, however, claimed dissatisfaction with both the Democrats and the Republicans, and he announced in September that he would be forming a new, independent Reform Party for the 1996 election.

In the first months of 1996, Perot again hinted that he would run for president if his name could be listed on the ballots of all fifty states. On July 11, two days after former Colorado governor Richard Lamm announced that he would seek the Reform Party's presidential nomination, Perot declared his own intention to seek the party's nomination. After bitter arguments between Lamm and Perot in the months leading to the August convention, Perot handily won the nomination with 65.2 percent of the vote, and he soon launched another series of television spots. In September, however, his campaign was crippled when the Commission on Presidential Debates barred him from participating in the televised debates between Clinton and Republican nominee Bob Dole; Perot then lost a court appeal to allow him to engage in the debates. Ultimately, Perot's campaign never gained the momentum of his 1992 effort, and he finished a distant third, with only 8 percent of the popular vote. Following the elections, he stated that his party would continue to pressure the government, but renewed divisions within the party led to questions about its direction and leadership.

Summary

A controversial figure throughout his life, H. Ross Perot used his early business success to allow him to bring certain issues, such as the status of American prisoners in Vietnam, into the national spotlight. He used the publicity generated by the Iran rescue to foster a positive public image, appearing as a national hero and a father figure determined to take care of his employees. All these factors played an important role when he decided to become involved in presidential politics.

Regardless of his motives, Perot has undeniably contributed a new popular vitality to politics that had been lacking in previous presidential elections. In 1992, he helped to turn the focus of the campaign from character questions to the American economy. In 1996, he forced the candidates to talk about political reform. Although many Americans disagreed with Perot's views, he did succeed in getting many people to start talking about the issues. More important, he also helped to empower many people, giving them the feeling that they could reclaim their government from special interests and regular party politics. In addition, although the Reform Party did not rival the strength of the Democratic or Republican Parties, his grassroots campaigns helped to strengthen and legitimize third-party politics.

Bibliography

Barta, Carolyn. *Perot and His People: Disrupting the Balance of Political Power*. Fort Worth, Tex.: The Summit Group, 1993. A lengthy and detailed account of Perot's 1992 presidential campaign. Besides narrating the campaign, the book critically examines Perot's influence in the election's outcome and weighs the possible positive and negative effects of Perot's bid on future elections. Charts list state-by-state election statistics.

Follett, Ken. *On Wings of Eagles*. New York: William Morrow, 1983. Commissioned by Perot to detail his and EDS's role in the rescue of two EDS employee hostages in Iran in 1979, this entertaining and popular work is decidedly biased in Perot's favor.

Levin, Doron P. *Irreconcilable Differences: Ross Perot vs. General Motors*. Boston: Little, Brown, 1989. An account of Perot's dealings with General Motors, particularly useful for its discussion of the formation of EDS and the personal disagreements that led to Perot's buyout at GM. Includes photographs of Perot and the major figures involved in the GM crisis.

Mason, Todd. *Perot: An Unauthorized Biography*. Homewood, Ill.: Irwin, 1990. As suggested by the subtitle, this business biography does not use interviews with Perot but depends on interviews with his competitors at GM and EDS. Covers Perot from his earliest years to the EDS suit against him in 1989.

Posner, Gerald. *Citizen Perot: His Life and Times*. New York: Random House, 1996. A relatively objective biography, with particular emphasis on Perot's formation of EDS and his dealings with GM. Especially useful for its balanced and unbiased account of the 1992 election.

Michael R. Nichols

FRANKLIN PIERCE

Born: November 23, 1804; Hillsborough, New Hampshire
Died: October 8, 1869; Concord, New Hampshire

After service in his state's legislature and in both houses of Congress, Pierce became the nation's fourteenth president, serving during the turbulent years between 1853 and 1857.

Early Life

Franklin Pierce was born on November 23, 1804, in Hillsborough, New Hampshire. His father, Benjamin, was an American Revolutionary War veteran and two-term state governor (1827-1828, 1829-1830). His mother, Anna Kendrick, was Benjamin's second wife. Frank, as family and friends called him, was the sixth of their eight children.

Frank attended local schools before enrolling in Bowdoin College. Overcoming homesickness and early academic nonchalance, he was graduated fifth in the class of 1824. Classmates there included John P. Hale, the 1852 Free-Soil Party's presidential candidate; Calvin Stowe, the husband of Harriet Beecher Stowe; and writers Henry Wadsworth Longfellow and Nathaniel Hawthorne. Pierce became close friends with Hawthorne, and the novelist later penned his campaign biography. Pierce taught school during semester breaks, but his major interest during his college years seemed to be the college battalion, in which he served as an officer.

After graduation, Pierce studied in several law offices including that of later United States Senator and Supreme Court Justice Levi Woodbury of Portsmouth. He was admitted to the bar in 1827 and immediately assisted in his father's successful bid for the governorship. When his father was reelected in 1829, he simultaneously gained a seat in the state legislature.

Life's Work

His political rise was steady. When first elected to the legislature, Pierce was named chairman of the Committee on Education. Later he served as chairman of the Committee on Towns and Parishes. In 1831, Governor Samuel Dinsmoor named him his military aide with the rank of

Franklin Pierce *(Library of Congress)*

colonel, and that same year and the next he served as Speaker of the House. In March, 1833, though he was not yet thirty years old, he was elected to the United States House of Representatives. By this time, his political course was already set. He had enjoyed rapid success because of his support for his father and the Democratic Party. From then on, he gave total loyalty to the party and to its experienced politicians.

Pierce served in the House from 1833 to 1837 before advancing to the Senate for one term (1837-1842). His service was undistinguished. He deferred to his elders (when he entered the Senate, he was its youngest member). He made no memorable speech and sponsored no key legislation. He served on several committees, eventually gaining the chairmanship of the Senate Pension Committee. He consistently accepted the Southern view on slavery, and was strongly antiabolitionist, a staunch defender of the Democratic Party, and a strong opponent of the Whig program. For example, he supported the Southern position on the Gag Rule and defended Andrew Jackson's opposition to internal improvements.

It was during these years that Pierce made the political contacts and created the impression that would result in his later nomination and election to the presidency. He came to be known as an accommodating person, fun loving, and always anxious to please. He seemed perfectly content to follow party policy, and he gave proper respect to his elders. He was a New Englander whom Southerners trusted. He formed a close friendship with Jefferson Davis during these years.

In 1834, Pierce married Jane Means Appleton, the daughter of a former Bowdoin College president and Congregational minister. Throughout their married life, she suffered from a variety of physical illnesses, anxiety, and depression; in addition, she held strict Calvinistic views on life. In contrast to her sociable husband, she felt very uncomfortable in social settings and consequently stayed away from Washington, D.C., as much as she could. Like many congressmen of that age, Pierce lived in a boardinghouse with several colleagues, and he joined them in drinking to try to compensate for the boredom of his existence. Pierce was no alcoholic, but he was incapable of holding any liquor. The smallest amount inebriated him. This problem, combined with his wife's unhappiness, which was exacerbated by the death of a newborn child, convinced Pierce in 1842 that he should go back to New Hampshire. There he promised his wife that he would never drink again or return to Washington.

In New Hampshire, Pierce became a successful lawyer. He did not spend much time analyzing legal principles because he was easily able to ingratiate himself with juries and win his cases that way. He was of medium height and military bearing, dark, handsome, and an excellent dresser. People who met him at social and political gatherings liked him immediately.

During these years, Pierce also played an active role in New Hampshire's Democratic politics. He was a driving force in most of the party's campaigns, achieving good success, though he lost out to college classmate Hale in a party dispute over Texas annexation. President James K. Polk offered him the attorney generalship, and his party wanted to return him to the Senate. He declined both offers.

When the Mexican War broke out, Pierce's long-held interest in military matters and his desire for more excitement than his Concord law practice provided caused him to volunteer as a private. Before he donned his uniform, he had gained the rank of brigadier general. He made many friends among the enlisted men, and General Winfield Scott named him one of the three commissioners who attempted to negotiate an unsuccessful truce. His combat record was much less sparkling. During his first combat in the Mexico City campaign, his horse stumbled, banging Pierce against the saddle horn and then falling on his leg. He fainted. Though still in pain when he was revived, he continued, only to twist his knee and faint again when he encountered the enemy. Later, he became bedridden with a severe case of diarrhea. He was happy when the conclusion of the war enabled him to return home.

Pierce resumed his legal and political pursuits. He supported the Compromise of 1850 and became president of the state constitutional convention. He helped rid the state party of an antislavery gubernatorial candidate and thereby improved his reputation in the South. When his former law tutor, Levi Woodbury, the state's choice for the 1852 Democratic presidential nomination, died in September, 1851, Pierce became New Hampshire's new favorite son. Remembering his promise to his wife, however, he said he would consider the nomination only in case the convention deadlocked. That was precisely what happened. None of the Democratic front-runners, James Buchanan, Lewis Cass, Stephen A. Douglas, and William L. Marcy, was able to obtain the necessary two-thirds of the convention ballots. On the thirty-fifth stalemated ballot, Pierce's name was introduced. He was a Northerner with Southern principles and a person everyone seemed to like. These characteristics carried the day. On the forty-ninth ballot, he gained the nomination. When his wife learned the news, she fainted from shock.

The 1852 presidential campaign between Pierce, Whig candidate

Winfield Scott, and Free-Soiler Hale was issueless. Pierce made no formal speeches; according to the custom of the time, he allowed his supporters to campaign for him. Hawthorne quickly wrote a laudatory biography, and others worked to overcome the accusation that Pierce was a drunkard, a coward, and an anti-Catholic. (The latter accusation came from an anti-Catholic provision remaining in the revised New Hampshire constitution.) In a Boston speech the previous year, he had called for the enforcement of the Fugitive Slave Law yet voiced his belief that it was inhuman, so he had to work hard to repair damage in the South from that remark. He never denied the statement but insisted he had been misrepresented, and this seemed to satisfy his critics. He won the general election 254 to 42 in electoral votes, although he had a popular margin of only forty-four thousand.

At first, Pierce made good progress in organizing his administration. Then tragedy struck. He, his wife, and their eleven-year-old son, Benjamin, were riding the train from Boston to Concord when, without warning, their car toppled off the embankment. Benjamin was killed. Neither Pierce nor his wife was ever able to recover from the shock. They vainly sought to find meaning in the freak accident. Pierce wondered if his son's death was God's punishment for his sins. Jane Pierce concluded that God had taken the boy so her husband could give his undivided attention to the presidency.

Pierce thus entered office in a state of turmoil. The feeling of insecurity that caused him to want to please others and follow his party's line now received further reinforcement from the guilt and self-doubts resulting from his son's death.

His wife's reaction only added to his burdens. Quite by accident, she learned from a friend that her husband, far from not wanting to return to Washington as he had insisted, had actually worked hard to get the nomination. She had lost her son; now she learned that her husband had deceived her. She locked the bedroom door, seldom even appearing for public functions. Eventually she spent most of her time writing little notes to her dead son, apologizing for her lack of affection during his life.

Pierce became president determined to adhere to old-line Democratic policy, with a strong dose of expansionist ideas. Unfortunately, everything he tried seemed to fail. He attempted to broaden the base of support for his administration by giving patronage to all segments of the party, but loyal supporters, especially Southerners, became angry. He made decisions on what he considered to be principle but lost political support in the process. Most significantly, he did not seem to understand that slavery, especially its expansion into the territories, was a powder keg. He had always considered public opinion to be the stuff of demagogues, so he believed he could ignore the strong negative feelings about slavery which were gaining ground in the North.

Pierce seemed incapable of providing effective direction to his administration. His cabinet, the only one in history to remain intact for an entire term, was weak, but its members had to exert their authority since he did not. Jefferson Davis, the secretary of war, emerged as the most powerful of the group.

The tragedy of Franklin Pierce was that he was president during a time of major crisis and conflict. Pierce's presidency was dominated by controversy and even violence: the Kansas-Nebraska Act, Bleeding Kansas, Bloody Sumner, the Ostend Manifesto, the Gadsden Purchase, the destruction of the Whig Party and the birth of the Republican Party. The nation cried out for leadership, for some kind of direction, but Pierce was unable to provide it. Events seemed to provide their own impetus, and he seemed incapable of directing them. His pro-Southern and antiabolitionist attitudes, his desire to please, and his uncertainty about his own capabilities did not allow him to act effectively.

The Kansas-Nebraska Act demonstrated the problem quite clearly. Pierce believed that this law providing for popular sovereignty would effectively solve the controversy over slavery in the territories. He never understood why it resulted in violence instead. Increasingly, slavery was becoming a moral issue, but he continued to treat it as merely another solvable disagreement. He and the nation paid the price.

Despite the ever more obvious failure of his presidency, Pierce hoped for renomination, authoring his 1855 annual address as a campaign document. He excoriated the new Republican Party. He reminded Americans about the need for compromise and recognition of the concept of states' rights. He claimed that despite the South's longtime willingness to compromise, as, for example, in the Missouri Compromise, the North now refused to respond in kind. The Kansas-Nebraska Act was good legislation, Pierce argued, and it could solve the problem of slavery in the territories if it were allowed to; Republicans and other antislavery fanatics had to recognize that the South had rights, too. No one could arbitrarily limit slavery. Pierce believed that such fanaticism would result only in national disruption, and did anyone really want to destroy the interests of twenty-five million Americans for the benefit of a few Africans?

Pierce's battle cry brought down a torrent of criticism. When the Democratic National Convention met in 1856, it chose James Buchanan as its candidate, snubbing Pierce and making him the only sitting president who wanted to run for reelection not to receive his party's renomination for a second term. He was bitterly disappointed and went on a three-year tour of Europe. When the Civil War erupted, Pierce first supported the Union effort, but he quickly reverted to his pro-Southern position. In a July 4, 1863, Concord speech, he blasted Lincoln's policy on civil rights and emancipation and proclaimed the attempt to preserve the Union by force to be futile. While he spoke, word filtered through the crowd of the Union victory at Gettysburg. Once again events had passed Pierce by. He lived another six years, but he played no further public role. He died on October 8, 1869, in Concord, New Hampshire.

Summary

Franklin Pierce's life was filled with contradiction. He was an outgoing man who married a recluse. He was a Northerner, but he held Southern attitudes on the major issue of the day, slavery. He gained the presidency because he seemed to be what the nation wanted: an amiable man whom neither Northerners nor Southerners found offensive. Yet it was this appealing inoffensiveness, actually a lack of firm purposefulness, which doomed his presidency from the start. The nation's problems needed determination and skill of the highest order; in Franklin Pierce, the nation gained an irresolute man, overcome with personal problems, who did not understand the crisis swirling around him and was carried along by events instead of directing them.

Bibliography

Bisson, Wilfred J., comp., with assistance from Gerry Hayden. *Franklin Pierce: A Bibliography*. Westport, Conn.: Greenwood Press, 1993.

Freehling, William W. "Franklin Pierce." In *The Presidents: A Reference History*, edited by Henry F. Graff. New York: Charles Scribner's Sons,

1984. A highly critical evaluation of Pierce. The New Hampshire politician is portrayed as a weak, vacillating individual whose mediocrity was the major reason why he was electable in 1852 and why he failed during his term.

Gara, Larry. *The Presidency of Franklin Pierce*. Lawrence: University Press of Kansas, 1991.

Kane, Joseph N. *Facts About the Presidents: A Compilation of Biographical and Historical Data*. 3d ed. New York: H. W. Wilson Co., 1974. A compilation of basic factual information on all the American presidents. Unusual or unique aspects about each president's administration are included.

Nevins, Allen. *Ordeal of the Union: A House Dividing, 1852-1857*. Vol. 2. New York: Charles Scribner's Sons, 1947. An excellent discussion of the Pierce years with insightful commentary on how his personality affected his policy. Nevins believes that Pierce's basic weaknesses doomed his presidency because they prevented him from taking the strong positions on national issues that the times required.

Nichols, Roy F. "The Causes of the Civil War." In *Interpreting American History: Conversations with Historians*, vol. 1, edited by John A. Garraty, 286-287. New York: Macmillan Publishing Co., 1970. A brief discussion of the White House relationship of Mr. and Mrs. Pierce. Nichols points out that Jane Pierce never recovered from the death of her son and became a virtual recluse in the White House.

__________. *Franklin Pierce: Young Hickory of the Granite Hills*. Philadelphia: University of Pennsylvania Press, 1931. This is the standard biography of the fourteenth president, detailed yet appealingly written. It emphasizes that, rather than outstanding ability, Pierce's physical attractiveness, his Mexican War military reputation, his ability to convince people with his oratory, his party regularity, and his pro-South policy gained him the 1852 Democratic nomination and eventually the presidency.

Taylor, Lloyd C., Jr. "Jane Means Appleton Pierce." In *Notable American Women, 1607-1950*, vol. 3, edited by Edward T. James. Cambridge, Mass.: The Belknap Press of Harvard University Press, 1971. A brief sketch of Pierce's wife which discusses how religious rigidity fostered a repressed personality which gave way under the strain of public life and the death of a young child.

John F. Marszalek

James K. Polk

Born: November 2, 1795; Mecklenburg County, North Carolina
Died: June 15, 1849; Nashville, Tennessee

A staunch nationalist, Polk used the authority of the presidency to bring about the expansion of the nation nearly to its continental limits. He added power as well as stature to the office.

Early Life

James Knox Polk was born in Mecklenburg County, North Carolina, on November 2, 1795. His parents, Samuel and Jane Knox Polk, were members of large Scotch-Irish families whose forebears began migrating to America late in the previous century. When James was eleven, Samuel moved the family westward to the Duck River Valley in middle Tennessee, where he became both a prosperous farmer and a prominent resident. The family was staunchly Jeffersonian in its politics, while Jane Polk was a rigid Presbyterian.

Young James was small in stature—of average height or less according to various accounts—and was never robust. At seventeen, he had a gallstone removed (without anesthesia), and thereafter his health improved somewhat. It became obvious early, however, that he would never be strong enough to farm, and contrary to his father's wish that he become a merchant, Polk decided on a law career with politics as his goal. For this goal, some education was necessary. He had been a studious youth but until the age of eighteen had had little formal schooling. Thereafter, he applied himself totally and entered the sophomore class at the University of North Carolina at the age of twenty. Two and a half years later, he was graduated with honors. Characteristically, he had worked diligently, but the drain on his physical reserves was so great that he was too ill to travel home for several months.

Upon his return to Columbia, Tennessee, Polk read law in the offices of one of the state's most prominent public figures, Felix Grundy. Through Grundy's sponsorship, Polk began his political career as clerk of the state senate in 1819 and was admitted to the bar the following year. Prospering as a lawyer, he was elected to the Tennessee legislature in 1823 and aligned himself with the supporters of the state's most famous citizen, Andrew Jackson. Soon he became friendly with Jackson, a presidential candidate in 1824, aided Old Hickory's election to the United States Senate, and thereafter was always associated with his fellow Tennessean.

On New Year's Day, 1824, Polk married Sarah Childress, a member of a prominent middle Tennessee family. Described as not particularly pretty, she was vivacious, friendly, and devoted, and the marriage, although childless, was apparently happy. By this time Polk's health

James K. Polk *(Library of Congress)*

had improved, but he remained slender, with an upright posture and a grim face below a broad forehead. According to contemporaries, he was always impeccably dressed, as befitted a promising young lawyer and sometime militia colonel on the governor's staff. Now nearly thirty, he was considered one of the state's rising Jacksonians.

Life's Work

Impressed with his legislative record and legal as well as martial success, in 1825 the Jackson faction supported Polk's bid for a seat in the House of Representatives against four opponents. His victory by a decisive plurality after a spirited campaign solidified his position among the followers of General Jackson. For the next four years, during the administration of President John Quincy Adams, Polk was in the forefront of the Jacksonians, who were determined to overturn the alleged "corrupt bargain" that had denied Jackson the presidency in 1824 and elect their man in 1828.

During the debates on the Adams program, considered too nationalistic by most congressmen, Polk seized numerous opportunities to express his opposition and to stand with the embryonic Democratic Party. He aided in reviving the "corrupt bargain" charge and spoke for economy, majority rule, and limited government. He embraced the party position against the protective tariff, internal improvements, and banks. Only on the question of slavery did he equivocate, as he would always do. Slavery was an evil, he believed, yet doing away with it was fraught with peril. It was best that all concerned recognize its existence and live with it as peacefully as possible.

The issues before Congress during the Adams term commanded less attention than the Jacksonians' primary goal—the election of Jackson. In this effort, Polk played an increasingly important part as his abilities and devotion to the cause became more evident. In the bitter campaign of 1828, he constantly defended Jackson and carried on an extensive correspondence with him at his home in the Hermitage. Victory for Jackson followed and, despite interparty infighting for the position of successor to the new president, the future of the Jacksonian party looked promising.

In the next decade, Polk's rise in the party hierarchy was steady. He served as chairman of the House Ways and Means Committee in Jackson's first term and played a leading role in the president's victory in the Bank War. He enjoyed a growing reputation for speeches and reports showing much preparation, logic, and clarity. In 1835, he was elected Speaker of the House, and was reelected two years later. His four years in the chair, where he was the first to function as a party leader and to attempt to guide through a program, proved to be trying. The Whig Party was gaining strength while the slavery issue was intruding in the House, resulting in the passage of the infamous "gag rule." In the middle of his second term as Speaker, Polk decided to become a candidate for governor of Tennessee rather than risk probable defeat for reelection. By now the recognized leader of the party forces in his home state, he won by a narrow margin in 1839.

Once again, Polk was the first incumbent to use an office for political purposes as a party leader. Yet since the governor had little real power and Whig opposition continued strong, Governor Polk was able to accomplish little in his single two-year term. When the victorious Whig presidential candidate, William Henry Harrison, easily carried Tennessee in 1840, Polk's chances for another gubernatorial term appeared to be slim. He was defeated for reelection in 1841 and failed again two years later. For the only time in his career, he was out of office.

On the national level, Polk's position in the party remained secure. In 1840, he was a leading candidate for the vice presidential nomination on the ticket with President Martin Van Buren but withdrew when the convention decided against making a nomination. Polk then began to work toward the nomination four years later, when it was expected that the former president would again contend for the top place. In the meantime, he repaired political fences and kept in touch with Van Buren and other party leaders.

Polk's comeback, which led to his nomination as the Democratic standard-bearer in 1844, is one of the best-known episodes in American political history. Expansionism, justified as "Manifest Destiny," was in the air as Texas clamored for admission to the Union while American eyes were on California and Oregon. It was expected that the presidential race would be between former president Van Buren and Whig Henry Clay. When both announced their opposition to the annexation of Texas, however, Van Buren's chances for the nomination faded. In the party convention in May, he withdrew when his cause looked hopeless, and on the ninth ballot delegates turned to Polk, who had declared for annexation weeks earlier. Although his nomination, recalled as the first "dark horse" selection, was a surprise to most voters, it was the result of much hard work and a correct recognition of the mood of the electorate.

In the ensuing campaign, Whig candidate Clay and his supporters obscured the issues by asking, "Who is James K. Polk?" Democrats responded by linking "Young Hickory" to the aged former president, vacillating on controversial matters such as the tariff and stressing annexation as a national, not sectional, question. After an exciting campaign, Polk won a narrow victory brought about in part because a number of potential Clay voters cast ballots for an antislavery candidate. In his inaugural address, President Polk announced a brief but positive program. He called for settling the Oregon question (Congress had voted to annex Texas by joint resolution a few days earlier) by its "reoccupation" and for the acquisition of California. The tariff was to be reduced to a revenue level, and the Independent Treasury, killed by the Whigs, would be reestablished. Unique among American chief executives, Polk carried out his entire program.

The new president assumed his duties, determined to be in control. He appointed able cabinet members, many of whom were friends, and he consulted them and Congress frequently, although he made his own decisions. Seldom away from his desk, he was constantly besieged by office seekers who placed an added drain on his limited strength and energy. Not surprisingly, his appointments were largely "deserving" Democrats.

Foreign affairs immediately commanded Polk's attention. Oregon, occupied jointly with England since 1818, was rapidly filling up with Americans who anticipated eventual absorption by the United States. It was "clear and unquestionable," the president declared in his inaugural, that Oregon belonged to the United States. Yet he revealed to the British minister his willingness to compromise at the forty-ninth parallel. A negative response evoked from Polk a hint of war and a request in his first annual message for congressional sanction for termination of joint occupation. For the first time, there was a presidential reference to the Monroe Doctrine as justification for action, and war talk, including demands for "Fifty-four Forty or Fight," was heard. Neither nation wanted war, so the British countered with Polk's original suggestion, it was accepted, and a treaty was completed, setting the boundary at the forty-ninth parallel, where it has remained.

In the meantime, the Mexicans had not accepted the loss of Texas, and they now maintained that the southern boundary was the Nueces River, not the Rio Grande, as the Texans claimed. Polk agreed with the Texans and also feared that the British might interfere there, as well as in California and New Mexico. As tensions increased, he sent to Mexico City an offer of some thirty million dollars for the entire area. When the offer was refused, he ordered General Zachary Taylor to move his troops into the disputed section. A predictable clash took place, but before word reached Washington, Polk had decided to ask for war. Congress responded with a declaration on May 13, 1846. Although American forces were victorious from the beginning, the Mexican War, called "Mr. Polk's War," was among the most unpopular in the nation's history. Opposition to it was voiced in Congress, in the press, and among the people. Even though the two leading generals professed to be members of the party, Whigs led the protests, which tended to increase Polk's strongly partisan attitudes.

To a greater extent than any previous chief executive, Polk took his role as commander in chief seriously. His military experience was meager, yet he planned grand strategy, was personally involved in military appointments and promotions, and took the lead in peacemaking. His emissary (although technically recalled) completed with a defeated Mexico a satisfactory treaty which ceded California and New Mexico to the United States and recognized the annexation of Texas in return for some fifteen million dollars. Polk decided to accept the offer. The Senate narrowly approved the treaty on February 2, 1848, and the continental limits of the nation had almost been reached. Near the end of his term, Polk looked longingly at other areas, such as Cuba, but nothing further was done.

In Congress, the remainder of Polk's limited program was approved. The Independent Treasury was reestablished and remained in existence into the next century. In addition, the tariff was reduced considerably. Although these successes seemed to indicate party harmony, the Democrats actually were engaged in much interparty wrangling, adding to the president's many problems.

Of more lasting effect was the revival of antislavery agitation as a result of the possible addition of territory. In the midst of the war, as an appropriations measure was debated in Congress, Representative

David Wilmot of Pennsylvania proposed an amendment banning slavery in any territory acquired from Mexico. This so-called Wilmot Proviso was never approved, yet it rekindled sectional animosities which finally led to secession some fifteen years later. Polk, a slaveholder who seldom thought of slavery in moral terms—he believed that the solution was the extension of the Missouri Compromise Line to the Pacific—was not directly involved in the ensuing agitation during the remainder of his term, yet the legacy of sectional bitterness continued to be linked to his administration.

In his acceptance letter in 1844, Polk declared that he would not be a candidate for a second time, the first nominee ever to do so. As his term drew to a close, he refused to reconsider. His health remained poor, and the split within his party was unsettling. Nor did his outlook improve with the election of one of the Mexican War generals, Zachary Taylor, as his successor.

Following Taylor's inauguration, the Polks slowly made their way home, often delayed by the poor health of the former president and well-meaning attempts by supporters to entertain them. Polk never fully recovered (his main complaint was chronic diarrhea) and he died June 15, 1849, slightly more than fourteen weeks after leaving office. His considerable estate, including a Mississippi plantation, was left to his widow, who lived until 1891, witnessing the tragic sectional split and devastating war brought about in part by the events associated with her husband's presidency.

Summary

The youngest presidential candidate elected up to that time and often called the strongest chief executive between Andrew Jackson and Abraham Lincoln, James K. Polk raised the presidency in public esteem. Although humorless, partisan, and totally without charisma, he was devoted to the office and impressed all those around him with his dedication and diligence. Nothing was allowed to interfere with the carrying out of his duties (except that no business was conducted on Sundays unless in an emergency). Unlike most occupants of the office, he seldom was away from the Capitol, absent a total of only six weeks in four years.

Under his leadership, a relatively brief, successful war was fought with Mexico, the annexation of Texas was completed, the most troublesome dispute with England was resolved, and the nation expanded almost to its continental limits. These accomplishments came about despite Polk's frail constitution and sharp political differences with the Whig Party and among his fellow Democrats. Unfortunately, his successes only added to the increasing sectional tensions which would soon tear the nation apart and cause a long, costly conflict.

Bibliography

Bassett, John Spencer, ed. *The Southern Plantation Overseer as Revealed in His Letters*. Westport, Conn.: Negro Universities Press, 1925. Most of these letters, from the Polk papers, were written by overseers on Polk's plantations in Tennessee (sold in 1834) and Mississippi (sold by Mrs. Polk in 1860). The correspondence indicates that the Polks, who were apparently benevolent owners, derived much of their income from the labor of slaves.

Bergeron, Paul H. *The Presidency of James K. Polk*. Lawrence: University Press of Kansas, 1987.

Cutler, Wayne, et al., eds. *Correspondence of James K. Polk*. 6 vols. to date. Nashville, Tenn.: Vanderbilt University Press, 1969-1983. A well-edited, complete publication of all extant Polk papers. Also includes many letters to Polk. An indispensable source for the history of the period.

Haynes, Sam W. *James K. Polk and the Expansionist Impulse*. Edited by Oscar Handlin. New York: Longman, 1997.

Johannsen, Robert W. *To the Halls of the Montezumas: The Mexican War in the American Imagination*. New York: Oxford University Press, 1985. An interesting study of how the American people viewed the Mexican War and its effects on their lives. Reaches the usual conclusion that the war, although immediately successful, presaged great trouble.

McCormac, Eugene Irving. *James K. Polk: A Political Biography*. Berkeley: University of California Press, 1922. Reprint. New York: Russell and Russell, 1965. First published in 1922 and somewhat dated, it was for many years the standard political biography of Polk. Still useful for an account of the political maneuvering in the Jackson years.

Mahin, Dean B. *Olive Branch and Sword: The United States and Mexico, 1845-1848*. Jefferson, N.C.: McFarland, 1997.

Quaife, Milo Milton, ed. *The Diary of James K. Polk.* 4 vols. Chicago: A. C. McClurg and Co., 1910. Reprint. *Polk: The Diary of a President, 1845-1849.* Edited by Allan Nevins. New York: Longmans, Green and Co., 1929. Only five hundred copies of the original diary were printed. Written between August 26, 1845, and June 2, 1849, it is highly personal and apparently was not written with an eye on future historians. As a result of the 1929 publication, in which selections of the earlier publication appeared, Polk's presidency was reassessed and his reputation considerably enhanced.

Schroeder, John H. *Mr. Polk's War: American Opposition and Dissent, 1846-1848.* Madison: University of Wisconsin Press, 1973. A provocative study of public opinion during the Mexican War. Conclusion is that Polk not only decided on the war before learning of the firing on American troops but also welcomed the conflict as a way to fulfill his expansionist plans.

Sellers, Charles Grier, Jr. *James K. Polk: Jacksonian, 1795-1843.* Princeton, N.J.: Princeton University Press, 1957.

__________. *James K. Polk: Continentalist, 1843-1846.* Princeton, N.J.: Princeton University Press, 1966. These volumes constitute the best treatment of Polk and his times up to the introduction of the Wilmot Proviso, a portent of things to come. Well-balanced and thoroughly researched, the study established Polk's claim to be considered one of the "near great" presidents.

Weems, John Edward. *To Conquer a Peace: The War Between the United States and Mexico.* Garden City, N.Y.: Doubleday, 1974. A popular treatment of the war. Largely undocumented but interesting and basically sound. Weems believes that Polk hoped to avoid war by making a show of force.

C. L. Grant

Colin L. Powell

Born: April 5, 1937; New York City

The first African American to become chairman of the Joint Chiefs of Staff, Colin Powell successfully organized and supervised American military operations in the Gulf War of 1991.

Early Life

Colin Powell was born in New York City on April 5, 1937. His parents, Luther Powell and Maud McKoy, were both immigrants from Jamaica who had come to the United States in the 1920's. Both worked in Manhattan's garment district. Their first child, a daughter, was born in 1931; five and a half years later, Colin Powell was born. In 1940, the Powells moved from Manhattan to the Bronx and settled in Hunt's Point, an ethnically mixed working-class section of the city. Colin's boyhood friendships reflected that ethnic mixture, experiences that may have contributed to his attitudes about race.

Powell attended neighborhood public schools. The New York City school system was then among the strongest in the country, and although Powell did not stand out scholastically, he benefited from the high quality of his teachers. In high school, he took the college preparatory program; as a senior, he applied for admission to New York University and to the City College of New York. Admitted to both, he elected to attend City College, at that time the only free public university in the United States.

CCNY, as City College was commonly known, was a remarkable school. It attracted first-and second-generation students from every immigrant group arriving in New York. Its alumni flocked to graduate and professional schools in greater numbers than from any other undergraduate institution. Powell began as an engineering student but switched to geology when, as he later put it, he could not manage to "visualize a plane intersecting a cone in space." The highlight of Powell's university career was his service in the Reserve Officers Training Corps (ROTC). In the ROTC, Powell found himself in his element. He enjoyed every aspect of his military training and became a member of the Pershing Rifles, an elite military fraternity. Powell was graduated in June, 1958, his degree in geology less important to him than his commission as a second lieutenant in the U.S. Army.

Colin Powell *(U.S. Air Force)*

Life's Work

A few days after his graduation, Powell traveled to Fort Benning, Georgia, for five more months of military training, including attendance at the Infantry Officer Basic Course. He volunteered for and successfully completed Ranger School and Airborne (parachute) training. His first full duty assignment was in Germany as a platoon leader in the Second Armored Rifle Battalion of the 48th Infantry. As the reports of his superiors confirmed, he was an able and adaptable officer from the beginning of his military career. His record was typical of officers who are on the "fast track"—that is, who are marked for early promotion because of their exceptional abilities.

On his return from Germany, Powell was assigned to the Fifth Infantry Division at Fort Devens, Massachusetts. While there, he met Alma Johnson, a young woman working as an audiologist with the Boston Guild for the Hard of Hearing. Johnson and Powell began dating, and they were married shortly before he received orders that would send him to Vietnam.

Powell served two tours of duty in Vietnam. During the first, in 1962 and 1963, he worked as adviser to a South Vietnamese army battalion in the A Shau Valley, one of the hottest areas of the war. His unit saw a great deal of action, and Powell suffered a wound from a Viet Cong booby trap. During his second Vietnam tour, in 1968 and 1969, Powell was already a major, senior enough to be a battalion executive officer in the Americal Division. When the division's commander, Major General Charles Gettys, learned that Powell had been the second-ranking graduate of the Army's Command and General Staff College at Fort Leavenworth, he assigned Powell to be the staff operations officer for the entire division. Powell was successful in this position, but his tour of duty ended when he suffered a broken ankle in a helicopter crash. His two tours in Vietnam persuaded him that war must have clear political and military objectives and a definable end—a belief that would help to shape his later service.

After Vietnam, Powell served in a variety of military and political positions. His introduction to the civilian side of senior leadership occurred when he was awarded a White House Fellowship in 1972. These fellowships are awarded on a competitive basis to a select group of young professionals. Powell's assignment as a White House Fellow was to the Office of Management and Budget under Caspar Weinberger, who later became secretary of defense; Weinberger's deputy, Frank Carlucci, also later went on to become secretary of defense. Powell learned about budgeting, the importance of press relations, and, more generally, how to handle himself in the senior political world. The White House Fellowship marked Powell, both in the Army and in the government, as a rising young officer. The contacts he made at the Office of Management and Budget were also to serve him well in later years.

After his fellowship year, Powell received assignments of increasing responsibility. He commanded a brigade of the 101st Airborne Division in 1976 and 1977. He was military assistant to the deputy secretary of defense from 1979 to 1981 and to the secretary of defense from 1983 to 1986. Later in 1986, he was given overall command of the Army's V Corps in Europe. From 1987 to 1989, he served as President Ronald Reagan's National Security Adviser, working on the most delicate matters of national security policy. Among these were such issues as nuclear disarmament and the U.S. stance toward the dissolution of the Soviet Union. During his service as National Security Adviser, Powell continued to impress those with whom he was working, among them Vice President George Bush.

In 1988, Bush was elected to succeed Reagan, and he became president in January, 1989. Powell refused several jobs in the new administration, including that of director of the Central Intelligence Agency (CIA). He preferred to return to the Army, and he was promoted to full general and put in charge of Forces Command. Ten months later, when Admiral William Crowe retired as chairman of the Joint Chiefs of Staff, Powell was the obvious choice for the position. Although he was the most junior of the fifteen existing four-star generals, he had a unique combination of civilian and military service, a record of success in every job he had undertaken, and excellent personal and professional relations with other senior members of the defense and foreign-policy establishment. After a brief period of consideration, President Bush nominated him for the chairmanship, and the appointment was quickly confirmed by the Senate.

Powell's new job did not involve the direct command of troops. The chairman, however, is the head of the Joint Chiefs of Staff and the principal military adviser to the president and the secretary of defense. It is a unique position; the chairman has immense power and influence. Powell determined to use this influence to prevent unwise military entanglements—the lesson of Vietnam remained vivid to him—and to promote his conception of the size and organization of the U.S. military establishment in the wake of the Soviet collapse.

He had hardly settled into his new office when a crisis developed in Panama. The Bush Administration had been awaiting an opportunity to depose Panamanian president General Manuel Noriega, who was deeply involved in the international drug business. On Powell's second day in office, reports were received that an anti-Noriega coup was imminent. Should the United States enter the fray? Powell and his senior colleagues decided that the reports were too fragmentary and the probability of success too remote. In the event, they were proved right; the coup collapsed after only a few hours.

Two months later, however, after Panamanian soldiers shot and killed an American serviceman and beat another, the Bush Administration acted. U.S. forces invaded Panama, routed the Panamanian military, and captured Noriega within a few days. The operation was conducted in compliance with Powell's prerequisites for the use of U.S. forces: There must be attainable military objectives and a way out of the commitment after the objectives are achieved.

Powell's greatest accomplishment as chairman of the Joint Chiefs of Staff was the successful organization and implementation of U.S. strategy during the 1991 Persian Gulf War. On August 2, 1990, Saddam Hussein's Iraqi forces invaded Kuwait and threatened the security of Saudi Arabia. For a variety of reasons, President Bush determined that the United States could not tolerate these extensions of Iraqi power. The U.S. military response, code-named "Operation Desert Shield," began almost immediately, and American forces were sent to Saudi Arabia to protect it from a potential Iraqi attack. Within a few months, the American commitment of forces to Desert Shield amounted to nearly 250,000 troops. Simultaneous economic and diplomatic pressures were applied to Iraq in order to persuade Hussein to withdraw from Kuwait. When it became clear that these were not succeeding, Bush ordered that preparations for "Operation Desert Storm"—the forcible expulsion of Iraqi troops from Kuwait—to begin. Overall responsibility for these operations fell to Colin Powell, and the buildup of U.S. forces continued. Eventually, half a million American troops reached Saudi Arabia, where they were joined by detachments sent by many U.S. allies, including a number of Arab countries.

Powell was instrumental in insisting to his superiors that the military and political objectives be clearly defined. Moreover, he worked closely with General Norman A. Schwarzkopf, the field commander, to assure that the strategy of attack did not involve costly frontal assaults on fortified positions. In January, 1991, air attacks began against Iraq and Iraqi forces. In February, a ground assault was launched. Four days of fighting were sufficient to clear Kuwait of the invaders and destroy most of Iraq's heavy armored divisions. President Bush, Secretary of Defense Dick Cheney, and Powell halted the war immediately thereafter to prevent further slaughter.

Powell's term as chairman lasted into the Bill Clinton Administration. When his term expired, he retired from the Army. In 1996, there was intense speculation about whether Powell would accept a vice-presidential nomination on the Republican presidential ticket, but he declined to be considered.

Summary

Colin Powell's career has been marked by a number of notable achievements. He was the first African American to achieve the highest position in the U.S. military. Some observers pointed to Powell's success as a sign that racial barriers were continuing to disappear; others remarked that the rise of an African American to the very top of the military establishment was appropriate for an Army that is disproportionately black. Powell also helped to restore confidence and pride in the American armed forces, among both the general public and the troops themselves, as the Gulf War victory helped to assuage the bitterness that had been the legacy of Vietnam. For this, some of the credit belongs to Powell, one of the principal architects of the resounding victory. In addition, his efforts to reduce the size of America's standing forces in the wake of the Soviet Union's collapse met with general approval as an appropriate step toward a more realistic and affordable military policy for the United States. Finally, Powell's insistence that military objectives be defined and attainable helped to put national foreign policy on a more realistic basis.

Bibliography

Means, Howard. *Colin Powell: Soldier/Statesman, Statesman/Soldier*. New

York: Donald I. Fine, 1992. Although marred by minor factual errors, this biography is based on interviews with many of Powell's closest associates and friends. Contains numerous quotations.

Powell, Colin L., with Joseph E. Persico. *My American Journey*. New York: Random House, 1995. Powell's own summation of his life. Especially strong on the details of his military career. Although Powell was assisted by Joseph Persico, enough of his own character and personality come through to make the book worthwhile.

Roth, David. *Sacred Honor: A Biography of Colin Powell*. San Francisco: HarperCollins, 1993. Roth, one of Powell's public affairs officers after the Gulf War, has prepared this admiring biography of the general. Contains discussions of Powell's character and religious views that are not found in other works about him.

Schwarzkopf, H. Norman. *It Doesn't Take a Hero*. New York: Bantam Doubleday Dell, 1993. General Schwarzkopf's autobiography is strong in its coverage of the relationship between the field commander—Schwarzkopf— and the overall strategist—Powell—in the planning and execution of the Gulf War, although Schwarzkopf naturally focuses on his own activities.

Woodward, Bob. *The Commanders*. New York: Simon & Schuster, 1991. Focuses on the decision-making process in Washington, especially regarding the Panamanian and Iraqi operations during Powell's tenure as chairman. Much of the material comes from anonymous sources.

Robert Jacobs

JEANNETTE RANKIN

Born: June 11, 1880; near Missoula, Montana
Died: May 18, 1973; Carmel, California

Rankin devoted her life to women's rights and peace. She was the first woman elected to Congress and the only member to vote against the entry of the United States into both world wars.

Early Life

Born near Missoula, Montana, in a ranch house on June 11, 1880, Jeannette Rankin was the eldest of seven children. Her father, John Rankin, the son of Scottish immigrants, moved into Montana in the late 1860's. After prospecting for gold, he settled in Missoula, became a builder and contractor, and played a central role in the town's political and economic development. Jeannette's mother, Olive Pickering, migrated from New Hampshire to Missoula in 1878 and served the town as its schoolteacher until her marriage to John Rankin the following year. John developed a lucrative business and purchased a ranch for cattle raising and farming.

The Rankin family was close-knit and loving but fostered each member's individuality. Evenings were often spent in lively discussion and hearing stories of gold prospecting and Indian warfare in the Montana Territory. The family was also very religious, and its beliefs formed the values by which Jeannette lived her entire life.

Although she loved to read, public school bored Jeannette. She found more satisfaction in learning practical skills from her parents. From her mother, Jeannette learned sewing, and she became an expert seamstress. She studied carpentry with her father and constructed a sidewalk in downtown Missoula.

Jeannette entered Montana State University in 1898, but her college experience was as frustrating as her earlier schooling. The university was located in Missoula, hence the change of scenery that she desired was impossible; the campus was regional, thus little opportunity existed to meet students from diverse backgrounds. Moreover, she frequently complained that her classes were uninteresting. She completed her studies, was graduated in 1902, and for a short time taught school.

Looking for something more challenging than teaching, Jeannette drifted from one job to another—dressmaker, sawmill supervisor, and furniture builder. In 1904, Jeannette visited her brother at Harvard College in Boston. She found the city exhilarating but was shocked by the slum conditions and the extent of poverty, overcrowded dwellings, and poor health among working-class residents. Repulsed by what she witnessed, Jeannette committed herself to social work.

Jeannette Rankin *(AP/Wide World Photos)*

Life's Work

In 1908, Jeannette Rankin enrolled in the New York School of Philanthropy to study social issues and social work. After completing the program in 1910, she secured employment in a Spokane, Washington, children's home. At that time the state of Washington was considering woman suffrage. Volunteering her services, she distributed leaflets, canvassed voters door-to-door, and delivered speeches in favor of the state suffrage amendment. Washington granted women the right to vote in November, and her participation sparked an enthusiasm that placed Jeannette on a crusade for woman suffrage and social reform.

Rankin returned to Montana in December, 1910, for the Christmas holidays and learned that her home state had scheduled debate on a suffrage amendment for January. She quickly organized the Equal Franchise Society, requested and received an invitation from the state assembly to speak on behalf of the amendment, and presented a well-received argument for woman suffrage. Although the amendment was not passed until 1913, Jeannette was instrumental in its eventual victory.

Having gained a taste for social reform politics, Jeannette Rankin became a member of the National American Woman Suffrage Association (NAWSA) and joined organizations in several states. By autumn of 1914, she had lobbied and spoken before the legislatures of ten states, marched in rallies in major cities, and petitioned Congress for a national woman suffrage amendment. Rankin was quickly becoming a national personality.

In 1914, war erupted in Europe. Although the United States was not involved, Rankin feared that it might be unable to remain neutral. War, she reasoned, would shift the public's attention from social issues and slow the movement for woman suffrage. While in New York, Rankin helped to form the Women's Peace Party in January, 1915, and lobbied Congress to stay out of the European conflict. Although she spent the next summer in Montana organizing "good government clubs" designed to eliminate corruption and to increase women's rights, she devoted most of her time to speaking and writing against American entry into World War I.

In 1916, the likelihood of war led Jeannette Rankin to take the boldest step of her career. Against the advice of Republican Party leaders, Rankin announced her candidacy for election to the U.S. House of Representatives. Her personal platform reflected her professional goals—an amendment to the U.S. Constitution for woman suffrage, child protection laws, social justice, and good government. She was most demanding regarding continued American neutrality. Her antiwar views, which most Montana voters shared, brought her victory in November. Jeannette Rankin was the only Republican to win office in Montana that year and the first woman in American history to take a seat in the United States Congress.

Jeannette Rankin took the oath of office on April 1, 1917, but the warm welcome she received did not last long. On April 5, the House of Representatives commenced debate on American entry into the Great War. Special attention was focused on Rankin. She symbolically represented all women in the nation. Her vote for or against war would be interpreted as a woman's ability to deal with political crises.

The House debated the war resolution throughout the night. Rankin chose to remain silent but listened intently to the heated arguments. Tensions rose as opponents of war were jeered, hissed, and verbally branded as unpatriotic. When the House voted, Jeannette Rankin rose to her feet. "I want to stand by my country," she said, "but I cannot vote for war. I vote no." She found herself in the minority. Three hundred seventy-four representatives supported the resolution, while only fifty voted against war. On April 7, 1917, President Woodrow Wilson declared war on Germany.

Hannah Josephson stated in her biography *Jeannette Rankin, First Lady in Congress* (1974) that Rankin was warned before the vote that she might lose reelection because of her antiwar stance. Her opposition to war was far more important to her than her concern for reelection. The public's response was swift. Rankin was labeled unpatriotic and a disgrace to women nationwide. Even the National-American Woman Suffrage Association claimed that her vote against war would lose supporters for a constitutional suffrage amendment. Rankin later said that her vote against war was the most significant one she ever made. Women, she believed, had to take the lead to end war.

Once the nation was committed to war, Jeannette Rankin supported American troops, worked in Congress to protect civil liberties, and pushed for social reform. She championed legislation authorizing the government to hire more women workers, to provide financial relief to families of soldiers, to improve conditions for imprisoned women, and to guarantee food, clothing, shelter, and health care for children living in poverty. She participated in congressional debates on a federal amendment for woman suffrage, which Congress finally sent to the states for approval in 1918. As her term in the House of Representatives ended, however, Rankin's antiwar vote resurfaced and caused her defeat for reelection.

During the twenty years which followed, Rankin toured the nation promoting feminist issues. She served the National Consumers' League, which advocated federal child labor laws, better working conditions, and increased women's rights. Most of her energy, however, was directed toward achieving international peace.

The horrors of World War I still vivid in her mind, and aware that social justice could never be attained as long as money was spent on defense and warfare, Rankin helped to form the Women's International League for Peace and Freedom and volunteered her services to numerous other peace organizations. She campaigned against Reserve Officers Training Corps programs on college campuses. She was a central figure at the Conference on the Cause and Cure for War, participated in the Peace March on Chicago, lobbied congressmen to introduce legislation to outlaw war, and advocated the creation of a National Peace Party to challenge both Republicans and Democrats in state and federal elections. As the 1930's drew to a close and the prospect for another world war seemed likely, Rankin intensified her efforts.

In November, 1940, at age sixty, Jeannette Rankin was again elected to Congress on a peace platform. She proposed bills to prevent the sending of American troops abroad and to require a national vote before war could be declared. Neither measure passed, but she persisted throughout 1941. Despite Japan's attack on Pearl Harbor on December 7, Rankin stood for peace regardless of personal consequences. On December 8, Congress voted for war. This time, Rankin cast the only vote in opposition. As before, Rankin received the brunt of public criticism and was not reelected the following year.

Until her death in 1973, Jeannette Rankin traveled the world. The extent of global poverty and injustice she witnessed intensified her belief that only in a peaceful world could social problems be resolved. Based on this view, she condemned America's war in Vietnam throughout the 1960's. In January, 1968, she participated in an antiwar march on Washington. The Jeannette Rankin Brigade, so named by her admirers, petitioned Congress to end the war and "heal a sick society at home."

Summary

Until her death on May 18, 1973, Jeannette Rankin pressed her demands for an end to war, protection of civil liberties, and direct popular vote on critical national issues. She never realized her dream to end war, but she was responsible, directly or indirectly, for the creation of many laws. Her efforts resulted in voting rights for women, support for dependents of servicemen, free postage for members of the armed forces, retention of citizenship for women who marry aliens, child labor and protection laws, and women's rights. Throughout her life she spoke on behalf of labor, for child welfare, for social justice and greater democracy, and against racial prejudice. She further advocated multimember congressional districts, a unicameral Congress, direct election of the president, and the restructuring of the U.S. military into a purely defensive force. Her two elections to Congress opened avenues for women nationally in politics and business. Although she was labeled an idealist and was criticized severely for her antiwar position, Jeannette Rankin possessed the courage to remain true to her convictions and dedicated her life to the betterment of American society and the human race.

Bibliography

Chafe, William H. *The American Woman: Her Changing Social, Economic, and Political Roles, 1920-1970*. New York: Oxford University Press, 1972. Chafe develops a thorough, detailed study of American feminism in the twentieth century, illuminating its development, course, and reception by American society. This work has become a standard in the field and accurately presents Rankin's era.

Davidson, Sue. *A Heart in Politics: Jeannette Rankin and Patsy T. Mink*. Seattle, Wash.: Seal Press, 1994.

Dedication of the Statue of Jeannette Rankin. Washington, D.C.: Government Printing Office, 1986. This publication includes a biographical sketch of Rankin and speeches given by prominent political figures in remembrance of her advocacy of women's rights and an end to war. Included is a time line of Jeannette Rankin's life.

Josephson, Hannah. *Jeannette Rankin, First Lady in Congress*. Indianapolis: Bobbs-Merrill, 1974. Although many prominent and influential women with whom Rankin worked receive limited attention and the broad context in which Rankin operated is somewhat vague, Josephson has presented a complete, well-researched biography of Jeannette Rankin. The author's twenty-year personal relationship with

Rankin makes the work most insightful and revealing.

Libby, Frederick J. *To End War*. Nyack, N.Y.: Fellowship Publications, 1969. Libby surveys the patterns of antiwar thought and peace organizations in twentieth century America.

Noble, David W. *The Progressive Mind, 1890-1917*. Rev. ed. Minneapolis, Minn.: Burgess, 1981. This work provides an overview of the intellectual foundations of the Progressive Era and the evolution in thought of Progressives themselves. One chapter devoted exclusively to women of the period adequately highlights the feminist movement.

Kenneth W. Townsend

Ronald Reagan

Born: February 6, 1911; Tampico, Illinois

After a succession of failed presidencies over two decades, Reagan stemmed the general feeling of instability that had begun to surround the office. Almost by sheer personality and by effortlessly exuding an enormous self-confidence, Reagan reversed many of the negative images of the presidency.

Early Life

Ronald Wilson Reagan was born February 6, 1911, in Tampico, Illinois. He was the younger of two sons; his brother John Neil Reagan was born on September 3, 1909. His father, John Edward Reagan, was born July 13, 1883, in Fulton, Illinois; his father's parents were born in County Cork, Ireland. His mother, Nelle Clyde Wilson Reagan, of English-Scottish ancestry, was born July 24, 1885, in Fulton, Illinois. When Reagan was ten years old, his family settled in Dixon, Illinois, after living in several other rural Illinois towns. Reagan's father was a shoe salesman who was troubled by alcoholism and had difficulty holding a job. His mother loved the theater, and it was in Dixon, while attending high school, that Reagan first participated in acting. In 1928, he was graduated from high school, where he played basketball and football and was on the track team; he was also president of the student body. For seven summers during his high school and college years, he worked as a lifeguard at Lowell Park near Dixon.

Reagan won a scholarship which paid half of his living expenses, tuition, and fees at Eureka College, where he majored in sociology and economics. At Eureka, he participated in student politics, athletics, and theater, playing the lead in several college productions and winning honorable mention in a drama competition sponsored by Northwestern University. He won varsity letters in football, swimming, and track, and, as in high school, was elected president of the student body. After receiving a B.A. degree on June 7, 1932, he was hired as a sports announcer for station WOC in Davenport, Iowa. WOC was a five-thousand-watt station which shared its wavelength with WHO in Des Moines; both stations became part of the NBC network within a year after Reagan's initial employment. By 1937, his coverage of major league baseball, Big Ten Conference football, and other sports events had earned for him a national reputation as a sportscaster. While covering the Chicago Cubs' training camp at Catalina Island, he was introduced to a Los Angeles motion picture agent who succeeded in getting him a screen test at the Warner Bros. studio. In 1937, he signed a two-hundred-dollar-per-week, seven-year contract with Warner Bros.

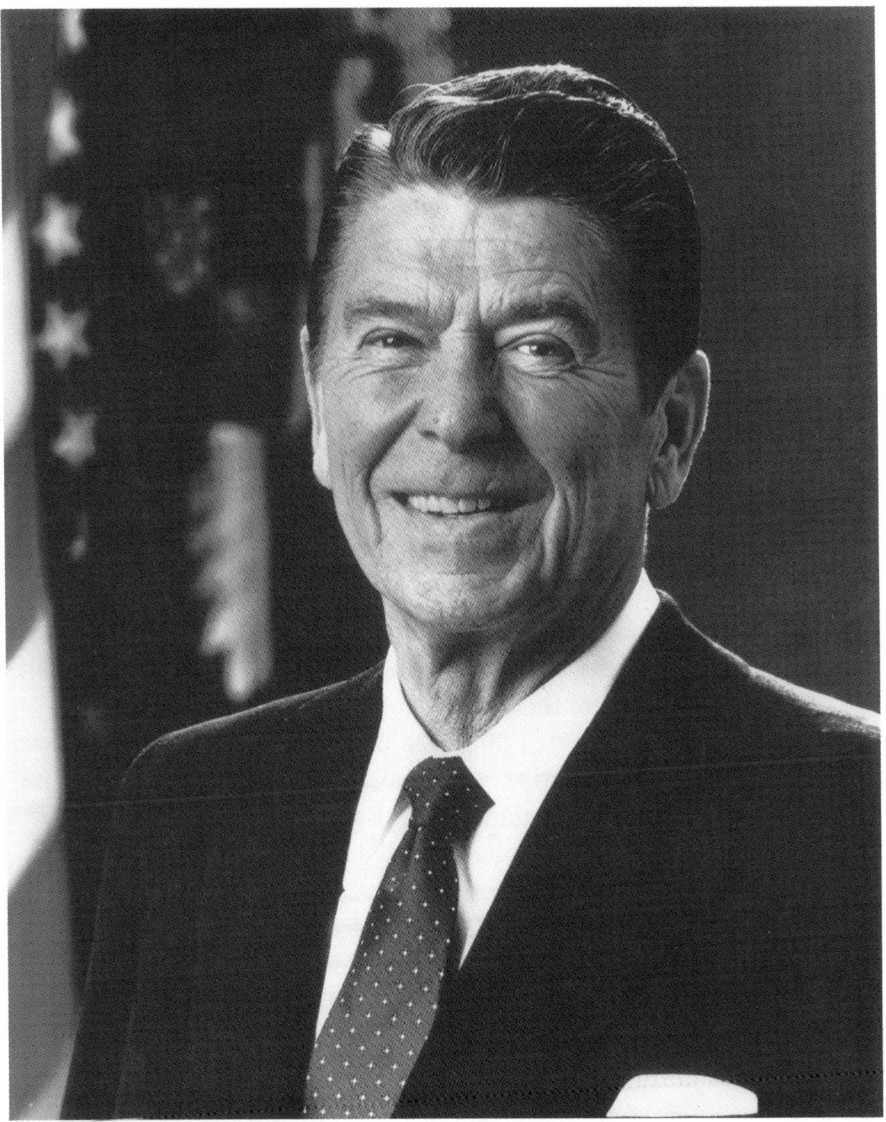

Ronald Reagan *(Library of Congress)*

Life's Work

Reagan's first film, the 1937 production *Love Is on the Air,* was well received, with Reagan cast as a radio commentator. He played in more than twenty B pictures before his performance as George Gipp, the famous Notre Dame football star, in *Knute Rockne, All American* (1940) established his reputation as a serious actor. In 1940-1941, he was chosen one of the "Stars of Tomorrow" in an exhibitor's poll. Reagan's most memorable film role was probably that of Drake McHugh, the victim of a sadistic surgeon, in *King's Row* in 1942. This was an excellent film, directed by Sam Wood, and Reagan's performance was generally described as excellent by reviewers. In all, Reagan, generally regarded as a competent but not outstanding actor, made fifty-five feature-length films, mostly for Warner Bros., between 1937 and 1964. Reagan left Warner Bros. in the 1950's and free-lanced among several studios for a few years; his career was to be rescued by television.

On April 14, 1942, Reagan had entered the United States Army as a second lieutenant of cavalry in reserve; poor eyesight disqualified him for combat duty. Until his discharge as a captain on December 9, 1945, he made training films for the army in California. It was after his three-year stint in the army that Reagan began to give serious attention to the politics of the film industry. He took fewer roles as an actor after he was elected as president of the Screen Actors Guild (SAG) in 1947. SAG was one of the major labor unions in the industry; Reagan was elected to six one-year terms as president, in which capacity he successfully negotiated several significant labor contracts. In October, 1947, he appeared before the House Committee on Un-American Activities (HUAC, as it became popularly known) as a friendly witness in its investigation of communist influence in the film industry. He came to view HUAC and its chairman, Congressman J. Parnell Thomas, and their questionable tactics, however, with enough wariness that he did not name names of suspected communists.

Reagan started his political life as a liberal Democrat who ardently supported Franklin D. Roosevelt. In the 1940's, however, his political outlook became much more conservative. His movement to the right of center politically came during his experience from 1954 to 1962 when he was employed by the General Electric Company, as host, program supervisor, and occasional actor on the weekly television show *General Electric Theater*. Between television appearances, Reagan traveled throughout the country for General Electric's personnel relations division. He spoke at the company's 135 plants and addressed thousands of its workers. In these speeches he often repeated the themes of the American need for free enterprise while warning against the evils of big government. In 1962, Reagan became the host of the weekly television program *Death Valley Days;* he remained with that show until he entered the race for governor of California in 1965.

Reagan switched to the Republican Party in 1962, although he had campaigned as a Democrat for Dwight Eisenhower in 1952 and 1956, and again for Richard Nixon in 1960. He had supported Harry S Truman in 1948. In October, 1964, Reagan's prerecorded speech on behalf of Barry Goldwater, "A Time for Choosing," was well received by viewers and resulted in a huge surge in campaign contributions. Reagan's friendly, low-key delivery suggested a reassuring, plain patriotism that became a hallmark of his appeal to voters in the future.

In November, 1966, Reagan defeated incumbent Democratic Governor Edward G. "Pat" Brown by more than a million votes. Reagan stumped the state with his basic speech, essentially unchanged from his days with General Electric. He called on voters to bring "common sense" back to government. He was reelected four years later when he defeated Democratic State Assembly Speaker Jesse Unruh by more than a half-million votes.

As governor, Reagan mastered the art of compromise with state legislators and was more restrained and pragmatic than his conservative rhetoric suggested. He took a hard line toward dissident students in the state's educational system, particularly at the University of California in Berkeley. He also reduced expenditures in a number of areas, including social services and education, in order to fulfill his campaign promise to reduce the size of government. These cuts, along with a prosperous state economy, resulted in substantial surpluses in the state government's revenues. In 1973, he was able to begin generous programs of income tax rebates and credits as well as significant property tax relief. A major tax law was passed during his tenure as governor which corrected a regressive state revenue system. A major achievement of Reagan's second term was the passage of the California Welfare Reform Act of 1971. This law reduced the numbers of people on the welfare rolls while increasing payments to those in need, notably those recipients of Aid for Families with Dependent Children. His successes as a governor led many political observers to regard him as a leading contender for the GOP presidential nomination in 1968.

Reagan's first run for the presidency, however, was too tentative to stop Richard M. Nixon in 1968, and he accordingly requested that the convention make Nixon's nomination unanimous. He next campaigned for the presidency against Gerald R. Ford, beginning with the New Hampshire primary in February, 1976. Reagan narrowly lost the nomination to Ford at the Republican Convention in Kansas City, Missouri; the delegate vote was 1,187 for Ford to Reagan's 1,070. Nevertheless, Reagan had laid the groundwork for 1980 by his strong showing, especially with voters in the South, and in July of that year he arrived unopposed at the Republican National Convention. In his acceptance speech, Reagan pledged to support a conservative platform which called for voluntary prayer in public schools, tuition credits for private school tuition, and strong opposition to school busing, abortion, and the Equal Rights Amendment. Reagan overcame questions about his age with a vigorous campaign against incumbent Jimmy Carter, and his disarming and engaging performance in televised debates helped him to defeat Carter at the polls on November 4, 1980. His margin in the popular vote was substantial, and he received 489 votes to Carter's 49 in the electoral college.

Ronald Wilson Reagan was inaugurated as the fortieth president of the United States at 11:57 A.M. on Tuesday, January 20, 1981, with Chief Justice Warren Burger administering the oath of office. For the first time, the ceremony was held at the West Front of the Capitol, in a symbolic allusion to Reagan's Western roots. The president gave a twenty-minute address calling for "an era of national renewal." Minutes afterward, he fulfilled a campaign promise by placing a freeze on government hiring. As the president concluded his address, at 12:33 P.M., the Iranian government released the American hostages whom they had held for 444 days. The news added to the festive spirit of the occasion.

Reagan is six feet, one inch tall and weighs 185 pounds, with light-brown hair and blue eyes. He has worn contact lenses for many years, is a nonsmoker, and drinks only on occasion. He retreats often to his ranch, Rancho del Cielo, near Santa Barbara, California. He enjoys horseback riding, chopping wood, and watching television and privately screened motion pictures. In 1994, he was diagnosed with Alzheimer's disease and has since made few public appearances.

Reagan was married for the first time on January 24, 1940, to actress Jane Wyman, whom he had met while they were both appearing in films for Warner Bros. From that marriage, which ended on July 19, 1949, they had a daughter, Maureen Elizabeth, and an adopted son, Michael Edward. On March 4, 1952, Reagan married actress Nancy Davis, the daughter of Dr. Loyal Davis, a prominent Chicago neurosurgeon. They had two children, Patrician Ann and Ronald Prescott. Reagan was the first president to have been divorced.

Reagan was shot in the chest as he left the Washington Hilton Hotel at about 2:30 P.M. on March 30, 1981, after addressing a group of union officials. His assailant, John Hinckley, Jr., was overpowered and arrested at the scene of the crime. The president was rushed to nearby George Washington University hospital, where he later was operated on to remove a bullet from his left lung. On April 11, 1981, after a remarkably quick recovery, he returned to the White House.

During his first term, Reagan concentrated on a strategy of cutting taxes for economic growth stimulation, holding back increases in government spending, and an expensive buildup of American defenses throughout the world. By 1984, inflation was under control, interest rates moved down, though not low enough, employment was up significantly, and generally the economy was upbeat. Difficult problems remained, however, such as the huge size of the federal deficit, a somewhat myopic view of government's role in domestic matters, and a Supreme Court which was perhaps too conservative in such a complex, modern world. Solutions for the plight of minorities and the American farmer remained to be found. Nevertheless, the Reagan presidency set standards against which present and future programs will be judged.

Summary

Ronald Reagan has fashioned two careers in his long years in the public eye. He has held only two public offices, first as governor of the largest state in the union, then as President of the United States; he began his second career at the top. His years in the governor's mansion in Sacramento coincided with an era of national protest, foreign war, and social change; his years in the White House have been marked by economic recession and recovery, problems of unemployment, complicated foreign affairs, and expanding American military buildup.

Yet Ronald Reagan was well known to the public before he undertook a career in public service in the 1960's. His first career was in film and television, and most voting-age Americans initially encountered him in the darkened film theater or at home on television. It was during the Hollywood years that Reagan's vision of America was formed. He learned more in the film world than simply acting: He acquired an easy way with an audience, and also experienced the competition and studio politics that led him into the larger arenas of the New Deal, SAG, and HUAC—all of which constituted the apprenticeship for his second career.

Reagan's optimistic attitude appealed to voters, and his conservatism produced a number of programs that have changed American government in fundamental ways. By June, 1986, public approval of President Reagan's performance was higher than ever before, according to a Gallup Poll. The poll also found that Reagan was more popular than any previous President in the second year of his second term since World War II. A crest of public support in 1981, when fifty-eight percent of Americans approved of his performance, had tapered off in 1982 and 1983 to forty-four percent, rising again in 1984 to fifty-six percent approval and sixty-one percent in 1985. Despite the Iranian arms crisis which marred the later half of his second term, few presidents in the twentieth century have demonstrated such staying power in the polls, including Dwight Eisenhower and Franklin D. Roosevelt. Indeed, perhaps Reagan's greatest achievement is to have restored the office of President of the United States to a position of power and prestige.

Bibliography

Adler, Bill. *Ronnie and Nancy: A Very Special Love Story*. New York: Crown Publishers, 1985. The most interesting part of this book follows Reagan's career from Hollywood actor and political activist to television personality and General Electric spokesman and on to governor of California and president. There are fascinating glimpses into the inside workings of campaigning and, to a lesser extent, life in the White House. There is also a frank discussion of the most successful public marriage in recent American history.

Cannon, Lou. *President Reagan: The Role of a Lifetime*. New York: Simon & Schuster, 1991.

__________. *Reagan*. New York: G. P. Putnam's Sons, 1982. This substantial and highly critical biography is the work of a veteran reporter and White House correspondent for *The Washington Post*. Although dated—writing his conclusion midway through his subject's first term, Cannon confidently assesses him as a one-term president—it provides a perspective on Reagan to be considered with other, more positive viewpoints. Illustrated and well documented, with an extensive bibliography.

Evans, Rowland, and Robert Novak. *The Reagan Revolution*. New York: E. P. Dutton, 1981. An informed analysis of the Reagan administration, which the authors portray as "revolutionary"; they favorably compare Reagan's first one hundred days in office to that celebrated span in Franklin D. Roosevelt's first term. In seeking the presidency, the authors suggest, Reagan hoped to restore the United States to world leadership, to halt the pervasive growth of government, and to revive free enterprise.

Gelb, Leslie H. "The Mind of the President." *The New York Times Magazine*, October 6, 1985, sec. 6: 20-24, 28-32, 103, 112-113. The author concludes that Reagan is unique in the history of American presidents because he alone possesses the mind of both an ideologue and a politician. Reagan "has all the moral force and power that swell from absolute conviction." His success stems from the fact that he is a "natural horsetrader" who has mastered the art of political compromise in order to achieve his own political ends.

Greenstein, Fred I., ed. *The Reagan Presidency: An Early Assessment*. Baltimore: The Johns Hopkins University Press, 1983. A collection of scholarly essays that came out of a November, 1982, conference at Princeton University on the first two years of the Reagan presidency. The authors attempt to judge Reagan's performance in four major policy areas—fiscal, foreign, defense, and domestic. They examine Reagan's ideological objectives and the ways in which they have been translated into public policy.

Hannaford, Peter. *The Reagans: A Political Portrait*. New York: Coward, McCann and Geoghegan, 1983. Written by a former aide, this book provides many details about Reagan's political life, including a thorough treatment of his days as Governor of California. The author reveals the intense struggle between Reagan's 1980 campaign manager John Sears and the others in the candidate's inner circle of advisers. An interesting portrait written from the standpoint of an "insider."

Johnson, Haynes Bonner. *Sleepwalking Through History: America in the Reagan Years*. New York: Norton, 1991.

Reagan, Ronald, with Richard G. Hubler. *Where's the Rest of Me?* New York: Dell, 1981. Reagan originally wrote this autobiography in 1965 long before he dreamed of becoming President of the United States. It is a frank, witty, and moving account of his life. The title comes from his most famous line from his best movie, *King's Row*, in 1942. The book reveals much of the charm, optimism, and common sense that made him such a phenomenally successful politician.

Ritter, Kurt W., and David Henry. *Ronald Reagan: The Great Communicator*. Foreword by Bernard K. Duffy. New York: Greenwood Press, 1992.

Schaller, Michael. *Reckoning with Reagan: America and its President in the 1980's*. New York: Oxford University Press, 1992.

Thomas, Tony. *The Films of Ronald Reagan*. Secaucas, N.J.: The Citadel Press, 1980. The only book-length study of Reagan's film career. Reagan took his acting seriously, in spite of what his political opponents may say. He was an able actor usually assigned to poor roles. Workmanlike in his professional duties, he was seldom criticized for being less than convincing within his acting range. The author concludes that Reagan's career was a respectable one.

Weintraub, Bernard. "The Reagan Legacy." *The New York Times Magazine*, June 22, 1986, sec. 6: 12-21. This article examines Reagan's firm belief that his impact on America will prove to be just as far-reaching as Franklin Roosevelt's. The author concludes that Reagan has reestablished the primacy of the presidency as an institution after nearly two decades of White House disarray. Weintraub quotes Senator Edward M. Kennedy, who, despite his frequent criticism of Reagan's economic, social, and civil-rights policies, acknowledges that "he has contributed a spirit of good will and grace to the presidency and American life generally and turned the presidency into a vigorous and forceful instrument of national policy."

Arthur F. McClure

Janet Reno

Born: July 21, 1938; Miami, Florida

As Florida's first female state attorney, Janet Reno focused on the root causes of criminal behavior, instituting programs to change the social and personal conditions that lead people to commit crimes. As the first woman attorney general of the United States, she declared her intention to reorient the national crime policy in the same way—toward prevention first, and then punishment.

Early Life

Janet Reno was born on July 21, 1938, in the Coconut Grove section of Miami, Florida. Her father, Henry Reno, was a Danish immigrant who worked as a police reporter for the *Miami Herald* for forty-three years until his death in 1967. Her mother, Jane Wood Reno, was an investigative reporter for the *Miami News*. Her maternal grandmother was Daisy Sloan Hunter Wood, a genteel southern lady who instilled in her children and grandchildren a passionate commitment to duty and family.

Janet was the oldest of the Renos' four children, each born a year apart. In 1946, the family bought twenty-one acres on what was then the edge of the Everglades, twenty miles outside Miami. Jane Reno built the family house, where Janet still lives and where she lived with her mother until the latter's death on December 21, 1992. The house became a symbol to Janet that she could do anything she really wanted, if it was right, and if she put her mind to it.

The house had no air conditioning or central heating, and no television. Janet spent much of her time outdoors and developed a love of camping and canoeing. Her family's love of books, poetry, world affairs, and music linked her to the outside world.

While Janet got much of her independent spirit from her mother, who did not tolerate cosmetics, organized religion, or racism, she was also greatly influenced by her father. He was a gentle man who understood protocol. He taught his children compassion and social justice, always treating people with respect and dignity. He told his children stories of police officers, judges, and officials, most of whom were wise, compassionate, and honorable. Janet was drawn to government by the

Janet Reno *(AP/Wide World Photos)*

judges and police officers Henry brought home.

Janet attended public schools in Dade County, Florida. In 1960, she graduated from Cornell University with a bachelor's degree in chemistry. At Cornell, she was president of the Women's Student Government and earned her spending money by working as a waitress. She received her LL.B. degree in 1963 from Harvard Law School, where she was one of sixteen women in a class of 500.

Denied a position in one of Miami's large law firms because she was a woman, she took a position in a smaller firm. In 1971, she received her first political appointment as staff director of the Judiciary Committee of the Florida House of Representatives. In 1972, she ran for a seat in the state legislature and lost, but cheered herself with the knowledge that Abraham Lincoln had also lost his first election.

Life's Work

Janet Reno's career in public service began to flourish when she joined the state attorney's office in Dade County, Florida, in 1973. While there, she was assigned to organize a juvenile division within the prosecutor's office. It was at this time that she began developing views about preventive crime-fighting through services to children and rehabilitating delinquent youths. From 1976 to 1978, she left public service briefly to become a partner in the Miami-based law firm of Steel, Hector and Davis, the same firm that refused to give her a job thirteen years earlier because she was a woman. In 1978 she was appointed by the governor of Florida to serve as Dade County State Attorney, becoming Florida's first female state attorney.

Janet Reno was elected five times to the post of state attorney for Dade County, running as a Democrat in a heavily Republican district. She believed that the first objective of a prosecutor should be to make sure innocent people do not get charged. The second objective should be to convict the guilty according to due process.

Reno took office when racial tension, drug trafficking, and illegal immigration from Cuba, Haiti, and South America were all on the rise. She gained widespread criticism in 1980, when her office failed to convict four white police officers who had been charged with beating to death a black insurance salesman. Miami's black community erupted into three days of rioting, and black community leaders called for her resignation.

Reno systematically set out to mend fences with the black community. She attended social functions and meetings, listened to their opinions as well as their anger, and took the time to explain her decisions. She marched in the Martin Luther King, Jr., Day Parade every year following the riots. Her office hired more blacks and Latinos and tackled issues important to minorities. Her policy of pursuing delinquent fathers for child support also helped her gain widespread respect in the black community. When she marched in the Martin Luther King, Jr., Day Parade five years after the Miami riots, she received a standing ovation.

As Dade state attorney she reformed the juvenile justice system, and she began aggressively prosecuting child abuse cases. She also instituted a domestic-violence intervention program that relied heavily on counseling for victims and abusers. Beginning in the mid-1980's, she advocated a new approach to the prosecutor's traditional mission, one best described as preventive crime-fighting by trying to get at the root cause of crime. Since most people who go to jail eventually return to their communities, Reno chose to emphasize the importance of rehabilitation. She stated her view that imprisonment cannot serve as the ultimate solution to crime, although she did support life imprisonment sentences for the most violent criminals.

During her term in office, Reno developed a community policing team that helped clean up a crime-ridden Miami housing project. In 1989, she established Miami's innovative drug court, which offered first-time drug offenders a chance to wipe their records clean if they completed a year-long treatment program. Approximately sixty percent of those who started the program finished it, and ninety percent of those who finished remained trouble-free a year later. The court became a model for dozens of others around the country.

In 1990, Reno extended her office's pioneering approach to justice still further, offering young, nonviolent offenders a chance to avoid confinement and a criminal record by undertaking a program of rehabilitation which may include making restitution to their victims.

Reno's accomplishments and support for law and order issues brought her to the attention of the Clinton Administration. On March 12, 1993, Janet Reno was sworn in as the seventy-eighth Attorney General of the United States, the first woman ever to hold that post. Following her swearing-in ceremony, in her first act as attorney general, she told reporters that she intended to protect women who sought abortions from harassment by antiabortion protesters.

She made what may turn out to be the most difficult decision of her career in April, 1993, when she ordered the Federal Bureau of Investigation (FBI) to launch an assault on the Branch Davidian cult compound outside Waco, Texas. The FBI and representatives of the Bureau of Alcohol, Tobacco, and Firearms (ATF) had been locked in a tense confrontation with the cult and its leader, David Koresh, for several weeks; Reno believed the children in the compound were being physically abused. In the end, eighty-six people, including seventeen children, died in the fire that followed. Shortly thereafter, Reno, visibly distraught, took full responsibility for the tragedy. Her earnest manner and the fact that she did not pass blame impressed both Washington officials and ordinary citizens.

As attorney general, Reno hopes to revolutionize how America thinks about law enforcement. She has encouraged government agencies, federal, state, and local, to work together to address the root causes of crime. She wants to start with good prenatal care, continuing to ensure that all children will have adequate health care, education, supervision, jobs, and job training. She has advocated flexible workdays so that parents can be home when their children get out of school, and plans to implement flex time at the Justice Department.

She has acknowledged that most of the country's successful crime programs come from local communities, not the federal government, but believes that one of her responsibilities is to keep talking about her crime prevention ideas in order to promote an ongoing, national dialogue. Her enormous influence on the criminal justice debate outside Washington cuts across the political spectrum. She has persuaded the American Bar Association to broaden its criminal studies by examining the needs of children.

Summary

In her years as Florida state attorney for Dade County, Janet Reno gained a reputation as a hard-working prosecutor with a social conscience and fought for better children's services as a way of preventing crime. In addition, she instituted innovative rehabilitation programs for first-time offenders.

As the first woman attorney general of the United States, Reno brought unquestioned integrity to the office and has been recognized nationally for her strength and honesty. She has become known as a direct, strong-willed, but compassionate politician with a record of attacking the root causes of criminal behavior. In a break with her Republican predecessors, Reno has envisioned her preeminent role as reorienting national crime policy, calling for comprehensive programs that provide a balance between punishment and prevention. Believing society's resources should go toward better education, housing, and health care, not more jails, Reno also has stated that she believes hardened criminals should be locked up permanently. As the people's lawyer, she has stated that she wants to be accessible to all citizens and to know what is happening on the streets of America, not just in the Justice Department. By implementing her plans to shift national crime-fighting priorities from punishment of crime to crime prevention, Reno has begun to establish her mark on law enforcement nationwide.

Bibliography

Anderson, Paul. *Janet Reno: Doing the Right Thing*. New York: John Wiley & Sons, 1994. Written by a reporter for the *Miami Herald* who observed Reno for many years, this first book-length biography chronicles Reno's lively family history (her immigrant grandfather discarded his Rasmussen surname in favor of "Reno" upon his arrival), her college and law school years, and her legal career. Emphasizes Reno's integrity, common sense, and strong work ethic.

Gibbs, Nancy. "Truth, Justice and the Reno Way." *Time* 142 (July 12, 1993): 20-27. Provides an in-depth overview of Reno's history and her plans for the Justice Department, specifically focusing on her advocacy for children and cooperation among government agencies as a way to prevent crime.

Laughlin, Meg. "Growing up Reno." *Lear's* 6 (July, 1993): 48-51. Written by a Miami-based writer, the article focuses on Reno's upbringing, yet also includes brief highlights of her career.

Reno, Janet. "A Common-Sense Approach to Justice." *Judicature* 77 (September, 1993): 66-67. An edited transcript of Reno's address to the annual dinner of the American Judicature Society, August 6, 1993. Reno discusses her goals as attorney general and the role of lawyers in society.

__________. "As State Prosecutor: Respected, Abused, Liked and Hated." In *Women Lawyers: Perspectives on Success*, edited by Emily Couric. New York: Law and Business/Harcourt Brace Jovanovich, 1984. Reno discusses her job as Florida state attorney for Dade County, covering the years 1978-1982. Readable, concise explanation of her thoughts and the philosophy behind some of her actions.

Simon, Charnan. *Janet Reno: First Woman Attorney General*. Chicago: Children's Press, 1994. One of the first juvenile biographies about Reno to appear in print, this work provides a useful introduction to Reno's life and career up through her first year as attorney general.

Wood, Chris. "World: America's Top Cop." *Maclean's* 106 (April 5, 1993): 18-20. Discussion of Reno as Florida state attorney for Dade County. Includes information on various programs instituted by Reno to prevent crime, such as Miami's drug court.

Sarah Thomas

Franklin D. Roosevelt

Born: January 30, 1882; Hyde Park, New York
Died: April 12, 1945; Warm Springs, Georgia

Displaying extraordinary personal courage and perhaps the most astute political leadership America has ever witnessed, Roosevelt dominated American government for a longer period than has any other president of the United States.

Early Life

Born in Hyde Park, New York, on January 30, 1882, Franklin Delano Roosevelt was a member of an American aristocratic family of great wealth. James and Sara Roosevelt, of Dutch and English ancestry, educated their only child with private tutors and European tours. At Groton School in Massachusetts, Roosevelt came under the influence of Rector Endicott Peabody, who prided himself on grooming future politicians and instilling in his charges a lifelong commitment to public service.

By 1900, when Franklin enrolled at Harvard University, he was an impressive young man—six feet two inches tall, handsome, with a patrician nose and majestically deep-set eyes. In his junior year, he fell in love with his fifth cousin, Eleanor Roosevelt, a tall, slender woman whose pleasing face was punctuated by a prominent set of Rooseveltian teeth. Eleanor was the daughter of President Theodore Roosevelt's younger brother, Elliott, who died from alcoholism when she was ten. In 1905, Franklin married Eleanor, over the objections of his mother, who tried to postpone the wedding.

Following Harvard, Roosevelt dabbled briefly with the practice of law before turning to the real love of his life: politics. In 1910, he entered the political arena for the first time, running for the New York State Senate. Fellow Democrats skeptically observed his entrance into the race for several reasons: his aristocratic bearing, his tendency to look down his nose at people, his unfamiliarity with working-class voters in the Hyde Park-Poughkeepsie area, and the fact that he was a former Republican. The political climate, however, demanded a reformer, and Roosevelt, following in the footsteps of his cousin Theodore, could fill the bill by pointing to the ugly specter of corruption within the opposition party. During the campaign, FDR (as he came to be known) showed he was different from the average "cheap-talking" politician, displaying a pragmatic unorthodoxy that later endeared him to the nation. He even campaigned for office in an automobile, an

Franklin D. Roosevelt *(White House Historical Society)*

unusual political act for a time when most people eyed the horseless carriage with suspicion. Victory was his, however, and FDR became only the second Democrat elected from his district to the New York State Senate since the Civil War. He was on his way.

It was not an easy path to success. Experiences in the New York senate taught him the limits of progressive, reformistic power. When he challenged Charles F. Murphy's Tammany machine of New York City over the Democratic nomination for the United States Senate, he met defeat. He gradually learned, however, to moderate his reform tendencies. This later proved to be his first major lesson in the school of politics. Following his reelection in 1912, Roosevelt jumped at the opportunity to join Woodrow Wilson's administration in the capacity of assistant secretary of the Navy under Josephus Daniels. In doing so, young FDR may have imagined himself following the example of Theodore, who had achieved the governorship of New York, the vice presidency, and the presidency after serving in the same position. The Navy Department afforded Roosevelt a chance to hone his administrative skills and strengthen his political ties throughout the Democratic Party to the point that, by 1920, delegates to the national convention were willing to exploit his famous name by nominating him for the vice presidency as James M. Cox's running mate. Cox and Roosevelt suffered defeat in the Republican landslide that swept Warren G. Harding and Calvin Coolidge into office. FDR remained basically unchanged throughout these events, still a somewhat immature young man who maintained very few strong convictions.

All this changed in August, 1921, when Roosevelt contracted polio while vacationing at Campobello Island, his family's resort off the Maine seacoast. His health was shattered, but a new Roosevelt slowly began to emerge. Paralyzed from the waist down, and wealthy enough to retire at the age of thirty-nine, he fought to regain his vigor. First, he had to overcome the frustration that resulted from the wearing of heavy steel braces which prohibited him from walking unaided. Second, he had to ignore the pleas of his mother (whom he worshiped but who urged him to withdraw from politics) and listen to his wife and his personal secretary, Louis McHenry Howe, who plotted to restore him to some semblance of health. During this period of recovery, Eleanor became his "legs," going where he could not go, doing what he could not do physically, and generally learning the art of politics.

Life's Work

In 1924, FDR showed that Roosevelt the fighter had superseded Roosevelt the dedicated aristocrat when he appeared at the Democratic National Convention to give his "Happy Warrior Speech" nominating Alfred E. Smith for president. Smith lost the nomination, but Roosevelt did not lose his political career to polio. Instead, it seemed to give him a strength of character he had rarely shown before the Campobello incident. In 1928, while Smith was losing his home state of New York by 100,000 votes to Herbert Hoover, FDR was winning the governorship by twenty-five thousand, thus becoming the front-runner for the 1932 Democratic presidential nomination. Reelected by an unprecedented 725,000 votes in 1930, Roosevelt, aided by his national campaign manager, James A. Farley, began his first run for the presidency. Capturing the nomination on the third ballot, Roosevelt pledged himself to create, if elected, a "new deal" for the American people.

The 1932 presidential campaign pitted FDR against the Republican incumbent, Herbert Hoover. With the country three years into the Great Depression, Roosevelt wisely ran a pragmatic campaign—fluctuating between alternative ideological positions, allowing Hoover's record to speak for itself, and leaving the decision to the American electorate. On November 8, 1932, the people spoke—giving him a 472-59 electoral victory over Hoover. When Roosevelt took office on March 4, 1933, the nation was mired in the worst depression in American history. There were approximately thirteen million unemployed people—25.2 percent of the work force. As a mood of apprehension gripped the country, Roosevelt tried to calm the panic-stricken populace:

> First of all, let me assert my firm belief that the only thing we have to fear is fear itself—nameless, unreasoning, unjustified terror which paralyzes needed efforts to convert retreat into advance. In every dark hour of our national life a leadership of frankness and vigor has met with that understanding and support of the people themselves which is essential to victory. I am convinced that you will again give that support to leadership in these critical days.

During the crucial one hundred days that followed his inaugural speech, Roosevelt began the New Deal. He quickly satisfied the public's overwhelming desire for leadership and action by issuing executive orders and introducing legislation which a frightened Congress quickly rubber-stamped. FDR acted in four critical areas: finance, industry, agriculture, and relief (welfare). In combating the Depression, Roosevelt gave the nation no panacea but offered the means through which it might be able to survive the crisis. He did not end the Depression—but many of his programs and the laws he signed got the country through the Depression and remained an effective part of the federal government long after his death. In finance, the Emergency Banking Act (1933) and the Glass-Steagall Banking Act (1933) saved the banking structure and helped prevent a future crisis by creating the Federal Deposit Insurance Corporation. The Truth-in-Securities Act (1933) and the Securities Exchange Act (1934) brought Wall Street under tighter public regulation. In industry, the National Industrial Recovery Act (1933) offered both business and labor opportunities for greater self-government. Later, through the National Labor Relations Act (1935), he concentrated more on allowing labor unions the right to organize. In agriculture, Roosevelt tried to restore farmers' prosperity through the Agriculture Adjustment Act (1933) by subsidizing certain farm products they could not afford to sell at market prices. In relief, FDR straddled the line between welfare and public works. At first, the New Deal doled out money to unemployed people through the Federal Emergency Relief Administration (1933) and sent young men to work camps through the Civilian Conservation Corps (1933).

After the one hundred days had passed, FDR turned away from welfare and made government jobs a primary goal of his administration. Listening to his advisers, Harry Hopkins and Harold L. Ickes, Roosevelt made the federal government the employer of the last resort through the Civil Works Administration (1933), the Public Works Administration (1933), and the Works Progress Administration (1935). In particular, the WPA, which averaged 2,112,000 on its monthly payrolls from 1935 to 1941, was the largest, most visionary, and probably most effective federal relief program ever created. Perhaps the most long-lasting reform achieved by FDR was the Social Security Administration (1935), granting unemployment compensation and old-age pensions.

Roosevelt's New Deal programs generated billions of new dollars throughout the American economy, increasing incomes and causing tax revenues to "trickle up" to the federal and state governments. The jobs also raised the hopes of millions of voters who came to believe that

FDR had saved them from financial disaster. He was the man who put food on their tables, shoes on their feet, and a roof over their heads. In brief, the New Deal was political dynamite, and Roosevelt was the New Deal. The president's charismatic leadership, his inspirational speeches and informal "fireside chats," made him an unbeatable campaigner, as his 1936 Republican opponent learned. Roosevelt crushed Kansas Governor Alfred M. Landon by the largest electoral margin in recent American history, 523 to 8.

In less than three years, Roosevelt created an imperial presidency and vastly enlarged the federal bureaucracy, thus prompting criticisms from conservatives and the Supreme Court. When the Court began invalidating some New Deal programs such as the National Industrial Recovery Act (*Schechter v. United States*, 1935) and the Agriculture Adjustment Act (*Butler v. United States*, 1936), he struck back. In 1937, FDR tried to pack the Court with New Dealers by introducing the Federal Judiciary Reorganization Bill. Although the bill failed to pass Congress, Roosevelt prevailed in this struggle, since the Court's later decisions proved more favorable to New Deal legislation. Still, the court-packing scheme suggested dictatorial ambitions and damaged FDR's reputation in some circles. His popularity further declined as the nation slid deeper into the Depression in 1938, and the president, determined to keep his working majority in Congress, attempted to purge conservative Democrats from his party. This tactic also failed. By 1939, the New Deal, for all practical purposes, was dead.

As the New Deal passed into history, new dangers loomed on the horizon. Totalitarian regimes in Germany, Japan, and Italy threatened America's position in the world. Roosevelt himself recognized that the leaders of these regimes, Adolf Hitler, Hideki Tojo, and Benito Mussolini, would necessitate some changes in American foreign policy when he said that "Dr. Win the War" would have to replace "Dr. New Deal." In this way, he reluctantly began to shift American diplomacy in the direction of confronting these aggressors. After Germany invaded Poland on September 1, 1939, precipitating a declaration of war by England and France, Americans debated whether their country should maintain its isolation or aid its British and French allies. While Roosevelt was preaching neutrality, he won an unprecedented third term, a 449-82 electoral victory over his 1940 Republican opponent, Wendell Willkie.

When the war came to America, it struck with a fury. Possibly no aspect of FDR's foreign policy has evoked more controversy than the role he played in leading the United States into World War II. On December 7, 1941, a little more than a year after he promised that "this country is not going to war," Japanese planes swept down on the American naval base at Pearl Harbor, Hawaii, nearly destroying the United States Pacific Fleet. The declaration of war that followed prompted his critics to complain that he had tricked his nation into war. While the Roosevelt Administration made numerous errors in judgment, FDR did not intentionally expose the military installation to attack in order to drag a reluctant and isolationistic American people into the war.

Shortly after the "day of infamy," Roosevelt met with British prime minister Winston Churchill in the first of several Washington conferences forming a "grand alliance" between the two world leaders and their nations. At the first meeting, Roosevelt agreed to the idea that the allies should place top priority on defeating Germany and Italy, while fighting a holding action against Japan in the Pacific theater. In fact, throughout the war, FDR actively planned and executed top military and diplomatic decisions that affected its outcome and the postwar world. Together with Churchill and Soviet premier Joseph Stalin, he agreed to the formulation of the United Nations. At the Yalta Conference (February, 1945), Roosevelt made another of his extremely controversial decisions that would affect public opinion long after he was gone. In return for Stalin's promise to enter the war against Japan and to allow free elections in the Soviet bloc nations, FDR acquiesced to Russia's hegemony in eastern Poland and other territories occupied by Soviet troops. Because these decisions were kept secret by the chief signatories, Roosevelt never felt the full fury of his critics before his death on April 12, 1945.

Summary

In electing Franklin D. Roosevelt to an unprecedented four terms of office, the American people lent credence to the belief that FDR was the greatest leader ever to hold the presidency. This view was further substantiated by the 1982 survey conducted by Professor Robert K. Murray of Pennsylvania State University among a thousand Ph.D. historians; only Abraham Lincoln ranked ahead of Roosevelt as the best president in American history. Nevertheless, Roosevelt certainly had his critics, and they made valid points: He seems to have had dictatorial ambitions when he circumvented the Constitution and tried to pack the Supreme Court. FDR may have gravely damaged the national economy by allowing the national debt to grow to astronomical proportions. Other presidents followed him down the path of "deficit spending," enlarging upon the problem that he had created in order to combat the Depression. Without a doubt, Roosevelt was one of the most controversial presidents in American history.

FDR created the imperial presidency, in the process setting a precedent for leadership by which all his successors have been evaluated. He took the executive branch, which had lost much of its power and glory, and expanded it beyond the limits achieved by any twentieth century American chief executive. Circumstances such as depression and war, and the force of his indomitable personal character shaped by the adversity of polio, allowed him to restructure the office into its present form—one that casually encroaches on the normal powers and functions of Congress and the Supreme Court. In 1939, for example, in an act that escaped virtually unnoticed by the nation's press, he issued Executive Order 8248, creating the Executive Office of the President and shifting the powerful Bureau of the Budget from the Treasury Department to the White House. Then, when the time came to run for an unprecedented third term in 1940, Roosevelt occupied a perfect position to manipulate the federal economy for reelection purposes, and manipulate it he did—setting another example that his successors have followed.

Although Roosevelt's primary claim to greatness lay in domestic achievements, he made major contributions in foreign policy as well. He was the president who led America to victory over the Axis powers and then achieved the first détente with the new superpower: Soviet Russia. It was in the arena of American politics and government, however, that FDR made his greatest imprint. Even his critics must concede that his impact on the nation was extraordinary.

Bibliography

Abbott, Philip. *The Exemplary Presidency: Franklin D. Roosevelt and the American Political Tradition*. Amherst: University of Massachusetts Press, 1990.

Burns, James MacGregor. *Roosevelt: The Lion and the Fox*. New York: Harcourt Brace, 1956. The best political biography of Roosevelt. Burns stresses FDR's Machiavellian tendencies and his failure to implement an enduring reform coalition.

__________. *Roosevelt: The Soldier of Freedom*. New York: Harcourt Brace Jovanovich, 1970. One of the best books analyzing Roosevelt's role as commander in chief during World War II.

Dallek, Robert. *Franklin D. Roosevelt and American Foreign Policy, 1932-1945*. New York: Oxford University Press, 1979. Dallek received the Bancroft Prize in history for this excellent analytical overview of FDR's foreign policy.

Davis, Kenneth Sydney. *FDR, Into the Storm, 1937-1940: A History*. New York: Random House, 1993.

Divine, Robert A., ed. *Causes and Consequences of World War II*. Chicago: Quadrangle Books, 1969. Very good historiographical collection of essays and accompanying bibliography focusing on the prelude to and aftermath of World War II.

Freidel, Frank. *The Apprenticeship*. Boston: Little, Brown and Co., 1952. The first of a projected six-volume biography. *The Apprenticeship* covers the period from Roosevelt's birth through his tenure as assistant secretary of the Navy. Some reviewers thought this volume suffered from an overemphasis on FDR's early life.

__________. *Franklin D. Roosevelt: A Rendezvous with Destiny*. Boston: Little, Brown, 1990.

__________. *The Ordeal*. Boston: Little, Brown and Co., 1952. The second volume covers the era from 1919 to 1928, including FDR's contracting polio in 1921, his comeback (firmly established by the "Happy Warrior Speech" in 1924), and his election as governor of New York in 1928.

__________. *The Triumph*. Boston: Little, Brown and Co., 1956. The third volume addresses the subject of Roosevelt's two terms as governor of New York, culminating with his election as president of the United States in 1932. This is a very dispassionate analysis of Roosevelt's emergence as the master politician who crushed Herbert Hoover's hopes in the 1932 presidential election.

__________. *Launching the New Deal*. Boston: Little, Brown and Co., 1973. Focuses on the winter of 1932-1933 through the completion of the "One Hundred Days" Congress of June, 1933. This is a very detailed, well-documented study of the early New Deal, although it omits Harry L. Hopkins' Federal Emergency Relief Administration. (Freidel's four-volume series on Roosevelt provides an unusually well-balanced account. The first three volumes constitute the definitive analysis of FDR's early years.)

Leuchtenburg, William E. *Franklin D. Roosevelt and the New Deal.* New York: Harper and Row, 1963. This overview of Roosevelt's foreign and domestic policy up to 1940, the best one-volume treatment of its subject, is scholarly yet highly readable.

Schlesinger, Arthur M., Jr. *The Age of Roosevelt: The Crisis of the Old Order, 1919-1933.* Boston: Houghton Mifflin Co., 1957. This is the first of four projected volumes focusing on the changes experienced by the United States during Franklin Roosevelt's career. Essentially, the first volume analyzes the political, economic, and social currents of the 1920's, culminating with FDR's first presidential election in 1932. Somewhat flawed by the author's tendency to allow his liberalism to prejudice his historical analysis of the period.

__________. *The Age of Roosevelt: The Coming of the New Deal.* Boston: Houghton Mifflin Co., 1959. The second volume of Schlesinger's series analyzes the first two years of Roosevelt's presidency and the New Deal from 1933-1935. The problem of Schlesinger's pro-Roosevelt bias is less serious in this work than in his first volume.

__________. *The Age of Roosevelt: The Politics of Upheaval.* Boston: Houghton Mifflin Co., 1960. The third volume (to date) of Schlesinger's multivolume study of Roosevelt carries the analysis of FDR through his reelection in 1936. As with the first and second volumes, this work is characterized by Schlesinger's highly subjective analysis of political, economic, and social history, but it solidifies Schlesinger's major contribution to the literature on Roosevelt.

J. Christopher Schnell

THEODORE ROOSEVELT

Born: October 27, 1858; New York, New York
Died: January 6, 1919; Oyster Bay, New York

As twenty-sixth president of the United States, Roosevelt energetically led America into the twentieth century. Popular and effective, he promoted major domestic reforms and a larger role for the United States in world affairs. In so doing, he added power to the presidential office.

Early Life

Theodore Roosevelt, twenty-sixth president of the United States, was born October 27, 1858, to a moderately wealthy mercantile family in New York City. His father, Theodore, Sr., was of mostly Dutch ancestry; his mother, Martha Bulloch of Georgia, came from a slaveholding family of Scots and Huguenot French. (During his political career, Roosevelt would claim an ethnic relationship with practically every white voter he met; among his nicknames—besides TR and Teddy—was Old Fifty-seven Varieties.) He was educated at home by tutors and traveled with his parents to the Middle East and Europe.

As a child, Roosevelt was puny, asthmatic, and unable to see much of the world until he was fitted with thick eyeglasses at the age of thirteen. He grew determined to "make" a powerful body, and by strenuous exercise and force of will, young Roosevelt gradually overcame most of his physical shortcomings. Shyness and fear were other weaknesses he conquered. "There were all kinds of things of which I was afraid at first," he later admitted in his *Theodore Roosevelt: An Autobiography* (1913). "But by acting as if I was not afraid I gradually ceased to be afraid." Insecurity, however, was one demon which he never exorcised.

While becoming athletic and assertive, young Roosevelt retained his wide-ranging intellectual curiosity. At Harvard, from which he was graduated in 1880, his absorption with both sports and books made him something of an oddity. Yet career plans remained uncertain. Dull science classes at Harvard dimmed his earlier interest in becoming a naturalist. A year at Columbia University Law School (1880-1881) did not stimulate him toward a legal career. While attending Columbia, he

Theodore Roosevelt *(Library of Congress)*

married Alice Lee, completed his first book, *The Naval War of 1812* (1882), and entered politics in the autumn of 1881 by election to the New York legislature as a Republican representative from Manhattan. For the remainder of his life, except for brief military glory in the Spanish-American War, writing and politics would absorb most of his overflowing energy.

Life's Work

At the age of twenty-three, Roosevelt, the youngest member of New York's legislature, attracted attention because of his anticorruption stance and his flair for the dramatic. He instinctively knew how to make his doings interesting to the press and the public. Personality flaws were obvious from the beginning of his political career (egotism, impulsiveness, a tendency to see everything in black or white, and occasional ruthlessness), yet Roosevelt's virtues were equally apparent and won for him far more admirers than enemies: extraordinary vitality and intelligence, courage, sincerity, conviviality, and, usually, a willingness to make reasonable compromises.

Family tragedy, the death of his young wife, prompted Roosevelt to retire from politics temporarily in 1884. During the next two years, he operated cattle ranches he owned in the badlands of the Dakota Territory, where he found time to write *Hunting Trips of a Ranchman* (1885), the first of a trilogy of books on his Western activities and observations. Ranching proved financially unprofitable, but outdoor life made Roosevelt physically more robust and helped ease the pain of Alice's death. In 1886, he returned to New York and married Edith Kermit Carow, who would bear him four sons and a daughter and rear the daughter, Alice, born to his first wife. That same year, Roosevelt was the unsuccessful Republican nominee for mayor of New York City; he also commenced work on a six-volume history of America's Western expansion, *The Winning of the West* (1889-1896).

Roosevelt did not seek another elective office until he won the governorship of New York in 1898, but in the meantime, he served in three appointive positions: member of the United States Civil Service Commission (1889-1895), president of New York City's Board of Police Commissioners (1895-1897), and assistant secretary of the navy (1897-1898). He resigned the latter post when war with Spain broke out in 1898. Eager for combat, he organized a volunteer cavalry regiment known as the Rough Riders. Most of the land fighting between the United States and Spain occurred in Cuba; the image of Colonel Roosevelt leading a charge up San Juan Hill (in actuality, Kettle Hill) became a public symbol of this brief, victorious war. "Teddy" was a national hero. In November of 1898, he was elected governor of New York and quickly published a new book, *The Rough Riders* (1899), which a humorous critic said should have been titled "Alone in Cuba."

As governor of New York (1899-1900), Roosevelt pursued a vigorous program of political reform. The Republican state machine, wanting him out of New York, promoted his nomination for vice president on the national ticket in 1900. With reluctance, thinking that office might be a dead end, Roosevelt was finally persuaded to accept the nomination, thus becoming President William McKinley's running mate in 1900.

Within a year, McKinley died by an assassin's bullet, and Theodore Roosevelt, at age forty-two, was sworn in as the youngest chief executive in the nation's history. Physically, the new president had an aura of strength despite his average height, spectacles, small hands and feet, and high-pitched voice. His wide, square face, prominent, firm teeth, and massive chest overrode any hint of weakness.

The presidency, Roosevelt once observed, was a "bully pulpit," and he wasted no time in exhorting America toward new horizons in both domestic and foreign policy. Yet Roosevelt was painfully aware that he had become president by mishap. Not until his overwhelming election to a full term in 1904 did he believe that the office was truly his.

Within the nation, President Roosevelt called for a Square Deal for both capital and labor. He saw himself as chief arbiter of conflicts between economic groups; government, he believed, should represent everyone equitably. Believing in capitalism yet convinced that big corporations were too powerful and arrogant, he began a policy of "trust busting." Roosevelt's administration was the first to use successfully the Sherman Anti-Trust Act (passed in 1890) to break up business monopolies. Actually, Roosevelt believed more in regulation than in "busting, " but he hoped to frighten big business into accepting regulation. Privately, he was convinced that, for modern America, industrial and financial combinations were inevitable; he desired to subordinate both big business and labor unions to a stronger central government, which he viewed as the proper instrument for protecting the general interest.

The Hepburn Act, which for the first time gave the Interstate Commerce Commission regulatory power over railroads, was a signal accomplishment of Roosevelt's presidency as were the Pure Food and Drug Act and the Meat Inspection Act, all passed in 1906. Conservation of natural resources was another Roosevelt goal. Over both Democratic and Republican opposition, he cajoled Congress into limiting private exploitation of the nation's wilderness, mineral, and water resources. His administration doubled the number of national parks and tripled the acreage of national forests. Fifty-one wildlife refuges were established. Conservation was probably Roosevelt's most passionate cause and one of his most enduring legacies.

In foreign policy, Roosevelt is remembered by the proverb he once used: "Speak softly and carry a big stick." In practice, however, he bifurcated that approach; he spoke softly toward nations whose power he respected, while saving the big stick for small or weak countries. High-handedly, he "took Panama"—to use his own words—away from the nation of Colombia in 1903, so as to build an isthmian canal; the next year, he proclaimed a protectorate over all of Latin America—the Roosevelt Corollary to the Monroe Doctrine. As for the Far East, Roosevelt worried over but respected the rising power of Japan. He wanted the Japanese to thwart Russian expansionism but not to dominate Asia. He assumed that Great Britain and the United States would draw closer in worldwide interests; he viewed Germany, Japan, and Russia as probable enemies of a future Anglo-American alliance.

Roosevelt did not run for reelection. He had pledged after his 1904 triumph that he would not seek or accept another nomination. It was a promise he later regretted. The Republican Party in 1908 chose Roosevelt's close personal friend William Howard Taft who, with Roosevelt's blessing, easily won the presidency. Yet Taft's troubled term (1909-1913) split the Republicans into Progressive and Old Guard wings, and by 1910, Roosevelt angrily decided that Taft had capitulated to the Old Guard. Consequently, Roosevelt attempted to regain the White House in 1912. After losing a bitter contest to Taft for the Republican nomination, Roosevelt burst into the general election as a third party (Progressive, or Bull Moose Party) candidate, thus virtually guaranteeing victory for Democratic nominee Woodrow Wilson. Roosevelt's personal popularity allowed him to finish second in the 1912 presidential election, but without a viable national organization, he lost heavily to Wilson in the electoral count. Taft ran third.

Roosevelt spent most of the remainder of his life writing books, exploring Brazil's backcountry, and criticizing President Wilson, whom he hated. He wanted to fight in World War I but was refused a commission. His health weakened by infections contracted in Brazil, Theodore Roosevelt died in his sleep on January 6, 1919, at the age of sixty.

Summary

"The Republican Roosevelt," as one historian termed him, is usually ranked among the best American presidents. An inspirational leader and superb administrator, he revitalized the presidency. His career seemed to defy the adage that power corrupts. In mental prowess, he had few equals in American political history; indeed, Roosevelt ranks among the rarest of human types: an intellectual who was also a man of action.

Ideologically, Roosevelt defies simple definition. Whether he was an "enlightened" conservative or a "Progressive liberal" remains in dispute. Roosevelt himself refused to accept pat labels. He viewed himself as a moral leader who combined practicality and idealism for the purpose of unifying the nation's opposing economic and social interests into a mutually beneficial synthesis.

Coming to the presidency at the dawn of the twentieth century, Roosevelt understood that America was fast becoming a complex urban, industrial nation and that a new balance was needed between individualism and the collective good. In foreign policy, Roosevelt acted upon his conviction that the old isolationism was no longer possible and that the United States, because of its growing strength, was destined to be a world power.

Bibliography

Beale, Howard K. *Theodore Roosevelt and the Rise of America to World Power*. Baltimore: The Johns Hopkins University Press, 1956. Best study of Roosevelt's foreign policy. Beale demonstrates that Roosevelt had prophetic insights yet was blind toward the nationalistic aspirations of "backward" colonial peoples.

Blum, John M. *The Republican Roosevelt*. Cambridge: Harvard University Press, 1954. "Brilliant" is the usual word for characterizing this book. Blum explains Roosevelt as an astute conservative who welcomed change as the only means of preserving what was vital from the past.

Chessman, G. Wallace. *Theodore Roosevelt and the Politics of Power*. Boston: Little, Brown, 1969. Most recommended brief biography of Roosevelt. Sympathetic to Roosevelt, it is a skillful blend of narrative and analysis.

Gould, Lewis L. *The Presidency of Theodore Roosevelt*. Lawrence: University Press of Kansas, 1991.

Harbaugh, William Henry. *Power and Responsibility: The Life and Times of Theodore Roosevelt*. Rev. ed. New York: Oxford University Press, 1975. The most thorough full-length biography of Roosevelt. Judiciously balances his virtues and limitations.

Miller, Nathan. *Theodore Roosevelt: A Life*. New York: Morrow, 1992.

Morris, Edmund. *The Rise of Theodore Roosevelt*. New York: Coward, McCann and Geoghegan, 1979. Splendidly written, insightful treatment of Roosevelt's life from birth to the beginning of his presidency in 1901. Especially good for Roosevelt's ranching days in the Dakota Territory and his exploits during the Spanish-American War.

Mowry, George E. *The Era of Theodore Roosevelt: 1900-1912*. New York: Harper and Row, 1958. The standard study of the first dozen years of twentieth century America, when Roosevelt was the central political figure. Invaluable for understanding Roosevelt's actions within the context of his time of ascendancy.

Pringle, Henry F. *Theodore Roosevelt: A Biography*. New York: Harcourt, Brace, 1931. This readable Pulitzer Prize biography of Roosevelt was long considered the definitive work, but later historians tended to fault Pringle for overemphasizing Roosevelt's immaturity and bellicosity.

Roosevelt, Theodore. *The Writings of Theodore Roosevelt*. Edited by William H. Harbaugh. Indianapolis: Bobbs-Merrill, 1967. An excellent one-volume anthology of Roosevelt's own words, including excerpts from his autobiography.

William I. Hair

ELIHU ROOT

Born: February 15, 1845; Clinton, New York
Died: February 7, 1937; New York, New York

As secretary of war under William McKinley and Theodore Roosevelt, Root administered territories gained at the end of the Spanish-American War and initiated reforms in army administration. He pursued a conservative line as secretary of state under Roosevelt and later as United States senator from New York, and argued for the value of international law as a political instrument.

Early Life

Born in Clinton, New York, on February 15, 1845, Elihu Root was the third of four sons of Oren and Nancy Buttrick Root. His father was professor of mathematics at Hamilton College in Clinton, and Elihu was valedictorian of the Hamilton class of 1864. He was graduated from New York University Law School in 1867. Root's legal career was successful from the start; in time he became one of the leading members of the American bar. Specializing in cases involving large corporations, he was labeled a Wall Street lawyer. Among his corporate clients were the Havemeyer Sugar Refining Company and the traction syndicate controlled by William C. Whitney and Thomas F. Ryan. Root's success as a lawyer and later as a member of McKinley's and Roosevelt's cabinets came from his capacity to master detail, the concise and logical qualities of his written arguments, and his ready wit. Reserved and a bit stiff with those he did not know well, Root formed strong friendships with men such as Theodore Roosevelt, William Howard Taft, and Henry Cabot Lodge.

Prior to his appointment as secretary of war in 1899, Root was involved in Republican Party politics on the local and state levels. He served from 1883 to 1885 as United States attorney for the district of Southern New York; he was a manager of the New York State constitutional convention of 1894. His association with Roosevelt began around 1882, when Root provided legal advice about an obstacle to Roosevelt's running for the state legislature. Root ran Roosevelt's unsuccessful campaign for mayor of New York City in 1886, he provided advice when Roosevelt served as city police commissioner, and in 1898 he resolved a question about Roosevelt's legal residence that enabled him to run for and be elected governor.

A thin, wiry man of average height, Root had closely clipped hair and a full mustache, both of which turned white in his old age. In 1878, he married Clara Frances Wales. An attentive husband and father to his daughter, Edith, and sons, Elihu and Edward Wales, Root often made decisions about his public career based upon his wife's distaste for life in Washington, D.C.

Life's Work

While Root declined President McKinley's offer to serve on the commission concluding a peace treaty with Spain, he accepted appointment as secretary of war in 1899. McKinley said that he wanted a lawyer in the job because of the need to administer the territories acquired during the war. The legal problems posed by the American occupation of Puerto Rico, Cuba, and the Philippines were complex, and the transition from military to civilian governments required a different solution in each case. In all three territories, however, Root favored improvements in education, health care, and transportation.

The absence of a strong movement for independence in Puerto Rico led Root to conclude that the best solution would be an indefinite period of American control. He proposed a highly centralized governmental structure centered on a governor and legislative council appointed by the president. Root persuaded McKinley that Puerto Rico's economic well-being depended upon an exemption from the Dingley Tariff rates, but the Administration accepted a temporary lower rate in the Foraker Act of 1900. Congress also provided for a popularly elected lower house in a bicameral Puerto Rican legislature, and Root accepted the change.

The terms of the peace treaty with Spain called for Cuban independence, and by 1902 Root had established a native government for Cuba and had withdrawn American military forces. He first replaced General John R. Brooke with General Leonard Wood as the military governor, and he instructed Wood to mount a program to repair war damage and to modernize schools, roads, and systems of sanitation. A constitutional convention met in 1901; the delegates were elected by Cubans, but Root had restricted the vote to property owners, former soldiers, and those who were literate. The constitution produced by the convention contained guarantees of American interests originally outlined in the Platt Amendment to the Army Appropriation Act of March 2, 1901. The government of the United States was granted the right to buy or lease bases on Cuban soil, and it was given the right to intervene with troops if Cuban independence or the stability of the Cuban government were threatened.

Root faced a more difficult task in dealing with the situation in the Philippines. Forces led by Emilio Aguinaldo were in revolt against the American military government, and Root, as secretary of war, had both to bring home the twenty-one thousand troops in the islands whose enlistments were running out and to replace them with an effectively trained force which eventually numbered seventy-four thousand. It took two years to end the guerrilla war, and in the interval the report of a commission headed by President Jacob Schurman of Cornell led Root to conclude that the Philippines were not ready for independence or for a great degree of self-government. In 1900, McKinley and Root sent Judge William Howard Taft to Manila at the head of a second commission charged with replacing the military government. Taft became governor general, and a bicameral legislature was created. Root's instructions to the Taft commission, adopted by Congress in the Organic Act of 1902, became the formula for government of the Philippines pursued by the Roosevelt Administration.

Partly as a result of his activities as a colonial administrator, Root saw the need for reforming the army bureaucracy. He instituted a general staff system headed by a chief of staff directly responsible to the secretary of war, and he ended the practice of making permanent army staff appointments in Washington. There was a regular rotation of officers from the staff to the line. Root called for legislation which established the Army War College and which made the national guard the country's militia. He took steps to see that the guard received the same training and equipment as the regular army.

Root resigned as secretary of war on February 1, 1904, despite the objections of President Roosevelt, but he returned to the cabinet as secretary of state on July 7, 1905. He played no part in Roosevelt's arbitration of an ending to the Russo-Japanese War by means of the Treaty of Portsmouth; nor did he have anything to do with securing for the United States the right to build a canal through the Isthmus of Panama. Root's chief actions as secretary of state were designed to bolster the fabric of international agreements ensuring world peace. He placed emphasis on friendly relationships with the nations of South America, and in 1906 he undertook a lengthy personal tour of that continent which led to Latin American participation in the Second Hague Peace Conference in 1907.

In the area of Canadian-American relations, Root resolved the North Atlantic coastal fisheries dispute. With the help of Lord Bryce, the British ambassador in Washington, he found a solution to the Alaska boundary issue. Root negotiated a voluntary immigration restriction agreement with Japan after the unrest in California over Japanese labor precipitated exclusion laws. By means of the Root-Takahira agreement and an arbitration treaty concluded in 1908, he established mechanisms for consultation between the governments of the United States and Japan. Root was committed to voluntary arbitration of international disputes, and during his tenure as secretary of state, he negotiated bilateral arbitration agreements with twenty-four foreign governments. In 1912, he was awarded the Nobel Peace Prize for these efforts to move international disagreements within a judicial framework.

In the instructions that were given to the American delegates to the 1907 Hague Peace Conference, Root outlined plans for a permanent court of arbitral justice and committed the American government to its establishment. The nations represented at the conference, however, could not agree on a procedure for selecting judges. The idea was put aside until 1920, when Root, invited by the League of Nations, served on the committee that drafted the statute establishing the World Court. Root worked with President Warren G. Harding and Secretary of State Charles Evans Hughes to gain approval for American membership in the court, but congressional opposition led by Senator Henry Cabot Lodge frustrated the effort. In 1929, Root returned to Geneva to serve on the committee revising the 1920 statute, and he devised a compromise on advisory opinions, usually termed the "Root formula," meeting United States objections to certain classes of cases coming before the World Court. Delays in submitting these changes to Congress and the changing political situation led to the treaty's eventual defeat in 1935.

By that time, Root was ninety years old, and his public career was behind him. He had resigned as secretary of state on March 5, 1909, before assuming the office of United States senator, to which he had been elected by the New York State legislature. Root's career as a senator was less significant than his previous career as a member of the McKinley and Roosevelt cabinets. Root lacked sympathy with the Progressive legislation supported by William Howard Taft, Roosevelt's successor, and he grew disenchanted with Woodrow Wilson's policy of neutrality toward the conflict in Europe that developed into World War 1.

Root supported Wilson's efforts to mobilize once the United States entered World War 1, and in 1917 he went to Russia as head of a mission to the Provisional Revolutionary Government. Wilson did not appoint Root as an American representative to the peace conference at Versailles, but the former secretary of state gave public support to Wilson's plan to join the League of Nations. He had reservations about Article X of the League Covenant and wanted modifications in the terms of the treaty, but he encouraged Senator Lodge to support American membership. Lodge, however, came out in opposition to both the Treaty of Versailles and membership in the League of Nations.

Elihu Root died in New York City on February 7, 1937. He was buried in the cemetery on the Hamilton College campus in Clinton, New York, his birthplace and family home.

Summary

The achievements of Elihu Root's long period of public service fall into two categories. The first is a set of pragmatic solutions to specific problems. His differing approaches to the governing of Puerto Rico, Cuba, and the Philippines, like the reforms he initiated in the structure and training of the army, testify to his skills as a lawyer. Root's work as secretary of war demonstrates the ability of the United States at the beginning of the twentieth century to take on the responsibilities of a global power. The second category of achievement is Root's consistent efforts to forge a judicial system to interpret a growing body of international law. His work as secretary of state on a series of bilateral arbitration treaties, his support of Wilson's call for a League of Nations, and his efforts to establish the World Court testify to his commitment. Root declined an appointment to the World Court itself. Given the fact that the United States was not a party to the treaty establishing the court, he believed that it was inappropriate for him to sit as a judge.

Root's skills were best suited to administration and negotiation. In addition to his work on behalf of the League of Nations and the World

Court, he was one of four American delegates to the Conference on the Limitation of Armaments held in Washington, D.C., between November 12, 1921, and February 6, 1922. He served as president or chairman of a number of the organizations founded by Andrew Carnegie, including the Carnegie Endowment for International Peace, and he advised every administration through that of Franklin D. Roosevelt in the area of foreign affairs.

Bibliography

Coletta, Paolo E. *The Presidency of William Howard Taft*. Lawrence: University Press of Kansas, 1973. Clear account of the Roosevelt-Taft split. Notes Root's ties to both men; examines the 1912 election campaign.

Gould, Lewis L. *The Presidency of William McKinley*. Lawrence: University Press of Kansas, 1981. Gould argues that McKinley shaped military and foreign policy more aggressively than previous scholars have believed.

Jessup, Philip C. *Elihu Root*. 2 vols. New York: Dodd, Mead, 1938. The most complete account of Root's public career and his political views, this book was begun during Root's lifetime and benefited from the use of his papers.

Leopold, Richard W. *Elihu Root and the Conservative Tradition*. Boston: Little, Brown, 1954. Leopold traces Root's political conservatism but also shows his pragmatic interest in international law.

Millett, Allan Reed. *The Politics of Intervention: The Military Occupation of Cuba, 1906-1909*. Columbus: Ohio State University Press, 1968. This study stresses the role of the United States Army in the policymaking process which determined the nature of the American occupation of Cuba.

Mowry, George E. *The Era of Theodore Roosevelt: 1900-1912*. New York: Harper and Row, 1958. Granting Root's service to Roosevelt, Mowry notes that the president's growing progressivism was matched by Root's increasing conservatism.

Pratt, Julius W. *America's Colonial Experiment: How the United States Gained, Governed, and in Part Gave Away a Colonial Empire*. Englewood Cliffs, N.J.: Prentice-Hall, 1951. Pratt's study pulls together the story of America's involvement in Cuba, the Philippines, Puerto Rico, Hawaii, and Central America.

Robert C. Petersen

Nellie Tayloe Ross

Born: November 29, 1876; St. Joseph, Missouri
Died: December 19, 1977; Washington, D.C.

The first woman governor of a state (Wyoming) in the United States, Ross later served as an officer in the Democratic Party and as a director of the U.S. Mint, one of the first women to head a federal agency.

Early Life

Nellie Davis Tayloe was born on November 29, 1876, in St. Joseph, Missouri. Her father, James Wynn Tayloe, was from a prominent Southern family, one of whose members had built the Octagon House in Washington, D.C., where President James Madison and his wife Dolley lived after the British burned the White House during the War of 1812. Her mother, Elizabeth Blair Green Tayloe, was descended from a family that claimed a distant kinship with George Washington.

Nellie attended public and private schools and had private instruction as well. Her family eventually moved to Omaha, Nebraska, where she completed a two-year program as a kindergarten teacher and taught briefly before her marriage.

While visiting relatives in Tennessee, she met and fell in love with a young lawyer, William Bradford Ross. He moved to Cheyenne, Wyoming, before marrying Nellie in 1902. The Rosses had four sons: the twins, George Tayloe and James Ambrose, born in 1903; Alfred Duff, born in 1905, who died at ten months of age; and William Bradford, born in 1912. Nellie devoted herself to her home and family during her marriage. She was active in the Cheyenne Woman's Club, which concentrated on intellectual self-improvement, and she often presented programs there.

William Ross practiced law and occasionally ran for political office. As a Democrat in a Republican state, however, he had little political success until, to his wife's dismay, he was elected governor of Wyoming in 1922 by a coalition of Democrats and Progressive Republicans. In September of 1924, he became ill and underwent an appendectomy. Complications from the surgery led to his death on October 2, 1924.

Life's Work

Because Governor Ross's death occurred close to the upcoming general election on November 4, 1924, Wyoming law required that his successor be elected then. Democratic Party leaders in Wyoming offered Nellie Tayloe Ross the nomination to fill the remainder of her husband's term. She did not reply and the party took her silence for acquiescence, nominating her on October 14. She had no political experience except for what she had acquired as her husband's confidant and in her tenure as the governor's wife. Although she lived in a state where women had voted since 1869, she had played no role in the woman suffrage campaign. She later indicated that she had accepted the nomination because she wished her husband's programs to continue and believed that she understood what he would have done better than anyone else; she also expressed the need for some purpose in her own life as she coped with the grief of widowhood. The Republicans nominated Eugene J. Sullivan of Casper, an attorney whose ties to the oil industry may have hurt his campaign since both Wyoming and the nation were immersed in the Teapot Dome scandal involving federal oil lands (including property located in Wyoming).

Nellie Ross did not campaign for office. Friends paid for a few political advertisements, and she wrote two open letters stating her intentions. She probably had two advantages in the election. The first was the sympathy of the voters for her widowhood. She indicated, and many people agreed, that a vote for her was a tribute to her deceased husband. The second advantage was the popular support among citizens for Wyoming to become the first state to elect a woman governor, since it had been first in 1869 to allow women to vote. This election would be the state's only chance to secure this distinction, since Miriam A. ("Ma") Ferguson, wife of impeached former governor James A. Ferguson, was likely to be elected governor of Texas in November. Although Ross won election easily, she did not help other Democrats in Wyoming in what was generally a catastrophic year for Democratic candidates nationwide in the wake of the crushing defeat of the party's presidential candidate by Republican Calvin Coolidge.

Nellie Tayloe Ross was inaugurated as the thirteenth governor of Wyoming on January 5, 1925, still wearing mourning clothes. In her brief address she stated that her administration would not be a new one, but rather a continuation of her husband's. She entered office with much popular sympathy and an administration in place. Since Ferguson was not sworn in as governor of Texas until January 25, Nellie Tayloe Ross was the nation's first woman governor.

When the Wyoming legislature convened in January of 1926, the new governor gave her first major speech, based on her husband's notes on his plans for that legislative session. She called for reductions in both state expenditures and taxes; for state assistance to the economically depressed agricultural industry; and for banking reform, noting the number of recently failed banks. She championed protective legislation for miners and for women and children, and she requested unsuccessfully that Wyoming ratify the federal amendment prohibiting child labor.

Ross recognized that the Republican-dominated legislature had little reason to cooperate with her. On some issues, such as banking reform, she was able to work out compromises with Republican leaders. In a few instances, she used the veto. She believed that her veto of a bill requiring a special election (rather than appointment by the governor) to fill a vacancy in Wyoming's delegation to the United States Senate caused her defeat in 1926. Wyoming's elderly Republican senator had been reelected only a short time earlier, and it was believed that he would not live to complete his term. Republicans did not want their Democratic governor to have the opportunity to appoint a Democrat to the position.

Ross was aware of the public's intense scrutiny of her actions and knew that if she made mistakes as governor, people would use them to claim that women should not hold high elective office. She found curiosity-seekers constantly in her office and on the porch of her home. Although she received invitations to speak all over the country, she declined them all. When she appeared in Calvin Coolidge's Inaugural Parade in Washington, D.C., she got the largest ovation. Many Easterners still thought of Wyoming as an uncivilized place, and its cultured, gracious governor attracted attention simply because she was so different from their expectations.

As an administrator, Ross received mixed reviews. She removed from office some administrators appointed by her husband who were not meeting her expectations. She lamented the difficulties of enforcing Prohibition and advocated better law enforcement. She stood up to the federal government on issues of federal lands and water allocation.

Nellie Ross was nominated by the Democrats for reelection in 1926, but was defeated in a close election by the Republican candidate, Frank C. Emerson. While her veto of the senatorial special election law was one issue, Republicans vaguely alluded to the idea that a man would be a better governor than a woman. Democrats tried unsuccessfully to win women voters by suggesting that a rejection of Ross would be a rejection of woman suffrage. Ultimately she probably was defeated because she was a Democrat in a Republican state and the sympathy issue that had helped her in 1924 was no longer a factor. As it was, she did better than any other statewide Democratic candidate in Wyoming.

Ross never again sought elective public office. Instead, she lectured and wrote articles for magazines. She became involved in national politics, serving as a Wyoming committeewoman to the Democratic National Committee (DNC) and then as vice chairman of the DNC, in charge of activities for women. In 1928, she seconded the presidential nomination of New York Governor Alfred E. Smith. With Eleanor Roosevelt, she headed the campaign drive launched by the party's Women's Division to generate support for Smith. Already a popular speaker, Ross traveled around the country making speeches tirelessly and unsuccessfully for Smith's election. Four years later, Ross was active in the Women's Speakers' Bureau, campaigning for the Democratic presidential nominee, Franklin D. Roosevelt.

With the election of Roosevelt as president in 1932, women became more visible in the federal government. Eleanor Roosevelt acted on her husband's behalf and publicly involved herself in policy issues to an unprecedented degree—one that was not duplicated until Hillary Rodham Clinton became First Lady in 1993.

Franklin D. Roosevelt decided that he wanted to be the first president to appoint a woman to the cabinet. Ross was considered for either secretary of the interior or secretary of labor, but Roosevelt selected Frances Perkins as secretary of labor instead. He appointed a number of women to federal office; among them were Ruth Bryan Owens as minister to Denmark (1933-1936), Josephine Roche as assistant secretary of the Treasury (1934-1937), and Nellie Tayloe Ross as director of the United States Mint.

As director of the Mint, Ross dealt with the American gold and silver bullion reserve and the minting of coins for the United States and several foreign governments. Appointed in 1933, she served as the Mint's first woman director. At that time, huge quantities of gold and silver poured into the U.S. government's coffers. Ross discovered that most of the work was still being done by hand and directed that the process be automated. She emphasized efficiency and was able to reduce the costs of her operation significantly. In 1950, she informed an astonished Congressional Appropriations Committee that she had not needed all of her previous year's appropriation and wanted to return about $1 million of her $4.8 million appropriation. Her efficiency plans reduced the labor needs of the mint and resulted in the discharge of about 3,000 of the Mint's 4,000 employees. She continued as director of the Mint in the Roosevelt and Truman administrations and was not replaced until the Republican administration of President Dwight D. Eisenhower came to power in 1952. Ross continued to make her home in Washington, D.C., until her death on December 19, 1977.

Summary

Nellie Tayloe Ross never intended to have a political career. She believed that women belonged at home and was content there until her husband's death thrust her into politics. Her election was probably attributable to public sympathy generated by her husband's death. She was the first of many women elected to fill out their husbands' unexpired terms in office.

As the nation's first woman governor, she did not have a tremendous impact. She was probably an average governor, although she was regarded more favorably than Texas governor Miriam A. Ferguson. She achieved few of her goals because of Republican control of the legislature. Her defeat for reelection was probably the result of being a Democrat in a predominantly Republican state.

After her defeat, she focused her attention on other political matters by becoming active in the Democratic National Committee and appearing as a popular and effective speaker. Her loyalty and support for Franklin D. Roosevelt led him to consider her for several offices before appointing her the first woman director of the United States Mint. She administered the Mint economically and efficiently for almost twenty years. Although she was not the most visible woman in the New Deal, Ross was one of the most durable and effective.

Bibliography

"First U.S. Woman Governor Celebrates Her Centennial During the Bicentennial." *Aging* 268 (February/March, 1977): 13-14. Aimed at a general audience, this biographical sketch provides a concise assessment of Ross's life and career. Discusses her activities after leaving office as governor, when she worked as a lecturer on the Chautauqua circuit and helped organize the women's division of the Democratic Party.

Huch, Ronald K. "Nellie Tayloe Ross of Wyoming Becomes First Female Governor." In *Great Events from History II: Human Rights*, edited by Frank N. Magill. Pasadena, Calif.: Salem Press, 1992. This is a brief, well-written account of her election as governor in 1924, with an analysis of its impact.

Othman, Frederick C. "She Makes Our Money." *Reader's Digest* 57 (November, 1950): 141-144. This condensation of a previously published newspaper article is a rare account of Ross's years as director of the Mint and is especially useful for information on her efforts to automate it.

Ross, Nellie Tayloe. "The Governor Lady." *Good Housekeeping* 85 (August, 1927), 30-31, 118-124; (September, 1927), 36-37, 206-218; (October, 1927), 72-73, 180-197. These articles provide Ross's own account of her years as governor. Except for Barbara Jean Aslakson's thesis, "Nellie Tayloe Ross: First Woman Governor" (University of Wyoming, 1960), these magazine pieces contain the best account of those years.

Scharff, Virginia. "Feminism, Femininity, and Power: Nellie Tayloe Ross and the Woman Politician's Dilemma." *Frontiers* 15, no. 3 (Spring, 1995): 87-107.

Ware, Susan. *Beyond Suffrage: Women in the New Deal*. Cambridge, Mass.: Harvard University Press, 1981. This is a well-researched account of influential women in the New Deal. It has information on Ross's activities in the Democratic National Committee, placing them in the context of women's roles in the New Deal.

__________. *Holding Their Own: American Women in the 1930s*. Boston: Twayne, 1982. This well-documented account is useful in placing Ross's activities in the context of her times, but it has only two direct references to her.

Judith A. Parsons

CARL SCHURZ

Born: March 2, 1829; Liblar, Prussia
Died: May 14, 1906; New York, New York

Recognized as a leader of the German-American community in the United States, this partisan of liberty fled Germany after the revolutions of 1848 and made a career as a journalist and politician, serving as a Union general in the Civil War, a senator from Missouri, and a secretary of the interior.

Early Life

Carl Schurz was born to Christian and Marianne (Jüssen) Schurz on March 2, 1829, in one of the outbuildings of a moated castle in the Prussian Rhineland (modern West Germany), where his grandfather worked for Baron Wolf von Metternich. His family was of humble origin but was respected in the local context of village life; his grandfather was the count's estate manager, one uncle was the mayor of a neighboring village, and his father was the Liblar schoolmaster. Schurz was reared a Roman Catholic, but with a strong dose of Enlightenment skepticism; as an adult, he considered himself a "freethinker." As a boy, he enjoyed the run of Metternich's estate, its formal gardens, its forests, and its farmlands. His parents noted his unusual intelligence and his musical skill and resolved to make sacrifices to give him a higher education. Thus he left his father's school in the village, going to preparatory school at neighboring Brühl and then at Cologne, several miles away. When he was seventeen, the family moved to the nearest university town, Bonn, so that the boy could study there, even though his parents had suffered financial reverses which temporarily put his father in debtors' prison.

At Bonn, Schurz began to make a name for himself both in the politically liberal fraternal organizations and as a budding scholar, under the tutelage of the young Romantic, Gottfried Kinkel. Then came the revolutionary fervor of 1848. Immediately, Schurz interrupted his formal education and turned to a life of political activity. Like many young men of his generation, he saw 1848 as the opportunity to achieve a unified German state with a liberal-democratic constitution. Too young to stand for election himself, he turned to journalism and popular agitation to support his goals. His zeal for freedom and justice, his skills as a writer and speaker, and his tireless and combative commitment to his cause were characteristics that would distinguish him as a prominent American statesman years later. He

Carl Schurz *(Library of Congress)*

joined the revolutionary army which fought against the old monarchies and barely escaped with his life when it was forced to surrender. In 1850, he returned to Prussia from exile in France and Switzerland in disguise and rescued Professor Kinkel from the prison to which the Prussians had condemned him. After spending a brief time in Paris and London, where he wooed and married Margarethe Meyer, daughter of a well-to-do Hamburg mercantile family, he decided to leave the Old World for America. If he could not be a citizen of a free Germany, he concluded, he would become a free citizen of the United States.

The tall, slim young man with thick glasses affected the flowing hair and mustache of a Romantic liberal in 1848; as he matured, he was recognizable for his bushy beard and sharp features, so often caricatured by Thomas Nast.

Life's Work

Schurz and his young wife arrived in the United States in 1852, staying first in Philadelphia and eventually settling in Watertown, Wisconsin, in 1855. As an immigrant, he was neither tired nor poor. His wife's dowry was enough to set him up in business. His fame as a daring fighter for freedom in Germany, his solid education, his gifts as a writer and speaker, and his political ambition combined to make him a well-known figure almost immediately. Although he rarely stood for election himself, his persuasiveness with German-American voters made him a force to be reckoned with in the ethnic politics of that age.

He led the Wisconsin delegation to the Republican National Convention in 1860. Though originally pledged to William H. Seward, he became an avid supporter of Abraham Lincoln once he had received the nomination. Schurz traveled more than twenty-one thousand miles campaigning for Lincoln, speaking in both English and German, and was credited with swinging much of the German-American vote away from its traditional inclination for the Democratic Party and into Lincoln's camp. In gratitude, Lincoln appointed him minister to Spain and, after the onset of the Civil War, brigadier and then major general in the Union army. Schurz's military career did little to enhance his reputation. He was only in his early thirties, and his high rank was clearly a result of political influence rather than demonstrated military skills. Schurz did his best, however, to contribute to the Union cause, seeing action at the Second Battle of Bull Run, Gettysburg, and Chancellorsville. Lincoln invited Schurz to report directly to him on the wartime situation, which Schurz did with great energy, pressing the president to emancipate the slaves.

After the war, Schurz settled in St. Louis as part owner and editor of the German language *Westliche Post*. His wife never liked the American Midwest, however, and so she spent much of her time in Europe. While visiting his family in Germany in 1868, Schurz made a widely reported visit to Berlin, where the onetime revolutionary was warmly received by Otto von Bismarck, now prime minister of Prussia and chancellor of the emerging German Empire.

Schurz was critical of President Andrew Johnson but enthusiastically supported Ulysses S. Grant in the 1868 elections. German-American forces were influential in Missouri politics, and the state legislature sent him to Washington, D.C., as a senator. Once there, he became disillusioned with the apparent corruption in the spoils system, and he turned his polemical skills to the issue of civil service reform. This challenge to the status quo alienated many of his party allies, and he was not returned to office in 1874. The Senate provided a platform for Schurz's oratorical skills, and he gained a national reputation as a spokesman for reform and for the German-American community. Because of his criticisms of United States politicians, some alleged that he was not a patriotic American. He responded with a turn of phrase which has become famous: "My country right or wrong: if right, to be kept right; and if wrong, to be set right."

No partisan loyalist, Schurz was active in founding the Liberal Republican Party, which supported Horace Greeley for president over Grant in 1872. With the election of 1876, however, he returned to the Republican Party, supporting Rutherford B. Hayes, and after Hayes's victory, Schurz was made secretary of the interior. He attempted to initiate environmental controls, particularly over forest lands, and to follow a humanitarian policy with respect to the Indians. Inevitably, his liberal idealism was unable to overcome deep-seated interests which opposed his policies. He left government office in 1881, never to serve again, and pursued his career as a journalist, author, and lecturer. He made New York his home, where he became editor in chief of the *Evening Post* and, eventually, *Harper's Weekly*.

As an independent, he found himself among the "Mugwumps," who were more committed to his liberal ideals, especially civil service reform, than to any political party. Looking at his record, one sees a man who supported James A. Garfield (Republican) in 1880, Grover Cleveland (Democrat) in 1884, 1888, and 1892, William McKinley (Republican) in 1896, William Jennings Bryan (Democrat) in 1900, and Alton B. Parker (Democrat) in 1904. In an age when corruption was often an accepted part of the political process, Schurz remained free of its taint. His nineteenth century liberalism has been criticized as being narrow and doctrinaire, a *laissez-faire* philosophy which had little room for labor unions and social programs. Yet his concepts of personal liberty, due process of law, and clean government surely put him in the mainstream of American political thought and action. He favored suffrage for blacks (but not for women) and spoke out strongly against anti-Semitism. In the 1890's, he looked with dismay upon American diplomatic and military expansion and, polemically as ever, crusaded as an anti-imperialist. The onetime general loathed war and its accompanying atrocities; moreover, he seemed to fear that an active policy overseas by the United States might at some time lead to a conflict with the land of his birth, Germany. As a man in his sixties and seventies, he traveled and spoke as avidly against an American empire as he had once fought for Lincoln's election and freedom for the slaves. Though he no longer was alleged to be able to swing the German-American vote in major elections, he was widely praised as that community's leader and was showered with honors. He died peacefully at his home in New York City at the age of seventy-seven.

Summary

Schurz saw himself as "the main intermediary between German and American culture." He continued to be equally fluent in German and English, writing his widely read memoirs in both languages. He traveled back and forth many times between the United States and the old country, filled with pride for both. When accused of mixed loyalties, he responded that he loved equally his "old mother" and his "new bride." Stalwart and eloquent, he vigorously defended the cause of freedom, as he saw it, in Germany and in the United States. His stubborn dedication to his principles and his combative temperament sometimes earned for him the enmity of political opponents. Surely not even all German-Americans supported him on every issue. As a group, however, they were proud of his accomplishments, the most impressive of any German immigrant at that time, and they agreed with him that fondness for their country of origin did not diminish their patriotism as Americans. Schurz would have been deeply saddened by the political and diplomatic events of the first half of the twentieth century which brought the United States and Germany into conflict, but much heartened by the development of a firm alliance between America and a liberal-democratic Germany after 1945.

Bibliography

Easum, Chester V. *The Americanization of Carl Schurz*. Chicago: University of Chicago Press, 1929. A brief, older work, upon which further scholarship on Schurz has depended.

Fuess, Claude M. *Carl Schurz, Reformer: 1829-1906*. Edited by Allan Nevins. New York: Dodd, Mead and Co., 1932. A gentlemanly biography by a scholar of German-American parentage.

Schurz, Carl. *Intimate Letters of Carl Schurz: 1841-1869*. Edited and translated by Joseph Schafer. Madison: State Historical Society of Wisconsin, 1928. Hitherto unpublished letters, mostly to members of his family, which shed light on Schurz's career and personal life beyond that shown in the six-volume set cited below.

__________. *The Reminiscences of Carl Schurz*. 3 vols. Garden City, N.Y.: Doubleday and Co., 1907-1908. An entertaining and enlightening view of Schurz as he saw himself, with insightful sketches of the great men he knew, especially Lincoln, Bismarck, and a long list of American political figures. A modern abridgment by Wayne Andrews (New York: Scribners, 1961) is available, with an introduction by Allan Nevins.

__________. *Speeches, Correspondence and Political Papers of Carl Schurz*. Edited by Frederic Bancroft. 6 vols. New York: G. P. Putnam's Sons, 1913. The vast array of Schurz's political output is set forth in this old, but well-edited, collection of his works.

Trefousse, Hans L. *Carl Schurz: A Biography*. Knoxville: University of Tennessee Press, 1982. A scholarly study of Schurz, based on exhaustive study of the printed and manuscript sources, in the United States and in Europe, including some private letters to his companion in later life, Fanny Chapman. Excellent notes and bibliography.

Gordon R. Mork

William H. Seward

Born: May 16, 1801; Florida, New York
Died: October 10, 1872; Auburn, New York

As an antislavery leader who helped to found the Republican Party during the 1850's, Seward, who contested Lincoln for the presidential nomination in 1860, went on to become one of the United States' greatest secretaries of state.

Early Life

The ancestors of William Henry Seward came to America from England during the early eighteenth century. His parents, Samuel and Mary Seward, reared five children. Young Seward was influenced mainly by his father, who valued discipline and wealth. At age fifteen, Seward left home for Union College in Schenectady, New York. A financial dispute with his father led him to leave Union College for Georgia, where he taught school (and observed slavery at first hand) for a short time. Returning to New York State, he completed his studies at Union College. He then worked for two law firms before being admitted to the bar in 1822. The following year, Seward moved to Auburn, near Syracuse, where he joined the law firm of Judge Elijah Miller. Judge Miller provided him not only a job but also a bride, for Seward married the judge's daughter, Frances, in 1824.

For men such as Seward, Auburn proved to be a great source of political opportunity. By the mid-1820's, Seward had already become very active in the National Republican Party, which supported John Quincy Adams, and he then became active in the Antimasonic Party, which not only challenged the "secret government" of the Masons but also advocated protective tariffs and government support for the construction of roads, canals, and railroads. It was as an Antimason that Seward launched his public career. He won a seat in the state senate, and he increasingly became a favorite of the leading political organizer of his party, Thurlow Weed (also of Auburn). The two men became close friends and established a lifelong political relationship which soon brought Seward to national prominence. Weed first carried Seward into the new Whig Party as it emerged during the winter of 1833-1834, then engineered Seward's nomination for governor. Although Seward lost when he first ran for the office in 1834, he triumphed four years later.

By the time he became governor, Seward had proven himself to be highly ambitious, often unprincipled, and tough. He stood for the Whig economic program of tariffs, internal improvements, and the national bank, and took a daring position in support of temperance, prison reform, and the abolition of jail sentences for debtors. On race issues, however, he was inconsistent. Although he detested slavery, he opposed, with equal vehemence, granting the right to vote to blacks. Yet he recognized that the controversy over slavery might offer him political opportunities, and he grabbed them during the next twenty-five years.

Life's Work

Portraits of Seward show a handsome man about five feet, six inches tall, with a graceful, thin face marked by an aquiline nose, a ruddy complexion, and wavy, red hair. Early photographs of Seward are not as flattering: The lines in his face are less graceful, his look less direct. This discrepancy can be observed also in his political career, for Seward often offered less than met the eye. As governor, he became well-known for his opposition to slavery and his support for the education of Catholic immigrant children in the face of nativist Protestant objections, and he continued to advocate high tariffs and internal improvements. Yet he took none of these positions without first having carefully assessed their potential impact on his career. When the Whigs in New York suffered reverses during the mid- and late-1840's, they turned to Seward as their best chance to regain a seat in the United States Senate. Their plan succeeded. In 1849, the Auburn lawyer moved to Washington, D.C.

The next twenty years witnessed the zenith of Seward's political career. Opposing the Compromise of 1850 because it did not end the expansion of slavery, Seward delivered his most famous speech. He argued before the Senate that there existed "a higher law than the Constitution" that prohibited the movement of slavery into free territory. This speech, which was reprinted thousands of times during the following decade, turned Seward into one of the leading symbols of the antislavery movement, a hero to Northerners, a demagogue to Southerners. Moreover, Seward's "higher law" speech guaranteed that when the Whig Party disintegrated during the period between 1852 and 1854, Seward would be called upon to lead the Republican Party, which replaced it. Seward in New York, Abraham Lincoln in Illinois, and Salmon Chase in Ohio all came to lead the new party that was both sectional (not national) and fundamentally opposed to the expansion of slavery into the territory acquired by the United States following the Mexican War.

Yet both Seward's friends and his foes exaggerated his opposition to slavery, for he was first and foremost a nationalist—and, as such, hardly a radical within the abolitionist cause. Slavery, he believed, would impede national development, but he was against so rapid and wrenching a transition away from slavery as might lead to war and destroy the Union. Seward favored gradual, not immediate, abolition. He advocated compensation for slaveholders who freed their slaves. A conservative and traditionalist, unlike many abolitionists, he continued to praise the Constitution. That Seward was a nationalist also explains his support of federal funding of internal improvements, tariffs, and development of the West. He remained suspicious of executive power, although not when it was used to assert the national interest against foreign competitors. Seward believed that, eventually, the United States would extend its boundaries from coast to coast and would encompass Canada and Mexico and Alaska (which he helped to purchase from Russia in 1867). As a nationalist, he believed, as did his hero John Quincy Adams, that Providence intended for the United States to dominate the Western Hemisphere. He believed that the political and moral contradictions of slavery would discredit this mission.

Seward viewed the systems of the nation's free and slave states and territories incompatible. This incompatibility would, he claimed in an 1858 speech, lead to "an irrepressible conflict," meaning that the United States would eventually have to extend either the free or the slave system to all of its borders. Lincoln shared this conviction, and the likelihood that either Lincoln or Seward would become the Republican Party nominee for president in 1860 led many influential Southerners to advocate secession.

Seward desperately wanted to become president, but, for a number of reasons, he failed to receive his party's nomination. The "irrepressible conflict" speech had become so notorious that many Republicans feared that its author could not win the election. Furthermore, Seward's long-standing support for Catholic education, stemming back to the New York education quarrels of the 1840's, left nativists in his party dissatisfied. (As for Thurlow Weed, another likely candidate that year of 1860, he was simply outmaneuvered by the opposition—a rare but important occurrence in his political career.) Thus, the Republican Party named Abraham Lincoln its candidate for the presidency. Seward's defeat was a bitter blow, yet—although he genuinely believed Lincoln to be less qualified than himself—Seward loyally supported Lincoln in the general election. Lincoln rewarded this loyalty, offering Seward the post of secretary of state following his electoral victory.

During the next eight years, Seward proved himself to be among the nation's most outstanding State Department chiefs, though it was not immediately apparent. He began his work in a provocative manner. He proposed that Lincoln, in effect, serve as a figurehead president while Seward assume the real powers of the presidency. He threatened war against England and France in order to motivate the South to return to the Union in a burst of nationalistic fervor. He insulted the British at a moment when the Union needed foreign support against the challenge of the Confederacy.

If his early diplomacy appeared belligerent, however, he quickly mended his ways. From the beginning of the Civil War in 1861, Seward's major task was to minimize foreign support for the Confederacy. The South not only sought diplomatic recognition from the Europeans; it also sought military aid in the form of loans and equipment, especially naval craft that could challenge the Union blockade of Southern ports.

Preoccupied with military and political matters, Lincoln gave Seward a free hand in the diplomatic arena. Seward played it well. When a Union naval captain plucked two Confederate officials off the *Trent*, a British frigate, officials in London threatened war. Seward avoided conflict in a very adroit maneuver in which the British, for the first time since the American Revolution, accepted the American view of neutral rights on the high seas. In like manner, Seward, through a combination of bluff, public appeal, and skillful negotiation, discouraged both the British and the French from aiding the Confederacy either diplomatically or materially.

Seward's skill was evident in more than simply wartime diplomacy. He shrewdly unveiled the Monroe Doctrine when the French installed a puppet regime in Mexico, and he effectively laid the foundation for

American financial claims against London stemming from damage inflicted on Union shipping by a Confederate cruiser, the *Alabama*, constructed in Great Britain. More important, his vision of an American continental empire culminated in his imaginative purchase of Alaska in 1867. "Seward's Folly," his critics called the acquisition, but even an unfriendly Congress recognized its potential value.

The plot to kill Lincoln also targeted Seward, who was severely wounded. He recovered to serve President Andrew Johnson as secretary of state, generally endorsing Johnson's Reconstruction policy. The fact is that Seward remained willing to subordinate black rights to what he believed to be the main task, that of the reconciliation of the North and the South.

Nevertheless, it was foreign policy, not Reconstruction politics, for which he would be remembered. Retiring from public life in 1869 and returning to Auburn, he died three years later, October 10, 1872.

Summary

William Seward's career touched upon virtually all the major issues of the pre-Civil War era. He became one of the country's leading Whig (and later Republican) leaders in part because he thoroughly supported the main Whig principles: nationalism, a limit on executive power, strict support for the Constitution, a high tariff to fund internal improvements, and low land prices in order to stimulate westward expansion. Yet it was antislavery that, above all, shaped his career. Seward became a leading opponent of the expansion of slavery, and he nearly rode this issue into the presidency.

What Seward lacked, however, was conviction. Seward never conveyed Lincoln's sense that slavery was a genuine American tragedy. To an extent, Seward was victimized by his evident ambition. He was not fully trusted, in large measure because he was not fully trustworthy. Too often he subordinated political principle to personal interest, a weakness which limited his effectiveness with allies and foes alike.

Nevertheless, his skepticism about principle allowed him to compromise where compromise was necessary and made him a particularly effective diplomat. Next to John Quincy Adams, he had the broadest vision of any secretary of state in American history. He was a practical man, a man of action rather than an intellectual. Whatever the flaws in his character, his record speaks for itself.

Bibliography

Adams, Ephraim D. *Great Britain and the American Civil War*. 2 vols. New York: Longmans, Green and Co., 1925. Adams, while very sympathetic toward the British, nevertheless provides a fair and detailed account of Seward's first four years as secretary of state.

Case, Lynn M., and Warren F. Spencer. *The United States and France: Civil War Diplomacy*. Philadelphia: University of Pennsylvania Press, 1970. An excellent survey of Seward's foreign policy from a Continental perspective. Seward is viewed with grudging respect.

Ferriss, Norman B. *Desperate Diplomacy: William H. Seward's Foreign Policy, 1861*. Knoxville: University of Tennessee Press, 1976. A sympathetic account of Seward's diplomacy, with a focus on the *Trent* affair.

__________. *The Trent Affair: A Diplomatic Crisis*. Knoxville: University of Tennessee Press, 1977. A thorough but dull account of the crisis that nearly brought Great Britain and the United States to war in 1861.

Paolino, Ernest N. *The Foundations of American Empire: William Henry Seward and U.S. Foreign Policy*. Ithaca, N.Y.: Cornell University Press, 1973. The author views Seward as defining a commercial imperial mission for the United States. Curiously, the book ignores the Civil War.

Seward, William H. *William H. Seward: An Autobiography from 1801-1834, With a Memoir of His Life, and Selections from His Letters*. 3 vols. Edited by Frederick Seward. New York: Derby and Miller, 1877. The editor was Seward's son. This volume provides a look at Seward's entire life from his own perspective.

Taylor, John M. *William Henry Seward: Lincoln's Right Hand*. New York: HarperCollins, 1991.

Van Deusen, Glyndon G. *William Henry Seward*. New York: Oxford University Press, 1967. The best one-volume biography. Van Deusen is sympathetic to but rarely uncritical of Seward, whom he views as a man both unprincipled and practical.

Warren, Gordon H. *Foundation of Discontent: The Trent Affair and Freedom of the Seas*. Boston: Northeastern University Press, 1981. This work is less kind to Seward than the work of Ferriss. It is very helpful in clarifying the complex legal issues of the affair.

Gary B. Ostrower

Roger Sherman

Born: April 19, 1721; Newton, Massachusetts
Died: July 23, 1793; New Haven, Connecticut

Sherman's political wisdom and facility for compromise helped create the United States Constitution. He also served ably as a Colonial leader in Connecticut during the American Revolution.

Early Life

Roger Sherman was born on April 19, 1721, in Newton, Massachusetts, outside of Boston. He was the second son born to William Sherman and Mehetabel Wellington Sherman; their family later grew to include seven children. The infant Roger was named for Roger Wellington, his maternal great-grandfather. The Sherman family had first arrived in America in 1636 when their ancestor, Captain John Sherman, migrated from Essex, England, to Watertown, Massachusetts.

In 1723, William Sherman moved his young family to a section of Dorchester, Massachusetts, that was incorporated as Stoughton in 1726. It was there that Roger Sherman was reared. He was taught by his father to be a cobbler, or shoemaker, and they also farmed the family land together. The latter work required Roger's full attention in the spring and summer months. When winter approached, he attended a one-room school located a mile and a quarter from his home. The education the boy received there was rudimentary, but he improved on it himself. When he traveled from house to house with his cobbler's tools, he also took along books to read while he made or repaired shoes. One of his earliest interests was mathematics; he also read widely in law, astronomy, history, philosophy, and theology. The last of these subjects probably became of interest to young Sherman from his association with the Reverend Samuel Dunbar, an influential Congregationalist preacher in Stoughton. Despite his curiosity about theological matters, Roger Sherman did not officially join Dunbar's congregation until he was twenty-one, on March 14, 1742. This delayed declaration of faith was rather unusual in Colonial America, where a person's religious affiliation was highly important in the community.

Sherman met his first wife, Elizabeth Hartwell, the daughter of a local church deacon, while he still resided in Stoughton, though Sherman did not marry her until a few years had passed. The death of his father intervened in 1741; Roger Sherman found himself suddenly responsible for the support and education of the younger children in his family. In order to facilitate family matters, Roger moved to New Milford, Connecticut, in 1742; he accomplished this by walking more than one hundred miles from his Massachusetts home. Once in New Milford, he helped his older brother William manage the general store he had already established in that farming community. On November 17, 1749, Roger Sherman married Elizabeth Hartwell. Their marriage would produce seven children, but only four survived infancy. Elizabeth herself died at age thirty-five in October of 1760.

Roger Sherman had varied interests in his first years in Connecticut. He produced an almanac (modeled after that of Benjamin Franklin) which predicted weather, gave advice to farmers, and quoted proverbs and poetry. Sherman continued this enterprise until 1761.

Roger Sherman found his most lucrative employment in 1745, when he was appointed as land surveyor for New Haven County; he received this position for his superb mathematical ability. At this time, surveyors were at a premium in the Colonies, and so, when Litchfield County was formed in northwestern Connecticut in 1752, Sherman became its surveyor as well. Because of these jobs, he was able to speculate in real estate dealings, much to his success. Also, his work in court to defend the land boundaries of plaintiffs drew Sherman more into an interest in law. He read more intensely in the law during these years, and in February of 1754, he was admitted to the bar. Because of his growing popularity and reputation for fairness, New Milford's citizens began electing Sherman to a series of political offices. He served on their grand jury, as selectman, as justice of the peace, and finally, as their delegate to the Connecticut General Assembly.

Life's Work

Sherman's life in New Milford, however, despite his popularity, became increasingly difficult after the death of his wife in 1760. The following year, he decided to move to New Haven, where he established a general store next to the Yale College campus. Because of his proximity to the college and local churches, Sherman sold many books; some of his best customers were students and ministers. Sherman's devotion to reading increased at this time; he also began to take more of an interest in Colonial politics. Sherman was still serving as a delegate to the Connecticut General Assembly, a position he first held in 1755 and (except for the years of 1756-1757) would continue to hold until 1761. In 1759, he had also been named a justice of the County Court of Litchfield. In 1766, he was appointed a judge in the State Superior Court of Connecticut. Connecticut's original charter from England had granted the colony the most carefully structured and autonomous government enjoyed by any colony. This is a fact that Sherman cherished and which he put to work in his later dealings in the congresses of the emerging nation.

Although Roger Sherman's record as an office holder in Connecticut's distinct government seems impressive in itself, his most valuable contributions to American society were yet to be made. With Sherman's selection to the First Continental Congress in August of 1774, his work as one of the Founding Fathers of the United States truly began. He served diligently in this congress, despite the fact that he was one of the oldest delegates. Sherman was also sent to represent Connecticut in the Second Continental Congress, which convened in May of 1775. It was becoming evident by the time of this second congress that a war for independence from England was inevitable for the thirteen colonies. Shots had been fired in Massachusetts between British redcoats and Colonial patriots in April of 1775. In this second congress, Sherman served on a committee of five men who drafted the Declaration of Independence, although most of the actual writing of the document was done by Thomas Jefferson. Once war had been declared, Sherman labored long hours on vital committees managing the Revolution. He headed efforts to raise ten million dollars to fund the war, and he organized the purchase of the Colonial army's supplies.

In his home state of Connecticut, Sherman also served on the Council of Safety during these years, and he stockpiled munitions at his New Haven store for the army. While at home in New Haven, he founded the New Haven Foot Guards, a unit of militiamen drawn together to defend the city and its residents. Despite these efforts, Sherman's house, as well as his son's, was raided by the British in an attack on New Haven in 1779.

Yet Sherman was not too weighed down by the burdens of his war work. He also enjoyed a happy family life during this period.

On May 12, 1763, he had married a beautiful young woman, Rebecca Prescott of Danvers, Massachusetts. Together they had eight children who kept Sherman's home life joyful and lively. One pretty young daughter's quick wit was commented on by a guest at their home: General George Washington.

Sherman, in the area of law and political compromise (an art he perfected), was to play an important role in the founding of the nation that Washington's army had fought to achieve. At the war's end, the thirteen colonies were rather loosely bound together by the Articles of Confederation, which Sherman had also worked to establish in the Grand Committee of the Continental Congress of 1776. It became evident, especially after Shays' Rebellion in Massachusetts, that a stronger central government was needed; powers the government had to have, such as taxation and treatymaking, were lacking. Sherman had served as a delegate to the Congress of the Confederation beginning in 1781. Then, he was also elected to represent Connecticut in the Constitutional Convention held in Philadelphia in the summer of 1787. It was there that Sherman made vital political compromises that helped establish the United States Constitution. Sherman, representing a middle-sized state, effected a successful compromise over an issue that had deadlocked this convention. He sought to establish a manner of legislative voting that would guarantee large states (such as New York and Virginia) and small states (such as Delaware and Rhode Island) an equal and fair voice in making laws. Sherman suggested the establishment of the two houses of the United States Congress as they now exist. The Senate has equal representation for each state, and the House of Representatives has representation proportionate to a state's population. Sherman's compromise was accepted on June 11, 1787; it is known by his name, as the Great Compromise, or as the Connecticut Compromise.

Sherman made other contributions to the founding of the American government. He favored the election of the president by the state legislatures, but he did not win this point. When the popular election of the president is held, however, the decisive recorded vote still comes in the electoral college, which Sherman was instrumental in establishing. He was also responsible for the concept of the congressional override on legislative bills vetoed by the president. Sherman also proposed that the trial for a president's impeachment be held in the

House and the Senate (instead of in the Supreme Court, as other delegates had suggested).

From records of his service in the various Colonial congresses, particularly the Constitutional Convention, one may draw a physical picture and character study of Sherman. His fellow delegates wrote in high praise of his conscientious work but also detailed his awkward physical and vocal mannerisms. From these Colonial leaders, one learns that Sherman was a tall man with broad shoulders; he was rugged-looking with a jutting jaw, wide mouth, and deep-socketed, piercing blue eyes, all set in a large head. He wore his brown hair cut close to his head in a conservative style and did not wear a powdered wig as did the men of the Colonial aristocracy. Sherman was one of the poorest delegates to the Constitutional Convention; he barely had enough money to feed his children during the difficult inflationary period caused by the war. Sherman's poverty and lack of a formal education were always evident in his speech, which contained slang terms and was delivered in a rustic accent.

Nevertheless, no one writing of Sherman for posterity denied his effectiveness as a statesman. He knew how to make his points in debates, and while he spoke very frequently, he was always concise. In committee work and in informal discussions among delegates, Sherman often saw the issues more clearly than anyone else. He had foresight as to what the United States Constitution had to include and what it had to avoid; here, he was a great advocate of states' rights. For all of his levelheadedness, earnestness in debate, dedication in his service, and honesty in his dealings, Sherman won the sincere praise of his peers.

Connecticut's citizens returned Sherman to serve as a United States congressman in the fall of 1789. He was also appointed to a seat in the Senate in 1791, an office which he held until his death. Sherman died from typhoid fever on the evening of July 23, 1793, in New Haven, Connecticut.

Summary

Sherman's distinguished career as a Colonial political leader and statesman afforded him the title the Great Signer. Because of his almost continual service in the various American congresses, Sherman was the only man to sign all the following major documents: the Articles of

Association of 1774, the Declaration of Independence, the Articles of Confederation, the Federal Constitution, the Declaration of Rights, and the Treaty of Paris (with Great Britain).

Sherman also enjoyed a prestigious career as a founding father of New Haven, Connecticut. He was the treasurer of Yale College from 1765 to 1776; in its early years, he often paid the school's bills with his own money to prevent its closing. He was elected the first mayor of New Haven, and while in office (from 1784 until his death), he built new schools and renamed the city streets for American patriots rather than British monarchs. He also built up the city's business and shipping enterprises by offering special loans to new merchants moving into New Haven.

The people of Connecticut expressed their gratitude to Roger Sherman for leading their state out of the struggles of a war for independence into the security of a new nation with a sound and wisely planned government—they named a city after him in 1802, Sherman, Connecticut.

Bibliography

Beals, Carleton. *Our Yankee Heritage: New England's Contribution to America's Civilization*. New York: David McKay Co., 1955. Beals entitles his chapter on Sherman "Shoemaker Statesman." In it, he emphasizes the patriot's early life as well as his political career. This chapter contains many details of Sherman's personal life not found in other sources. Beals also provides a thoughtful analysis of Sherman's character traits.

Boardman, Roger S. *Roger Sherman: Signer and Statesman*. Philadelphia: University of Pennsylvania Press, 1938. A readable, carefully researched study of Sherman's life and career, with much documentation—such as a full listing of the committees on which he served. A bibliography lists other important references. Focuses on Sherman's public career rather than on his personal life.

Bowen, Catherine D. *Miracle at Philadelphia: The Story of the Constitutional Convention, May to September, 1787*. Boston: Little, Brown and Co., 1966. Bowen describes the daily workings of the Constitutional Convention in great detail. A helpful item for the reader is the inclusion of a full text of the United States Constitution, as well as a bibliography. The text is readable and enlightening. The Founding

Fathers come through as human beings with distinct personalities and interests.

Collier, Christopher. *Roger Sherman's Connecticut: Yankee Politics and the American Revolution*. Middletown, Conn.: Wesleyan University Press, 1971. The book's title accurately reflects its dual subjects—Roger Sherman and the Connecticut of his era. Collier notes the lack of personal materials available on Sherman; only his public life is recorded in any detail. Thus, Collier's well-documented study covers the broader range of the statesman in his native state. A substantial bibliography is provided.

Gerber, Scott D. "Roger Sherman and the Bill of Rights." *Polity* 28, no. 4 (Summer, 1996): 521-541.

Rommel, John G. *Connecticut's Yankee Patriot: Roger Sherman*. Hartford, Conn.: American Bicentennial Commission of Connecticut, 1979. This is a slender but useful volume; it was prepared as one in a series of historical works on Connecticut topics for the two hundredth anniversary of the Declaration of Independence. It re-creates Sherman's political career accurately and concisely, concentrating on his work during and after the Revolutionary War. A small reading list is included.

Rossiter, Clinton. *1787: The Grand Convention*. New York: Macmillan Publishing Co., 1966. This book covers fully the 1787 convention, focusing on the men present and the work achieved there; Rossiter details also the later lives of the convention delegates. A careful factual accounting of a fateful political convention and the government it established. The Founding Founders are somewhat idealized here.

Van Doren, Carl. *The Great Rehearsal: The Story of the Making and Ratifying of the Constitution of the United States*. New York: Viking Press, 1948. A classic book on how the United States government was founded. Since no formal record was kept for much of the 1787 convention, the author works from the delegates' diaries and notes. Accuracy is a primary feature here, but the narrative remains lively and interesting. The author shows the delegates' personalities as well as their contributions to the final document. An informative appendix is included.

Patricia E. Sweeney

ALFRED E. SMITH

Born: December 30, 1873; New York, New York
Died: October 4, 1944; New York, New York

Smith was a leading figure in the Democratic Party during the Progressive Era and the 1920's. He represented the urban, immigrant Roman Catholic, and relatively liberal interests of the party at a time when it was deeply divided along regional, cultural, and ideological lines.

Early Life

Alfred Emanuel Smith was born the first of two children to a poor but not impoverished Irish-American family on the Lower East Side of New York City, in 1873. His sister Mary was born two years later. Smith's father, also named Alfred Emanuel Smith, was a "truckman" (driver of a horse-drawn wagon); he and Smith's mother, Catherine Mulvehill Smith, were the New York-born children of Irish immigrants.

Smith grew up in a mixed though primarily Irish and German neighborhood in the Battery section of New York, on the banks of the East River. His early youth was a happy one, although never without money worries, revolving around his close and warm family and the Roman Catholic Church. Smith served as an altar boy throughout his adolescence and was educated at the local parish school. His parents, particularly his mother, worked hard at rearing a "respectable" boy who was immune to the bad influences common in their kind of neighborhood.

Smith was not a particularly strong student; books would never play an important role in his life. He did like elocution, however, a not unusual interest among those who would ultimately enter politics. Nevertheless, young Smith stayed in school until completing the eighth grade. His father having recently died, Smith went to work at a wide variety of jobs over, roughly, the next six years. At seventeen, he got a job at the Fulton Fish Market as "assistant bookkeeper," and despite its title, much of the work was hard labor. At the same time, he expanded his interest in amateur drama and considered a career on the stage. Ultimately, however, this was neither respectable enough nor sufficiently sure as an escape from poverty.

Politics pervaded Smith's neighborhood, centering on Tammany Hall, the leading Democratic organization in New York City. Tammany's reputation for corruption went against Smith's strong personal ethical sense, but it was the only route to political preferment available to a young man with his lower-class, Irish Catholic background.

Smith began active political participation before he could vote, rapidly developing a reputation as a popular speaker, a reputation which his dramatic background served well. He steadily increased his involvement in party and Tammany activities and was rewarded, at twenty-one, with his first political job, as an investigator in the office of the commissioner of jurors. It paid eight hundred dollars per year and was his first white-collar job. During this period, Smith also courted a young woman of a middle-class Irish family from the Bronx, Catherine Dunn, whom he married in 1900. It was a strong, happy marriage, blessed with five children: Emily, Catherine, Arthur, Alfred, Jr., and Walter.

Tammany Hall was in disarray in the 1890's. Scandals associated with Boss Richard Croker not only permitted the reformers to take over City Hall but divided the Democratic Party and Tammany itself into bitterly opposed factions. Smith, through both good luck and his own sense of propriety, ended up on the right side among these factions, so that in the post-Croker period, when Charles Francis Murphy came to rule Tammany Hall, his reputation and potential were unblemished.

Finally, after loyal party work for more than a decade, Smith got what he wanted: party nomination for the state assembly in 1903. Once nominated, he easily won the election with seventy-seven percent of the vote in his overwhelmingly Democratic district. His electoral career had begun.

Life's Work

Smith found legislative life difficult, given his lack of schooling and of social contact outside his narrow Lower East Side milieu. He was a hard worker, however, and a quick learner. He taught himself both sufficient law and sufficient social graces to be able to fit in and function well in the Albany environment. He became a close friend of another Tammany legislator, future New York State and United States senator Robert F. Wagner, and both of them gradually developed reputations as unusually honest and competent Tammany legislators. Smith also developed a sense of bipartisanship and was able to work well with the Republicans, who generally controlled the assembly at the time.

The early twentieth century was still a period of much corruption in New York politics but also of increasing interest in reform. Smith, while maintaining his loyalty to Tammany, began to develop an identification with reform as well, particularly in the area of controlling large business interests, such as the utility companies, and defending the "little man." Steadily, his reputation grew and he became a leader of the Democratic Party in the legislature, straddling the growing division between Tammany and the reform Democrats, who were led by a new breed such as State Senator Franklin D. Roosevelt. In 1911, Smith became the Democratic leader of the assembly.

Smith's career continued to progress as he became steadily closer to the political and social reformers of the day. A highlight of this period was his leading role in the state constitutional convention of 1915, in which he demonstrated his expertise in state government and won the praise of both parties and numerous interests. Smith's contribution to the convention led to his nomination and election as sheriff of New York County in 1915, an extremely lucrative post that provided him with financial security for the first time in his life; it also widened his recognition among voters. In 1917, Smith ran for and was elected president of the Board of Aldermen, New York City's second most powerful position.

Smith ran for and was elected governor of New York in 1918. He was defeated for reelection in the Republican landslide year of 1920 but came back two years later and won three gubernatorial elections in a row; Smith completed a total of four terms as New York's governor. His gubernatorial years were successful, as he continued to use bipartisanship and negotiation among Democratic factions to create effective coalitions in the legislature.

Always a fiscal conservative, Governor Smith pared government finances. At the same time, however, he pursued an ambitious legislative program. Most notable was a spate of administrative reform and social legislation, which put his administration clearly in the progressive mainstream of the time. Financial reform, conservation, public health laws, workmen's compensation, and child labor reform were all among the measures of his governorship. He filled the state's administrative apparatus with first-rate personnel, a number of whom, such as Frances Perkins, would later distinguish themselves in Roosevelt's New Deal.

In 1924, Smith campaigned for the Democratic presidential nomination. The national convention saw bitter division between the more rural, Protestant, prohibitionist South and West, on the one hand, and the urban, ethnically heterogeneous, antiprohibitionist Northeast, on the other. Smith, representing the latter and being the first serious Roman Catholic candidate for a presidential nomination, was able to stalemate the former's candidate, William Gibbs McAdoo, but could not get the requisite two-thirds majority for himself.

In 1928, Smith once again fought for the nomination and got it. His unsuccessful campaign against Republican Herbert Hoover was an emotional one; his Tammany and New York background, opposition to Prohibition, and, especially, his Catholicism, alienated many voters. These same characteristics were very attractive to voters in the cities, however, and among newer Americans and the working class. Consequently, Smith's candidacy was important in beginning the swing of those groups toward the Democratic Party, groups which Roosevelt would soon turn into a Democratic majority.

After the 1928 campaign, Smith entered private business, serving as president of the Empire State Building and in a number of other ventures. He prospered but still sought the presidency, and contested Roosevelt in the 1932 Democratic National Convention. Beaten badly there, his long friendship with Roosevelt came to an end, the break exacerbated by Roosevelt's failure to request Smith's involvement in the New Deal.

Both his personal alienation from the Administration and his traditional fiscal conservatism rendered Smith less and less happy with the New Deal as its programs developed. By the mid-1930's, he became a leading figure in the virulently anti-Roosevelt Liberty League, which was trounced by the president in the elections of 1936. Smith remained moderately active in Democratic conservative politics for a few more years, but his public life had really come to an end with the election of 1936. In the spring of 1944, Smith's beloved wife died, and he followed her to the grave six months later.

Summary

In his early public years, Smith was one of those Democrats who brought their party into the mainstream of political reform that had been primarily the province of the Republicans. Throughout his career, he represented, and to some degree sought to enhance the position of, the newer elements in American society: workers, immigrants, Catholics and Jews, and the nonpowerful generally. This was, however, always within the constraints of a cautious, even conservative ideology.

Smith's presidential campaigns highlighted the contemporary divisions between newer and older groups of Americans and were a frustration to the former. At the same time, they illustrated the rising power of the cities and their people, whose political time did in fact come in 1932. Smith played an important role in the development of that voter coalition, which would dominate American politics from the Great Depression through the 1970's.

Smith's alienation from the New Deal was typical of old Progressives of both parties—their definition of reform did not include all the elements of mid-twentieth century American liberalism. By the 1930's, Smith was politically outmoded, but his role in the political developments of the 1910's and 1920's was considerable.

Bibliography

Allswang, John M. *A House for All Peoples: Ethnic Politics in Chicago, 1896-1936*. Lexington: University Press of Kentucky, 1971. A case study of Smith's role in the development of the "Roosevelt coalition" of urban, ethnic, and working-class voters in the Democratic Party.

Handlin, Oscar. *Al Smith and His America*. Boston: Little, Brown and Co., 1958. An interpretive biography, sketchy in some parts, but also perceptive. Focuses on the religious and ethnic aspects of Smith's career and his presidential campaign.

Hapgood, Norman, and Henry Moskowitz. *Up from the City Streets: A Biographical Study in Contemporary Politics*. New York: Grosset and Dunlap, 1927. A laudatory study by two men who worked with Smith in New York. Useful for its contemporary nature, and because of the authors' closeness to Smith.

Josephson, Matthew, and Hannah Josephson. *Al Smith: Hero of the Cities*. Boston: Houghton Mifflin Co., 1960. Based primarily on the

Frances Perkins papers and research Perkins had done for a planned Smith biography. Well researched and interesting reading.

O'Connor, Richard. *The First Hurrah: A Biography of Alfred E. Smith*. New York: G. P. Putnam's Sons, 1970. A general but fairly thorough biography. Based primarily on secondary materials but balanced and informative.

Pringle, Henry F. *Alfred E. Smith: A Critical Study*. New York: Macy-Masius, 1927. Reprint. New York: AMS Press, 1970. Written before the 1928 presidential race; Pringle was a poor predictor. The book is quite personal and interpretive, balanced in its view of Smith, and still worth reading.

Smith, Alfred E. *Up to Now*. New York: Viking Press, 1929. A straightforward autobiographical narrative for the period through the 1928 presidential campaign. Not overly critical but honest and factually reliable.

Voth, Ben. "The Smith 'Heat': Alfred E. Smith and the 'Catholic' Issue." *Southern Communication Journal* 59, no. 4 (Summer, 1994): 333-342.

Warner, Emily Smith. *The Happy Warrior*. Garden City, N.Y.: Doubleday and Co., 1956. An affectionate and approving biography by a devoted daughter. It is worth reading, as she was close to her father and was in his confidence.

John M. Allswang

MARGARET CHASE SMITH

Born: December 14, 1897; Skowhegan, Maine
Died: May 29, 1995; Skowhegan, Maine

As the first leading American stateswoman to be elected in her own right to both houses of the United States Congress, Margaret Chase Smith focused her attention on improving the status of women, military preparedness, and defense of free speech and democratic values.

Early Life

Margaret Madeline Chase was born in Skowhegan, Maine, on December 14, 1897. Skowhegan, a mill and factory town in west-central Maine, provided a small-town atmosphere in which her parents George Emery and Carrie Murray Chase reared their six children. Margaret was the eldest of the four who survived. Her father, a barber from Irish and English background, was a hardworking family man whose own father had fought in the Civil War before taking his position as a Methodist minister in Skowhegan. Her mother took jobs occasionally to supplement family income while instilling in her children the importance of family life and independence.

While pursuing a commercial course of study in high school, Margaret worked as a clerk in the local five-and-dime store, was employed as a telephone operator, and was hired to record tax payments in the town books during her senior year. She shook hands with President Woodrow Wilson on her senior class trip to Washington, D.C. After her graduation from Skowhegan High School in 1916, Margaret taught in the one-room Pitts School outside Skowhegan. Seven months later she returned to Skowhegan to accept a full-time telephone operator's job for Maine Telephone and Telegraph Company.

In 1919, she began an eight-year job at the town's weekly newspaper, the *Independent Reporter*, which Clyde Smith (her future husband) coowned. Rising to circulation manager, she continued to meet influential people and cultivate her skills in public relations. She drew on these skills in 1922, when she organized the Skowhegan chapter of Business and Professional Women's Club. Margaret was named president of the Maine Federation of the Business and Professional

Women's Clubs the following year. In 1928, she served as Office Manager for the Daniel E. Cummings Company, a Skowhegan woolen mill. Her early working experiences not only taught her how to get along with people but also instilled in her a respect for working people that influenced her subsequent pro-labor record in the United States Congress.

In 1930, Margaret Chase married Clyde H. Smith, a respected and experienced Maine politician who was twenty-two years her senior. From 1930 to 1936, she supported his energetic public career while learning the basic skills for campaigning and public service. During this period, she also served as a member of the Maine Republican State Committee. Clyde Smith was elected to the United States House of Representatives in 1936. Margaret served as his secretary in Washington, D.C., until his death in April, 1940.

Life's Work

Margaret Chase Smith won a special election in the spring of 1940 to fill her husband's vacated seat in the House of Representatives. As a candidate for the succeeding full term in office, Smith scored an impressive electoral victory in the September general election. Her eight years as the congresswoman from Maine's Second Congressional District are highlighted by her interest in military affairs. In her first term she broke with the Republican party and voted for the Selective Training and Service Act to draft men for the upcoming war. She was the only member of the Maine delegation to vote for Lend Lease in 1941, and she broke with her party to support a bill to arm American merchant ships. In 1943 she was appointed to the House Naval Affairs Committee, which was later merged into the Armed Services Committee.

Many of Smith's concerns focused on the status of women in the civilian workforce and in the military. In 1944, she was appointed by Secretary of Labor Frances Perkins to serve as technical adviser to the International Labor Organization, which explored the role of women in employment planning after World War II. Smith worked to improve the status of women in the military by introducing the Army-Navy Permanent Nurse Corps Bill to grant women permanent status in the military. This bill was signed into law by President Harry S Truman in April of 1947. Smith toured the South Pacific naval bases and sponsored legislation which would permit women to serve overseas during war. She gained passage for the Women's Armed Services Integration Act of 1948, which gave women equal pay, rank, and privileges. Her desire to see the United States exert leadership in world affairs enabled her to support U.S. membership in the United Nations and the European Recovery Plan.

Senator Smith favored domestic legislation to improve the conditions of the working class and women. She helped to defeat the Tabor Amendment, which had proposed to halve the funds designated for community service programs such as child care. In 1945 and 1949 she cosponsored a proposed Equal Rights Amendment which did not get the necessary two-thirds majority vote in Congress to be submitted to the states for ratification. She voted with the Democrats against the Smith-Connally Anti-Strike bill. In economic matters she opposed a bill to freeze the social security tax and voted for federal pay raises. In 1947 she voted against a Republican proposal to cut President Truman's budget. That same year she voted with her party in supporting the Taft-Hartley Act, which placed specific limits on labor. She had been named chair of the Maine State Republican Convention in 1944 to prepare her to chair the national Republican Party conference in 1967.

Margaret Chase Smith ran for election to the U.S. Senate in 1948, winning by a record plurality. Though her opponents charged her with being a party maverick by calling attention to the votes that she cast contrary to her party, she produced a House voting record that aligned with her party ninety-five percent of the time. Her election to the United States Senate in 1948 made her the first woman in United States history to be elected in her own right without prior service by appointment to serve in the U.S. Senate and the first woman to be elected to both houses of Congress. Her four terms in the Senate from 1948 to 1972 acquainted her with six presidents among whom were Eisenhower and Kennedy.

In 1949 Senator Smith began a daily newspaper column, *Washington and You*, which was syndicated nationally for five years. She was named to the prestigious Senate Republican Policy Committee. She won the Associated Press award for Woman of the Year in politics in 1948, 1949, 1950, and 1957. She delivered her famous "Declaration of Conscience" speech on June 1, 1950, as a response to the abuses of Senator Joseph R. McCarthy's inquisitions into communism in the

United States. She courageously opposed McCarthy's negativism and demeaning of Americans at a time when most Republicans in the Senate were either too afraid to oppose him or somewhat supportive of his extremist anticommunist activities. Her "Declaration of Conscience" speech still has appeal as a defense of American values and the importance of free speech to the maintenance of American democratic processes.

She traveled to Florence, Italy, in 1950 as U.S. delegate to the UNESCO conference. She was also appointed as a lieutenant colonel in the U.S. Air Force Reserves. After winning reelection to the Senate in 1954 she embarked on a twenty-three nation world tour to see how U.S. foreign aid money was being used. She interrupted her trip to return to the United States to cast her censure vote on Joseph R. McCarthy. In 1956 Senator Smith campaigned for Dwight Eisenhower, the Republican presidential candidate. She debated in his defense with Eleanor Roosevelt on CBS television's *Face the Nation*. As someone who enjoyed new experiences, Smith had by this time been the first woman to ride on an American destroyer in wartime, spend a day on an aircraft carrier at sea, and in 1957 to fly as a passenger in a F-100 jet fighter which broke the sound barrier.

In 1960, Smith won a hotly contested election over another female candidate, the first time two women had run against each other for a senate seat. That same year she won *Newsweek* magazine's press poll rating as Most Valuable Senator. Upon resuming her duties in the Senate, she agonized over her vote on Kennedy's Limited Nuclear Test Ban Treaty. Her concern for national security won out in her vote against both the treaty and most of her party. Her vote put her on the same side as Barry Goldwater, who became the Republican party presidential nominee for 1964. Although Margaret Chase Smith was touted as a potential candidate for vice president in 1964, she earned the distinction that year of becoming the first woman nominated for president by a major U.S. political party.

She supported the 1964 Civil Rights Act using her influence in the Republican Conference to keep the provision barring sex discrimination in employment in Title VII intact. Smith won an unprecedented fourth term for a woman to the Senate in 1966. In 1967 she was elected chair of the Conference of Republican Senators. The next year she had to miss her first roll call vote in her thirteen years in Congress because of hip surgery. She held the record for 2,941 consecutive roll call votes. In the remaining two years of her tenure in the Senate, Margaret Chase Smith cast important votes against President Richard Nixon's nominations of Clement F. Haynesworth and G. Harold Carswell for the U.S. Supreme Court. Demonstrations protesting the Vietnam War, especially on college campuses, led her to make her second "Declaration of Conscience" speech on June 1, 1970.

In her final campaign for reelection to the Senate in 1972, Smith was defeated by her Democratic opponent, William D. Hathaway. During her Senate career she served on the powerful Armed Forces, Appropriations, Government Operations, and Rules Committees and showed strong support for the space program as a charter member of the Senate Aeronautical and Space Committee. She also sponsored legislation for government support of medical research. Senator Smith used her considerable influence to look out for the seafaring interests and industries of the state of Maine and to cast votes on issues critical to the well-being of the Republican Party and the future course in world politics for the United States.

After she left public office, Smith focused on a second career as a visiting professor and lecturer with the Woodrow Wilson National Fellowship Foundation and at numerous college and university campuses. In the course of her career, she received ninety-five honorary doctoral degrees and more than 270 other awards and honors. In 1989, she was awarded the Presidential Medal of Freedom, the nation's highest civilian honor. The Northwood Institute, Margaret Chase Smith Library in Skowhegan, Maine, was dedicated in 1982 to serve as a congressional research library and archives. This library houses the papers, political memorabilia, and documents that Smith accrued in her thirty-two years in Congress. Her private residence adjoins the library on the historic Kennebec River. In 1990 she was honored by the dedication of the Margaret Chase Smith Center for Public Policy at the University of Maine.

Summary

Margaret Chase Smith's long and distinguished public service career furthered the interests of national security, especially military affairs. She pioneered legislation to further the status of women in domestic issues, military status, and internationally. She was a model of decorum and earned a reputation for integrity, honesty, and independence of judgment. As a servant of the people in Congress, she put first priority on her duties in office. She campaigned vigorously and without accepting campaign contributions.

Bibliography

Fleming, Alice. *The Senator from Maine*. New York: Thomas Y. Crowell, 1969. This is a well-written book highlighting the life of Margaret Chase Smith from childhood through her activities in Congress. Somewhat historically fictionalized, the book is suitable for grades six through eight.

Gould, Alberta. *First Lady of the Senate: Life of Margaret Chase Smith*. Mt. Desert, Maine: Windswept House, 1990. This work presents a juvenile level review of the public career of Margaret Chase Smith. The author emphasizes Smith's personal values, public integrity, independent judgment, and contributions to public life.

Graham, Frank, Jr. *Margaret Chase Smith: Woman of Courage*. New York: John Day, 1964. This readable biography describes Smith's professional life in the Senate. The author emphasizes her accomplishments as a woman in national politics—at that time, an arena dominated almost exclusively by men. Presents clear explanations of how the U.S. government works.

Meisler, Stanley. "Margaret Chase Smith: The Nation's First Woman Senator Reflects Back over a Capitol Life." *Los Angeles Times*, December 8, 1991, p. M3. A brief interview with Smith in which she reminisces about her experiences as a politician in Washington, D.C. Places her accomplishments within the context of women's efforts to gain greater political representation during the 1990's.

Schmidt, Patricia L. *Margaret Chase Smith: Beyond Convention*. Orono: University of Maine Press, 1996.

Sherman, Janann. " 'They Either Need These Women or They Do Not': Margaret Chase Smith and the Fight for Regular Status for Women in the Military." *Journal of Military History* 54 (January, 1990): 47-78. A scholarly analysis of Smith's stance on the issue of equitable status and treatment for women in the military. Amplifies her views on a topic that continues to generate interest among American military leaders and the general public.

Smith, Margaret Chase. *Declaration of Conscience*. New York: Doubleday, 1972. This book, composed by Smith with the assistance of her legislative aide, William C. Lewis, Jr., focuses on her three decades of public service. It contains important source material, including the text of her famous speeches and other important legislative statements.

Schmidt, Patricia L. *Margaret Chase Smith: Beyond Convention*. Orono: University of Maine Press, 1996.

Wallace, Patricia Ward. *Politics of Conscience: A Biography of Margaret Chase Smith*. Westport, Conn.: Praeger, 1995.

Witt, Linda, Karen M. Paget, and Glenna Matthews. *Running as a Woman: Gender and Power in American Politics*. New York: Free Press, 1993. A journalist, a political scientist, and a historian collaborated on this sweeping narrative of the experiences of female candidates in American politics. Written from the vantage point of 1992's "Year of the Woman," the book contains various references to Smith's trailblazing efforts in Congress and a telling assessment of public opinion regarding her chances of becoming president in 1964.

Willoughby G. Jarrell

EDWIN M. STANTON

Born: December 19, 1814; Steubenville, Ohio
Died: December 24, 1869; Washington, D.C.

Combining excellent administrative skills with attention to detail, Stanton as secretary of war made a major contribution to Union victory during the Civil War.

Early Life

Edwin McMasters Stanton, born on December 19, 1814, in Steubenville, Ohio, was the eldest child of a physician descended from a Quaker family. When Stanton's father died, the thirteen-year-old had to leave school to help support his family. He worked in a local bookstore and continued his education during his spare time.

His guardian and mother's attorney, Daniel L. Collier, impressed by the young man's ambition, loaned him money in 1831 so that he could attend Kenyon College at Gambier, Ohio. A year later, however, worsening family finances forced Stanton to withdraw from school. His former employer contracted with Stanton to manage a bookstore in Columbus, Ohio. After a disagreement with his employer, Stanton asked Collier for loans to study law in Columbus. Collier, however, suggested that Stanton return to Steubenville to study with him. Stanton passed the bar in 1836 and practiced in Cadiz, Ohio, as a partner of an established attorney and also formed an association with Judge Benjamin Tappan. In 1838, Stanton returned to Steubenville to oversee the practice of Senator-elect Tappan.

Stanton proved to be an extremely hardworking attorney. He spent hours preparing cases and consequently was often better prepared than his colleagues. By 1840, Stanton had established himself as a lawyer, had managed to repay all of his debts to Collier, and for the first time was providing a financially secure environment for his family. He married Mary Lamson of Columbus on December 31, 1836. Stanton and his wife shared a love for contemporary literature and often spent evenings reading aloud and discussing current events. The Stantons had two children, Lucy Lamson and Edwin Lamson. The death of Lucy was a terrible blow to the Stantons, and in March, 1844, the death of his wife nearly drove Stanton insane. In 1846, his brother Darwin, whom Stanton had put through medical school, committed suicide.

These personal tragedies completely changed Stanton's personality. He had been sickly as a child and, because of his health and his need to work, was isolated from others. Even so, he had a pleasant demeanor and enjoyed socializing, but now he became withdrawn and suffered from a deep depression. He disliked social events and was often rude and quarrelsome. He exhibited these traits for the remainder of his life.

Lonely and unhappy, Stanton decided to seek new opportunities in Pittsburgh, Pennsylvania, in the fall of 1847. He maintained residency in Ohio, however, and kept in touch with state affairs. His law practice bloomed in Pittsburgh, and he achieved national recognition. He represented the state of Pennsylvania against the Wheeling and Belmont Bridge Company, a company in Wheeling, Virginia, which had obtained permission from the state of Ohio to build a suspension bridge across the Ohio River. The proposed bridge, too low to permit existing steamboats to cross under the structure, would cut off Pittsburgh from river commerce. Pennsylvania sued either to stop construction of the bridge or to force the company to build a higher bridge. Stanton proved his point when he hired a steamboat to run at full speed under the bridge. When the steamboat's smokestack and superstructure were destroyed, Stanton won a favorable judgment.

The bridge case brought Stanton numerous clients, and he also worked as a junior counsel in the patent infringement case of *McCormick v. Manny*. Stanton's client, John H. Manny, lost, but Stanton performed ably in the case. During the trial, he met Abraham Lincoln briefly for the first time.

On June 25, 1856, Stanton married Ellen Hutchinson of Pittsburgh, and moved to Washington, D.C., to devote his time to practicing before the United States Supreme Court. Stanton found happiness with his new wife, and they had four children, but he never recovered the more congenial demeanor so manifest during earlier days. The ambitious attorney did well in the new environment. In 1858, Stanton was selected as a special United States attorney to represent the government in numerous fraudulent land claims in California arising from land deeded to individuals before the Mexican war. He spent most of the year in California laboring to reconstruct the necessary records. Stanton's attention to detail allowed him to win a number of victories and saved the government millions of dollars.

Although Stanton devoted his energies to civil law, he also proved himself to be an able criminal lawyer. Daniel E. Sickles, a New York congressman, scandalized the country in February, 1859, when he murdered Philip B. Key. United States Attorney for the District of Columbia and son of Francis Scott Key, best-known as the author of "The Star-Spangled Banner," Key had been carrying on an affair with Sickles' wife, and the congressman acted while in a rage. Stanton and his associates used the plea of temporary insanity for the first time in the United States. The jury acquitted Sickles, and Stanton's fame grew.

Life's Work

Stanton had not been actively engaged in politics before the Civil War. He was a Jacksonian Democrat who opposed slavery. He accepted the Dred Scott decision, however, and believed that constitutional provisions regarding slavery had to be enforced. He disliked Southern Democrats and fervently supported the Union as the crisis atmosphere grew in 1859 and 1860. After Lincoln's election in November, 1860, the nation faced a crisis of immense magnitude. Stanton believed in the Union and on December 20 agreed to serve in President James Buchanan's cabinet as attorney general for the short time before Lincoln assumed office. Stanton worked hard to preserve the Union and to stiffen Buchanan's resolve to keep the country together. Stanton joined others in the cabinet in opposing the abandonment of Fort Sumter, South Carolina, and kept an eye on individuals he believed were plotting against the government.

Stanton distrusted Lincoln's administration during the early months of the Civil War. Highly critical of Lincoln, Stanton became a friend and adviser of Major General George B. McClellan after he took command of the Army of the Potomac and then became general in chief.

Lincoln needed a new manager for the War Department capable of handling the massive mobilization of men and resources needed to fight to preserve the fractured Union. Secretary of War Simon Cameron, however, had turned out to be both inept and corrupt. It is not clear why Lincoln decided to appoint Stanton, but the Republican president needed support from War Democrats. For whatever reason, on January 15, 1862, Stanton was confirmed as secretary of war; the

War Department and the United States Army had found a master.

Stanton acted immediately by reorganizing the War Department, hiring new and better qualified personnel, and carefully investigating existing contracts. Contractors were pressured to deliver needed supplies, but supplies had to arrive on time and be of proper quality. He often worked far into the night, and he expected the same of his subordinates. Stanton efficiently managed a large-scale enterprise, and the Union armies never lost a battle for lack of supplies or equipment.

The war secretary also understood the importance of communications and transportation. Acting through Congress, he took over telegraph and railroad lines essential to carrying on the war. Stanton created a military telegraph system operated by the civilian-controlled War Department, not the army. Consequently, all information flowed through Stanton's office, enabling him to manage the flow of news and to censor anything of value to the South. The press criticized Stanton for censorship, but his actions were a sound and necessary wartime measure.

The railroad was equally important to the war effort. On one occasion, Stanton moved two army corps from the Eastern theater to Chattanooga, Tennessee, complete with arms, equipment, and supplies, in less than a week. Government control of the railroads in military areas proved to be a key factor in the war. Stanton established a railroad building program to repair and build new rail lines at an unprecedented rate. The war secretary clearly understood the technology of modern war.

In his early months as secretary, Stanton maintained a close relationship with McClellan. The general and Lincoln, however, had never agreed on strategy. Stanton soon realized that McClellan was a brilliant organizer but no fighter. The secretary's views may also have been colored by his improving relationship with Lincoln. The president wanted a fighting general who understood the political and military realities of the war. In August, 1862, Stanton worked to remove McClellan from command, although the general was briefly returned to duty during the fall.

Both Stanton and Lincoln sought a general who acted rather than one who simply asked for more men and supplies. Consequently, both often interfered with military operations early in the war when they thought generals were not doing enough. They maintained civilian control of the war effort in the face of a real danger that armies and generals might become too powerful and gain the upper hand in government.

In 1863, Major General Ulysses S. Grant, with his victories at Vicksburg and Chattanooga, emerged as the general both Lincoln and Stanton had sought. In March, 1864, Lincoln appointed Grant to the newly created rank of lieutenant general and gave him command of the entire one-million-man Union army. Grant found no cause to complain about Stanton. Stanton did all in his power to procure what Grant needed, but Grant never asked for more than could be realistically delivered. The combination of Stanton, Lincoln, and Grant brought Union victory when General Robert E. Lee surrendered to Grant at Appomattox Court House on April 9, 1865.

Stanton was shattered by Lincoln's assassination on April 14. The two men had developed a close working relationship, making it possible to wage an immense war. Stanton's anger never really abated, and he sought and prosecuted the assassins with a vengeance.

Grant's terms to Lee had been generous, but within political limits set by Lincoln. Major General William Tecumseh Sherman, however, fearing a bloodbath in the wake of Lincoln's death, negotiated a much broader surrender agreement with Confederate General Joseph E. Johnston in North Carolina two weeks after Appomattox. Sherman's terms enraged Stanton, who leaked them in garbled terms to the press and who privately accused Sherman of disloyalty. Sherman had certainly exceeded his authority, and after a cabinet meeting, Grant went to North Carolina and quietly supervised new terms. Sherman never forgave Stanton for his behavior. Ironically, both men probably acted out of grief over Lincoln's death.

President Andrew Johnson asked Stanton to stay in his cabinet. During the war he had left the Democratic Party, and by 1865 he fully sympathized with the Radical Republicans. Johnson's view of Reconstruction turned out to be far different from that of the Radical Republicans and of Stanton. The war secretary from the summer of 1865 onward differed with the president, wanting harsher terms imposed on the South. He approved of the Freedmen's Bureau and the Civil Rights Act of 1866, although both were enacted over Johnson's veto. He supported the Military Reconstruction Act, which passed over Johnson's veto on March 2, 1867, and assisted Radicals in formulating additional Reconstruction legislation that summer.

Johnson decided to remove Stanton from office early in August and demanded Stanton's resignation. The war secretary refused, however, on the grounds that the Tenure of Office Act gave Congress control over his removal. He used this pretext even though he himself believed that the act was unconstitutional. Johnson then suspended Stanton, making Grant secretary of war *ad interim*, until Congress could act. When the Senate refused Johnson's request, Stanton returned to office, and Johnson decided to remove him anyway. Impeachment proceedings against the president followed, failing by one vote on May 26, 1868. At that point, Stanton stepped down.

The tension-filled years had damaged his health, and he never fully recovered. Stanton had abandoned his law practice to serve his country and, without the energy to reestablish it, faced serious financial difficulties. When Grant assumed the presidency, he gave Stanton an appointment to the United States Supreme Court, which was quickly confirmed by the Senate. Stanton, however, died before taking office, on December 24, 1869.

Summary

Stanton faced many adversities early in life. He struggled to get an education because of his family responsibilities. Even so, he appears to have been a cheerful and congenial youth with a taste for literature and political discussion.

His great ability as an attorney gave him national prominence. By 1859, Stanton was on the road to great wealth with an annual income in excess of forty thousand dollars. Personal tragedies, however, altered Stanton's personality. The death of his first child followed by the death of his first wife and the suicide of his younger brother had a profound effect on the man. He had always been demanding, but with personal tragedy he became rude and quarrelsome, and his relations with others remained cold and distant.

He gave up wealth and security for public office, apparently with patriotic motives. A Democrat who opposed slavery, he fervently supported the Union. He joined Buchanan's cabinet in its waning months to help keep the nation together. With the onset of the Civil War, while critical of the Republican Party, he supported the Union.

Stanton proved to be an able secretary of war and thus a key to Union victory. The ability to act quickly while at the same time paying attention to the smallest detail made him a good administrator. He expected the best from subordinates and replaced those who did not measure up. Along with Lincoln, he ensured the maintenance of civilian control over an enormous army during a revolutionary time.

After the war, Stanton opposed readmission of the South to the Union without guarantee of full freedom to the former slaves. Stanton disagreed with Johnson's lenient Reconstruction policy. He fought hard to retain his position in the government for the simple reason that he believed himself to be right and Johnson to be wrong. Too much blood had been shed for him to do otherwise. A truly remarkable man, Stanton certainly deserves to be remembered as one of the great war secretaries, perhaps even the greatest.

Bibliography

Flower, Frank Abial. *Edwin McMasters Stanton: The Autocrat of Rebellion, Emancipation, and Reconstruction*. New York: Saalfield Publishing Co., 1905. A laudatory biography that has some value because of the author's access to papers no longer available.

Gorham, George C. *Life and Public Service of Edwin M. Stanton*. 2 vols. Boston: Houghton, Mifflin and Co., 1899. Gorham was commissioned by Stanton's family to prepare this biography. The author also had access to family papers that have since been scattered.

Hyman, Harold M. "Johnson, Stanton, and Grant: A Reconsideration of the Army's Role in the Events Leading to Impeachment." *American Historical Review* 66 (October, 1960): 85-100. This is an excellent discussion of the clash between Stanton and Johnson.

Pratt, Fletcher. *Stanton: Lincoln's Secretary of War*. New York: W. W. Norton and Co., 1953. A readable treatment of Stanton, but unequal to Thomas and Hyman.

Thomas, Benjamin P., and Harold M. Hyman. *Stanton: The Life and Times of Lincoln's Secretary of War*. New York: Alfred A. Knopf, 1962. A beautifully written biography based on massive research. It is unlikely that a more balanced treatment will appear.

United States War Department. *The War of the Rebellion: A Compilation of the Official Records of the Union and Confederate Armies*. 128 vols. Washington, D.C.: Government Printing Office, 1880-1901. These volumes contain the essential documents covering Stanton's work in wartime.

David L. Wilson

THADDEUS STEVENS

Born: April 4, 1792; Danville, Vermont
Died: August 11, 1868; Washington, D.C.

Although greatly disliked during his lifetime and by some later historians, Stevens was the leading advocate of a just policy for former slaves; his program was only a part of his larger commitment to equality for all people.

Early Life

Thaddeus Stevens was born April 4, 1792, in Danville, Vermont, to Sally and Joshua Stevens. His mother, who had the greatest influence on Thaddeus' personality, was a Baptist. Her Calvinism, evangelism, and piety contributed to his later devotion to principle and duty. Born with a club foot, Thaddeus was the last child in a family of four children. Sally worked, saved money, and taught young Stevens; she wanted him to have the finest available education, and she succeeded. Joshua, his father, was a generally unsuccessful shoemaker. The family was poor. Thaddeus was close to his mother since she provided most of his elementary education. She discouraged him from playing or associating with the local boys because of his physical handicap. Under her guidance, at a very young age Thaddeus learned to read the Bible.

Intellectually, Thaddeus was not disadvantaged. Although he had various run-ins with those in authority, at the age of twenty-two he was graduated from Dartmouth College. He was a shy young man who nevertheless often spoke his mind on issues and situations throughout his long life. Undoubtedly, his verbal skills were compensation for his physical disability; his wit and scorn became legendary.

In 1814, Stevens moved to York, Pennsylvania, to begin his law practice. He soon moved to the village of Gettysburg and became a leading lawyer in the area and a partner in the James D. Paxton Iron Works. Stevens served on the Gettysburg town council. His earlier political activity was with the Federalist Party, but as that party declined, Stevens became a leader in the Anti-Masonic movement because he distrusted the influence of secret societies in a republic. He believed that secret societies were elitist and created aristocracies of special privilege for their membership. Though the Anti-Masons generally became Whigs, Stevens was never popular with that party's leadership despite his strong opposition to Andrew Jackson and his policies. From his first political experience, Stevens was a strong nationalist whose program included the belief that government could create opportunities for all men. He never retreated from that general belief.

In 1833, Stevens was elected to the Pennsylvania house of representatives. During the next ten years, Stevens was politically active. He opposed any propositions based on class distinctions or any discrimination based on race or color. For example, Stevens in 1835 saved the principle of free public schools for all in Pennsylvania by defeating a proposed charity or pauper-school law. He also supported state aid to higher education. Stevens was a member of the Board of Canal Commissions, a powerful state planning agency. Unfortunately, his party, the Whigs, greatly influenced by Stevens' leadership, lost the dispute over control of the state house of representatives known as the Buckshot War. Discouraged, after another election, Stevens retired from party politics. He also needed to repair his personal fortune; his iron works had put Stevens more than $200,000 in debt. By 1842, Stevens was practicing law in Lancaster, Pennsylvania. He was fifty years old, and his prospects appeared to be limited; he was, however, on the eve of his greatest contribution to American history.

Life's Work

From 1848 to 1853, Stevens served in the House of Representatives as a Whig. His strong opposition to the Fugitive Slave Law, as part of the Compromise of 1850, contributed to his defeat. He returned to Lancaster, working to save his failing iron business. An important figure in the creation of the Republican Party in Pennsylvania, he was returned to the House in 1858, where he served until his death ten years later.

Despite his age and poor health, Stevens played a major role in the dramatic Civil War decade. He opposed any concession to the threat of secession from the Southern states. Early in the war, Stevens clearly stated his belief that the rebel states, by their behavior, had placed themselves beyond the pale of the Constitution; therefore Congress would determine their future status in any program of reconstruction.

In 1861, he became the chairman of the Ways and Means Committee and helped formulate the government's fiscal policy during the war, supporting the distribution of greenbacks, for example. Unlike many of his fellow Americans, Stevens recognized that slavery and the Union's fate were intermingled. He argued that any slave used in any military capacity should be freed, and he urged confiscation of all property used for insurrectionary purposes. Despite his contemporary and historical reputation for harshness, he never advocated execution for any rebel leaders. In fact, he opposed capital punishment. Nevertheless, he pushed for a punitive program against the Confederacy.

On March 28, 1864, he introduced the Thirteenth Amendment in Congress. As chairman of the House group of the Joint Committee on Reconstruction, he was a key member of the Radical Republicans. He contributed to the writing of the Fourteenth Amendment, and he supported it as part of the Reconstruction Act. He broke with President Andrew Johnson over his veto of the Freedmen's Bureau Bill. The alienation increased as Johnson pardoned more and more Confederates. On March 19, 1867, Stevens introduced a bill to confiscate all public land in the South, including individual rebel property. He wanted "forty acres and a mule" for every freedman and planned to use the money from the sale of rebel lands to finance military pensions and to retire the national debt. The bill was not passed. A milder form of Reconstruction prevailed.

Although he personally doubted its success, Thaddeus Stevens introduced the resolution for the impeachment of President Andrew Johnson. He was chairman of the managers who argued for impeachment before the Senate, but his failing health limited his contribution to the proceedings. The vote for removal failed by one vote. As a practical matter, the president now controlled Reconstruction.

Exhausted by his age and his activities, Stevens died on August 11, 1868, in Washington, D.C. As a matter of honor, the Republicans in his district kept his name on the ballot in the fall election.

Summary

Praised and cursed during his lifetime and after, Stevens nevertheless was one of the few politicians to see how slavery and the Union were combined. A strong abolitionist, Stevens believed that the federal government should ensure civil rights and just economic opportunities for freedmen. Although in the minority during his lifetime because of prevalent racism and because of his contemporaries' belief in limited government, Stevens' ideas were later vindicated by historical developments. Without any reservation, Thaddeus Stevens was an egalitarian. He recognized that class and class origins were key elements in determining a person's chances in life. He believed that government could balance the equitable opportunities between the rich and the poor. In his own way, Stevens' ideas anticipated the creation of the modern welfare state. Because the cemeteries of Lancaster were for whites only, Stevens, on his deathbed, ordered that he be buried in a black graveyard. In death as in life, Thaddeus Stevens continued questioning the status quo and thereby became one of America's greatest reformers.

Bibliography

Belz, Herman. *Emancipation and Equal Rights: Politics and Constitutionalism in the Civil War Era*. New York: W. W. Norton and Co., 1978. Good overview of the complex issues facing the United States during the Civil War.

Brodie, Fawn M. *Thaddeus Stevens, Scourge of the South*. New York: W. W. Norton and Co., 1966. The most balanced biography. The author still views Stevens' motivation in terms of punishment and hostility.

Current, Richard N. *Old Thad Stevens: A Story of Ambition*. Madison: University of Wisconsin Press, 1942. Highly critical. Stevens is depicted as ambitious for power and is held responsible for many evils, including the rise of big business.

Foner, Eric. *Free Soil, Free Labor, Free Men: The Ideology of the Republican Party Before the Civil War*. New York: Oxford University Press, 1970. A basic study for understanding the varied ideologies that influenced Stevens' life and thought.

Korngold, Ralph. *Thaddeus Stevens: A Being Darkly Wise and Rudely Great*. New York: Harcourt, Brace and Co., 1955. In this biography, Stevens is heroic in stature, pure in motive. Tends to overstate his many achievements.

McCall, Samuel W. *Thaddeus Stevens*. Boston: Houghton Mifflin Co., 1899. The best of the biographies written in the nineteenth century. It dwells on the public life of Stevens.

McPherson, James M. *Ordeal by Fire: The Civil War and Reconstruction*.

New York: Alfred A. Knopf, 1982. With a massive bibliography, broad chronological scope, and illuminating details, this book is the best available volume on the subject.

Pickens, Donald K. "The Republican Synthesis and Thaddeus Stevens." *Civil War History* 31 (March, 1985): 57-73. Places Stevens' ideas in the context of recent historiographic developments.

Trefousse, Hans L. *The Radical Republicans: Lincoln's Vanguard for Racial Justice*. New York: Alfred A. Knopf, 1970. In a revision of the traditional argument, this book claims that Radicals led Lincoln to positions which he was inclined to take in the first place but had regarded as politically risky.

Vaughn, William P. *The Antimasonic Party in the United States: 1826-1843*. Lexington: University Press of Kentucky, 1983. An insightful history of political Anti-Masonry. Balanced. Explains why an egalitarian such as Stevens could be attracted to such a cause.

Donald K. Pickens

Adlai E. Stevenson

Born: February 5, 1900; Los Angeles, California
Died: July 14, 1965; London, England

Although unsuccessful in his repeated bids for the presidency, Stevenson inspired a new generation of liberals who would write the agenda for the New Frontier and Great Society during the 1960's; he brought to the American political scene an all too uncommon blend of integrity, high intelligence, and humane values.

Early Life

Adlai Ewing Stevenson II was born on February 5, 1900, in Los Angeles, California, where his father, Lewis Stevenson, managed the Hearst mining and newspaper interests. Stevenson's family, however, was based in Bloomington, Illinois, and the marriage of his parents had united the town's leading Republican and Democratic families. The Stevensons and their relatives had long been active in Illinois political affairs. His great-grandfather, Jesse Fell, was a founder of the Republican Party and a political confidant of Abraham Lincoln. His grandfather, after whom he was named, was an Illinois Democrat who had served as Grover Cleveland's vice president during the 1890's.

This family history influenced Stevenson's formative years. In 1906, his family returned to Bloomington, where his father owned and managed several farms, became a noted agricultural reformer, and was active in state and national politics. Consequently, Adlai became acquainted with such political giants as William Jennings Bryan and, most notably, Woodrow Wilson, whose moral vision and internationalism became guideposts for his subsequent political career. Although he enjoyed a happy childhood in Bloomington, he became an indifferent student in the town's primary and secondary schools. This idyllic period was shattered in December, 1912, when he accidentally shot and killed his cousin. Stevenson was so shattered by the tragedy that he could never speak of it until it became part of the 1952 presidential campaign.

In 1916, Stevenson attended Choate School in Connecticut in order to prepare for the entrance examinations for Princeton University. He entered Princeton in 1918 and was graduated four years later with average grades. He was very active in student affairs and was managing editor of *The Princetonian*. At his father's insistence, Stevenson enrolled at Harvard Law School, where he was miserable; his grades declined accordingly. In 1926, he completed his legal training at Northwestern Law School. During this period, he met with Supreme Court Justice Oliver Wendell Holmes, Jr., which proved to be one of the most satisfying experiences of his life.

By this time, Stevenson had decided to make law his life's work. He had been considering seriously becoming a newspaper publisher, and he enjoyed working on the school press in Choate and Princeton as well as editing the family's Bloomington newspaper. In 1926, Stevenson made one last effort in the newspaper business by hiring out as a reporter for the International News Service to enter the Soviet Union and obtain an interview with Foreign Minister Georgi Chicherin. Stevenson traveled by train from the Black Sea through Kharkov and Kiev to Moscow, and his observations of life under the Bolshevik regime colored his attitude toward the Soviet system for the remainder of his life.

In 1927, Stevenson became a member of a prestigious Chicago law firm, and in the following year, he married Ellen Borden, a Chicago heiress with literary interests. They produced three sons, Adlai III, Borden, and John Fell, and established a home in the small community of Libertyville, Illinois.

Life's Work

In 1929, the United States suffered the greatest economic contraction in its history, with devastating social, economic, and political consequences. In 1932, voters turned to the Democratic Party under Franklin D. Roosevelt, who promised the country a "new deal." Stevenson became one of the New Deal's bright young attorneys who swarmed into Washington, D.C., to write, enact, and administer myriad administration programs. In 1933, he served as special counsel to the Agricultural Adjustment Administration under George Peek; then, a few months later, he joined the Alcohol Control Administration as special counsel to handle price codes and tax problems following the repeal of Prohibition. During the course of his brief service, Stevenson became acquainted with such figures as George Ball, Alger Hiss, James Rowe, and Tommy Corcoran, who played significant roles in American history.

Although Stevenson had left government service, he became increasingly active in politics. In 1930, he had joined the Council on Foreign Relations, where he honed his oratorical skills on behalf of Wilsonian internationalist principles. In 1939, he joined the Committee to Defend America by Aiding the Allies to counter the isolationist mood of the country. His support of Roosevelt's mobilization efforts, including the "destroyer deal" and the Lend-Lease program, reflected his belief that Great Britain was fighting the American fight against totalitarian aggression.

After the United States entered World War II in December, 1941, Stevenson became assistant secretary of the navy under his close friend Frank Knox, a Republican newspaper publisher from Chicago. Stevenson handled the press, wrote Knox's speeches, and promoted desegregation of the navy. In 1943, he led a mission to Italy to plan the Allied occupation of that country. As the war concluded, he was made a member of the United States Strategic Bombing Survey and then became assistant secretary of state under Edward L. Stettinius and James F. Byrnes, Jr. Finally, he became press officer of the United States delegation to the United Nations conference at San Francisco in 1945.

These posts served as a proving ground for Stevenson's meteoric rise in Illinois and national politics during the late 1940's and the 1950's. In Illinois, the incumbent Republican governor had been compromised by corruption in his administration, and Democratic boss Colonel Jacob M. Arvey of Cook County needed strong reform candidates to capture the state house and the Senate seat. Arvey selected Stevenson for governor and Paul H. Douglas for the Senate. In 1948, Stevenson campaigned as a political amateur and pledged honest government. He won by more than 500,000 votes, helping to bring in not only Douglas but also President Truman in one of the country's greatest political upsets. This victory made Stevenson one of the "class of '48," a group of moderates and liberals who would dominate national politics into the 1970's.

Although his political career led to the breakup of his marriage, Stevenson was an effective liberal governor during a period of anti-Communist hysteria known as McCarthyism. Stevenson appointed businessmen, Republican and Democratic, to state positions, terminated commercial gambling, placed the Illinois state police on civil service, built new highways, streamlined state government, and increased education appropriations. On the debit side, however, was his failure to persuade the state legislature to enact a permanent fair employment practices commission and to authorize a state convention to revise an archaic state constitution.

As a result of his gubernatorial performance, Stevenson became a favorite for the Democratic presidential nomination in 1952. The Democrats had been in power since 1933, and its domestic record and Cold War policies made it vulnerable to a conservative attack. The Truman Administration, in fact, had become so unpopular that the president declined to seek reelection. Instead, Truman placed strong private and public pressure on Stevenson to make the race. The problem was that Stevenson did not want the position; he wanted to be reelected governor of Illinois. Moreover, he believed himself to be too inexperienced for the office. Stevenson's hesitation led to the charge that he was indecisive, which was to haunt him for the rest of his career. In the end, he was nominated for president in a movement that came as close to a draft as any in the twentieth century.

The 1952 campaign between Stevenson and General Dwight D. Eisenhower, an enormously popular war hero, became a classic confrontation. Behind in the polls from the beginning, Stevenson pledged to "talk sense" to the American people and offered no panaceas for the nation's troubles. His position on the issues revealed him to be a moderate liberal on domestic matters and a cold warrior in foreign affairs. His penchant for writing his own speeches, his wit and erudition, his use of Lincolnian and Holmesian anecdotes, and his humility charmed millions of voters. When his opponents condemned him for appealing to intellectuals, he responded, "Eggheads of the world, unite! You have nothing to lose but your yolks!"

Although the early stages of the campaign showed promise, a number of factors combined to bring the Stevenson effort to a bitter conclusion. Stevenson's humor, intellectualism, and Hamlet-like posturing before the nominating convention made many voters suspect that he did not lust for the office. Moreover, the Republican attack of "K_1C_2" (Korea, Communism, corruption) proved to be very effective with the voters. Stevenson's entanglement with the Alger Hiss controversy did nothing to refute the charge that he was "soft on Communism." Additionally, his support for federal over states' rights on the tidelands issue cost him significant support in such states as Louisiana, Texas, and California. The *coup de grace* to the campaign, however, proved to be Eisenhower's pledge to "go to Korea" and bring that stalemated conflict to an end. On election day, Stevenson lost by 33,936,252 to 27,314,992 votes, including the electoral votes of four Southern states.

Stevenson declined to disappear from public view during the 1950's. He became a world traveler, met world leaders, and solidified his credentials in foreign affairs. He also maintained a rigorous speaking schedule at home, campaigned for Democrats in the congressional elections of 1954 and 1958, and published several books on contemporary issues. In 1956, he was renominated for president by his party and campaigned on the theme of a "New America." Although he proved to be more liberal on civil rights than Eisenhower, he badly mishandled the *Brown v. Board of Education* decision (1954), which struck down segregation. Seeking to prevent national divisiveness on this issue, he declared that he would not use federal troops to desegregate public schools. He later recovered somewhat by pledging to enforce the decision if it was defied by state authorities. More controversial, however, were his proposals to end the draft and nuclear testing. Whatever chance he had for success was undermined in late October and November, 1956, by the Suez Canal and Hungarian crises. The electorate declined to change leaders, and Stevenson lost by an even greater margin, by 35,590,472 votes to 26,029,752.

By now, Stevenson's career had crested. In 1960, die-hard Stevenson loyalists made a "last hurrah" for their hero at the Democratic National Convention in Los Angeles, but the party turned to John F. Kennedy and a younger generation for leadership. Following Kennedy's narrow election victory, Stevenson hoped to be appointed secretary of state, only to be bitterly disappointed by his nomination for ambassador to the United Nations. Kennedy softened the disappointment by making the position cabinet-level and promising Stevenson a role in the National Security Council.

Stevenson's expertise on world affairs and his relationships with world leaders made him a popular and effective representative for the United States. His confrontations with his Soviet counterpart, Valerian Zorin, were tough and dramatic. In April, 1961, Stevenson's prestige tumbled when he denied that the United States had aided the Bay of Pigs invasion in Cuba by Cuban exiles. When President Kennedy took full responsibility for the incident, Stevenson was badly embarrassed and contemplated resignation. This action was averted when Kennedy promised to keep him fully informed on foreign policy decisions and even to seek his counsel.

This led to Ambassador Stevenson's superb performance in October, 1962, over the Cuban missile crisis when he successfully challenged Zorin's denial of Soviet insertion of missiles inside Cuba. His calm presentation of the evidence and his vow to wait until "hell freezes over" for the Soviet response won for him great praise at home and abroad. Unfortunately, this bravura performance was tarnished by administration insiders who leaked to journalists that Stevenson had acted the role of appeaser toward the Soviets. Although Stevenson and the Kennedy Administration denied the story, it once again reinforced the public's perception of Stevenson's passivity.

Stevenson clearly was unhappy serving under Kennedy and Johnson. His admirers encouraged him to resign with a denunciation of their foreign policies, but he could not bring himself to take that step. While he did criticize Johnson's intervention in the Dominican Republic in 1965, he continued to support the containment, limited war, and collaborative aspects of American diplomacy developed during the Truman Administration. He even supported basic American policies in South Vietnam. On the afternoon of July 14, 1965, Stevenson collapsed and died of a heart attack on a street in London.

Summary

Adlai Stevenson had acquired the reputation of a political loser, but his career should elicit admiration rather than contempt. He brought to public life the highest ideals and standards and never wavered in their defense. He did not seek easy answers to complex issues. He was an enigmatic political leader, a man who sought the nation's highest office yet appeared indifferent when it was within his grasp. It has been said that Stevenson lacked the ruthlessness to become president, but it may also be that he wanted the office on his terms. It seems ironic that he received his highest accolades not from his fellow citizens but from the people of the world who saw him as the best that America could produce.

A politician's success can be measured in many ways. Stevenson's "New America" campaign of 1956 anticipated much of the social and economic legislation of the New Frontier and Great Society in the 1960's. He inspired and brought into the political system millions of voters who had never before participated. He stood up to McCarthyism and practiced a disciplined civility in politics to which all politicians should aspire.

Stevenson belongs to the tradition of pragmatic reform characteristic of the twentieth century. His admirers saw him as a political leader with a moral vision for economic and social justice at home and abroad. In foreign affairs, he represented the tradition of Wilsonian internationalism, with its respect for international law, collective security, nuclear arms limitation, and human rights. He was, at heart, an optimist, a gentle and wise man who believed in strong and compassionate government and the nurturing of democratic principles throughout the world.

Bibliography

Baker, Jean H. *The Stevensons: A Biography of an American Family*. New York: W. W. Norton, 1996.

Brown, Stuart Gerry. *Adlai E. Stevenson, a Short Biography: The Conscience of the Country*. Woodbury, N.Y.: Barron's Woodbury Press, 1965. A popular biography by a Stevenson admirer. Based on secondary sources as well as interviews with the subject and his friends and colleagues.

Cochran, Bert. *Adlai Stevenson: Patrician Among the Politicians*. New York: Funk and Wagnalls, 1969. Interprets Stevenson's life and career within the context of upper-class reform dating to the Gilded Age. Includes commentary on the role of intellectuals in the Cold War era.

Johnson, Wallace, and Carol Evans, eds. *The Papers of Adlai E. Stevenson, 1900-1965*. 8 vols. Boston: Little, Brown and Co., 1972-1979. Correspondence and papers dealing with the life and career of Stevenson. Reflects Stevenson's wit, intelligence, and character. A significant source of primary materials for students of post-World War II politics.

McKeever, Porter. *Adlai Stevenson: His Life and Legacy*. New York: Morrow, 1989.

Martin, John Bartlow. *Adlai Stevenson of Illinois: The Life of Adlai Steven-*

son. Garden City, N.Y.: Doubleday and Co., 1976.

__________. *Adlai Stevenson and the World: The Life of Adlai Stevenson.* Garden City, N.Y.: Doubleday and Co., 1977. An objective and scholarly two-volume biography of Stevenson by a longtime friend and associate. Volume 1 covers the formative years through the 1952 presidential campaign. Volume 2 discusses Stevenson's political decline and his influence in world affairs. A sympathetic portrait.

Severn, Bill. *Adlai Stevenson: Citizen of the World*. New York: David McKay Co., 1966. A popular biography useful for readers with little background in modern American political history. An admiring treatment.

Stevenson, Adlai E. *Call to Greatness*. New York: Harper and Brothers, Publishers, 1954. A candid nonpartisan assessment of the United States' position in world affairs during the 1950's. Emphasizes the destabilizing impact of nationalist and independence movements in the underdeveloped world. Urges Americans to be more mature in their hopes and aspirations for a stable and peaceful world order.

__________. *Friends and Enemies: What I Learned in Russia*. New York: Harper and Brothers, Publishers, 1959. Commentary on his observations while in the Soviet Union in 1958. Notes that the Soviet regime is here to stay but states that the Soviet Union and the United States can maintain a peaceful coexistence. Typical of Stevenson's elegance of expression and clarity of style.

Whitman, Alden, and *The New York Times*. *Portrait: Adlai E. Stevenson, Politician, Diplomat, Friend*. New York: Harper and Row, Publishers, 1965. Drawn largely from the files of *The New York Times*. A flattering account of Stevenson's career, especially from his Illinois gubernatorial campaign until his death. Views Stevenson as a great, but flawed, man and emphasizes his growing estrangement from the Kennedy and Johnson administrations.

Stephen P. Sayles

Henry L. Stimson

Born: September 21, 1867; New York, New York
Died: October 20, 1950; Huntington, New York

Serving as secretary of war during the years 1909 to 1913 and again during World War II, and serving as secretary of state from 1929 to 1933, Stimson helped to define the United States' transition from isolationism to world responsibility.

Early Life

Henry L. Stimson's ancestors arrived in the New World from England as part of the Massachusetts migration of the seventeenth century. From his father, who made and lost a fortune on Wall Street before devoting the remainder of his career to surgery, Stimson learned the Presbyterian values of simplicity, hard work, and frugality. Stimson's mother died when he was nine. He spent the next four years living with his grandparents. At thirteen, his father sent him to private schools that profoundly shaped his outlook: Phillips Academy, Yale, and finally Harvard Law School. Stimson credited Yale with giving him an appreciation for corporate class spirit and democracy; Harvard, with impressing upon him the values of individualism and competition.

Leaving law school in 1890, Stimson joined a firm headed by Elihu Root (who later joined President Theodore Roosevelt's cabinet). He soon entered local politics. Disgusted with what he considered to be the low ethical level of party leaders, Stimson helped to engineer a minor political revolt in 1897. This included attempts to eliminate financial corruption, to reform primary and election laws, and to select honest men to run for public office. Stimson's efforts brought him considerable influence in a revitalized Republican Party. His work was typical of Progressive reformers of that period.

Stimson's stern Presbyterian background helped to make him a patriot as well as a reformer. To his dying day, Stimson, like his hero Theodore Roosevelt, admired the military virtues. He joined the National Guard at the outbreak of the Spanish-American War in 1898. Sent to Puerto Rico, he arrived too late to see active service; nevertheless, he remained in his squadron for nine years after returning to the practice of law. In 1905, in part because of his association with Root, who had just become secretary of state, and in part because of his friendship with President Roosevelt, which began during his reform period in New York, Stimson was appointed United States attorney for the Southern District of New York (which included New York City). At age thirty-eight, the national phase of his career was about to begin.

Life's Work

Stimson's work as United States attorney involved prosecutions of many corporations during a period when the government began to serve as a counterweight to the influence of big business. By the time he resigned in 1909, he had gained both a zest for public life and a modest national reputation.

He also had gained Roosevelt's admiration, and in 1910 the former president handpicked Stimson to run as the Republican candidate for governor of New York. This was Stimson's one campaign for elective office. He did not enjoy the experience, and he lost the election. Stimson was ill-suited to popular campaigns. He was erect, mustasched, conservatively dressed, and self-consciously dignified; in fact, Stimson was rather cold and reserved. He resented telling crowds what they wanted to hear. Those who worked with him often found him distant and domineering, even arrogant.

His conservative brand of Progressive politics, however, met with the approval of both Roosevelt and his successor, William H. Taft, leading to Stimson's appointment as secretary of war in 1911. He served in the office for two years, initiating changes in the army that proved of value during World War I. Most notably, he increased the authority of the General Staff over the politically sensitive bureaus, and he modernized training procedures.

The political and administrative skirmishes that characterized Stimson's tenure in the War Department were forgotten when World War I arrived. Stimson had admired President Woodrow Wilson's domestic program, and he supported Wilson's defense of American neutrality. Stimson, however, increasingly deplored Wilson's refusal to prepare for war and openly opposed sending American troops to Mexico in 1915 because, he felt, the real enemy was in Europe. Only Wilson's Declaration of War ended Stimson's anger. He applied for a commission in the army and went to Europe as a colonel in the artillery. "Wonderfully happy," he later recalled of these days. His friends called him "Colonel" for the remainder of his life.

After the war, Stimson returned to the practice of law. His developing interest in international affairs was greatly sharpened by the debate over American membership in the League of Nations. Together with Elihu Root, who authored the charter of the World Court, Stimson became a leading Republican supporter of international organization. Regretting the Senate's rejection of League membership, Stimson in 1922 helped to found the Council on Foreign Relations in order to stem a national return to isolationism.

It is not surprising, therefore, that Stimson's subsequent public service occurred in the area of international affairs. During 1927, he accepted a presidential appointment as a special envoy to Nicaragua. He helped to protect American economic interests by ending a revolutionary challenge to the authority of the government, a process aided by the presence of American Marines. During the next two years, he accepted appointment as governor general of the Philippines. There he encouraged programs of economic development and became an influential opponent of those who wanted to grant independence to the islands.

Shortly after Stimson returned home, President-elect Herbert Hoover offered him the post of secretary of state. It was in the State Department that Stimson learned the lessons that shaped his approach to foreign policy for the rest of his life. The American public's preoccupation with the Great Depression, reinforcing popular disillusionment with the United States' involvement in World War I, undermined his efforts to generate a policy of international cooperation. Moreover, Stimson's own plans concerning the American role in both Europe and the Far East were much less clear than he later suggested in his memoirs.

These matters were not academic. In 1931, Japanese army units began the occupation of Manchuria in China, undermining the post-World War I peace settlement and beginning the process that led to World War II. In the years after he left the State Department, Stimson became one of the most articulate champions of collective security (that is, the use of collective force to keep the peace).

Just before the Manchurian Crisis, however, Stimson had been ambivalent about the League of Nations and collective security, preferring to see the League as useful in Europe alone. Even as he brought the United States into closer cooperation with the League following the Japanese occupation of Manchuria, he did so with a divided mind. He was fearful about becoming involved in war against Japan and uneasy about the isolationist sentiments of both President Hoover and the American public. Moreover, he was troubled by his own failure to reconcile conflicts among his Far Eastern priorities—protection of American economic interests, preservation of the postwar treaties and the League, and maintenance of peace with Japan. Even his greatest accomplishment—the famous Non-Recognition Doctrine of 1932, which held that the United States would not recognize political change made in violation of existing treaties—illustrated his failure: Japan subsequently ignored this doctrine, and friendly countries such as Great Britain and France viewed it as overly moralistic and rhetorical.

Henry Stimson learned from his failures. Between 1933 and 1939, while out of public office, he strongly advocated a policy of collective security that went far beyond nonrecognition. These were years that witnessed the rule of Adolf Hitler in Germany, the invasion of Ethiopia by Italy, and the expansion of Japanese control over China. Consequently, when the Democratic President Franklin D. Roosevelt in mid-1940 needed to personify his own commitment to the principles of bipartisanship and collective security after Hitler's armies invaded France, he invited a Republican, Stimson, to serve again as secretary of war.

Stimson headed the War Department from 1940 to 1945. He helped to streamline the lines of military command and brought a number of extraordinary subordinates into the War Department at a critical time in the nation's history. He worked well with Chief of Staff George C. Marshall, and he maintained a trusted relationship with President Roosevelt, whose domestic policies were at odds with his own. Stimson did not always prevail on issues of policy. He favored opening a second front in France in 1943 rather than 1944, as was finally done, and he respected General Charles de Gaulle more than did Roosevelt, who distrusted the leader of the Free French forces. He was rebuffed on strategic issues related to such things as his advocacy, in 1942, of the use of Army Air Forces for antisubmarine duty and his proposals in 1944 to increase the size of the army rather than merely replace units in the field.

Most of his recommendations, however, were accepted. He fully supported the "Europe first" strategy of defeating Germany before turning the weight of American military might against Japan. He reluctantly approved the removal of Japanese Americans from their homes on the West Coast, and he prevailed in his opposition to Secretary of the Treasury Henry Morgenthau's plan to convert postwar Germany into a strictly agricultural society. He oversaw the Manhattan Project, which produced the first atom bomb, and successfully chaired the Interim Committee that devised the strategy for using that terrible new instrument of war. Stimson understood the implications of the bomb better than most officials, and in 1946 he called for international cooperation regarding its development. In this quest he failed. Out of this failure would, in part, grow the Cold War.

Summary

Stimson left government service in 1945. His direct influence on military and foreign policy thereby ended, but his indirect influence as embodied in the work of his subordinates continued to affect policy for many more years. In many ways, Stimson's early contributions were made possible by his well-placed connections with men such as Elihu Root and Theodore Roosevelt. He did the rest on his own. Stimson was neither brilliant nor charismatic. He was, however, loyal, forceful, and strong-minded. His failures were often the product of an overly moralistic approach to politics, a trait that was especially evident in his service as secretary of state during the Manchurian Crisis.

Yet Stimson's failures prepared the way for his successes. If he failed in diplomacy, he came to symbolize collective security during a period when the diplomacy of appeasement gradually yielded to a recognition of the need for military defense. As secretary of war a second time, his administrative and military talents paid great dividends. There is no reason to think that the outcome of World War II would have been any different had someone other than Henry Stimson headed the War Department. Nevertheless, there is every reason to think that he effectively administered both the hugely complex war machinery between 1940 and 1945 and the planning for the postwar period, in which his moralism gave way to a more realistic appreciation of the behavior of great powers.

Bibliography

Bernstein, Barton J. "Seizing the Contested Terrain of Early Nuclear History: Stimson, Conant, and Their Allies Explain the Decision to Use the Atomic Bomb." *Diplomatic History* 17, no. 1 (Winter, 1993): 35-73.

Current, Richard N. "Henry L. Stimson." In *An Uncertain Tradition: American Secretaries of State in the Twentieth Century*, edited by Norman A. Graebner, 168-183. New York: McGraw-Hill Book Co., 1961. This is the best short overview of Stimson in the State Department. The author views Stimson's moralistic approach to diplomacy as creating more problems than it solved, and emphasizes the differences between Stimson and President Hoover.

__________. *Secretary Stimson: A Study in Statecraft*. New Brunswick, N.J.: Rutgers University Press, 1954. This critical appraisal faults Stimson for pursuing a policy that the author views as erratic and excessively moralistic.

Ferrell, Robert H. *American Diplomacy in the Great Depression: Hoover-Stimson Foreign Policy, 1929-1933*. New Haven, Conn.: Yale University Press, 1957. The author contends that the Depression prevented Hoover and Stimson from taking an assertive stance against the enemies of peace.

__________. *Frank Kellogg and Henry L. Stimson*. New York: Cooper Square Publishers, 1953. The author views Stimson as unnecessarily accommodating in respect to the action of Japan in Manchuria.

Hodgson, Godfrey. *The Colonel: The Life and Wars of Henry Stimson, 1867-1950*. New York: Knopf, 1990.

Morison, Elting E. *Turmoil and Tradition: A Study of the Life and Times of Henry L. Stimson*. New York: Houghton Mifflin Co., 1960. In the most comprehensive biography of Stimson, Morison provides a somewhat uncritical account of his career. The author relies heavily on the material in Stimson's own memoirs.

Ostrower, Gary B. *Collective Insecurity: The United States and the League of Nations During the Early Thirties*. Lewisburg, Pa.: Bucknell University Press, 1979. This work focuses on Stimson as the key figure in the transition of American diplomacy from isolationism to collective security.

__________. "Henry L. Stimson and the League of Nations." *Historian* 41 (1979): 467-482. The author argues that Stimson was less consistent in his support for the League than his memoirs and most conventional accounts suggest.

Sherwin, Martin J. *A World Destroyed: The Atomic Bomb and the Grand Alliance*. New York: Alfred A. Knopf, 1975. A brilliant analysis of the way in which the Bomb affected wartime diplomacy, and the part Stimson played in this drama.

Stimson, Henry L. *The Far-Eastern Crisis: Recollections and Observations*. New York: Harper and Brothers, 1936. Stimson wrote this book as a lesson for those who would deal with aggression in the future. His book is a plea for the democratic states to cooperate within the framework of a collective-security system.

Stimson, Henry L., and McGeorge Bundy. *On Active Service in Peace and War*. New York: Harper, 1948. A gracefully written memoir which benefited greatly from the existence of extensive diaries composed by Stimson. This volume emphasizes the period since 1929.

Gary B. Ostrower

CHARLES SUMNER

Born: January 6, 1811; Boston, Massachusetts
Died: March 11, 1874; Washington, D.C.

For a quarter of a century, Sumner was the most significant proponent in high public office of equal rights and equal opportunities for black Americans.

Early Life

In youth, Charles Sumner received little affection from his puritanical father, a Boston lawyer and politician, and his severe, distant mother, who was preoccupied with rearing his eight younger brothers and sisters. Shy and inhibited, young Sumner avoided outdoor games in favor of solitude and books. After studying at the Boston Latin School in the early 1820's, he attended Harvard College, from which he was graduated in 1830 at age nineteen. At six feet, two inches in height, weighing only 120 pounds, Sumner was ungainly, amiable, studious, humorless, and nervous near women.

Sumner was graduated from the Harvard Law School in 1834, but, temperamentally unsuited to his father's profession, he was unable to establish a successful practice. In December, 1837, he abruptly left Boston for Europe, where he spent three years in travel, living mostly on borrowed money. Letters of introduction from friends of his father procured for him invitations to visit eminent jurists, writers, and political leaders in Great Britain and France, many of whom were favorably impressed by the young New Englander's good manners and eager idealism.

Arriving home in May, 1840, Sumner gloried in his sudden prominence as one of the few Americans during that era who had enjoyed social success in Europe. He volubly recapitulated his triumphs in Boston drawing rooms while his law practice languished. As his celebrity diminished during the early 1840's, however, Sumner became increasingly moody, suspicious, and sensitive. In 1844, he suffered a physical breakdown.

Life's Work

The crisis eventually passed. Ardent involvement in social reform movements was Sumner's therapy for recovering from his depression. Embracing the cause of prison reform, he soon divided the local penal improvement society into warring factions when he tried to replace its longtime secretary with his friend Francis Lieber. As a member of the Peace Society, he used an Independence Day address in 1845 not only to denounce all wars but also to attack personally the uniformed militia members in his audience. Such exhibitions of tactless self-righteousness soon made Sumner a social outcast in Boston. Nevertheless, the pugnacious eloquence with which he assailed estab-

Charles Sumner *(The Associated Publishers)*

lished institutions brought him many admirers outside his immediate circle.

In time, Sumner confined his attempts at social regeneration almost exclusively to the antislavery movement. By the mid-1840's, he had begun to give speeches and publish articles condemning the South's peculiar institution as a national evil, which Congress ought eventually to abolish. Following the admission of Texas to the Union in 1845, Sumner joined a group of "Young Whigs" in Massachusetts, including Charles F. Adams, Richard H. Dana, Jr., John G. Palfrey, and Henry Wilson, who challenged the Boston Whig oligarchy, led by Congressman Robert Winthrop and Senator Daniel Webster, for collaborating in the aggrandizements of Southern slaveholders. Joining for the first time in party politics, Sumner helped to edit the antislavery newspaper published by this group. His bitter denunciations of the Mexican War further alienated the Boston Brahmins but drew praise from Northern abolitionists and peace advocates, who characterized their new spokesman's relentless vituperation as high moral courage.

After the Mexican War, Sumner became a candidate for Congress on the ticket of the Free-Soil Party, but he lost the 1848 election to Winthrop by a large margin. Two years later, running for the same office, he received less than five hundred votes. Once again, he seemed a failure.

Early in 1851, however, a coalition of Democrats and Free-Soil Party members in the Massachusetts legislature elected Sumner to the United States Senate. Cautious at first, he did not make the first of many Senate speeches against slavery until August 26, 1852. Soon, however, he was trading denunciations and insults with spokesmen for the slaveholding aristocracy, while other Northern senators spoke circumspectly or remained silent. His combativeness produced a surge of sentiment in his favor throughout the North, while he became a hated symbol of radical abolitionism in the South. In 1855, seeking political allies, he joined the Massachusetts Republican Party, recently established.

Sumner's most famous Senate speech, which was delivered on May 19, 1856, was entitled "The Crime Against Kansas." For three hours, he denounced what he called Stephen Douglas' swindle, the Kansas-Nebraska Act of 1854, and berated both its author and his former Senate seatmate, Andrew P. Butler of South Carolina. Continuing his indictment on the following day, he labeled Douglas a loathsome animal, and he called Butler a liar and a madman. On May 22, South Carolina congressman Preston Brooks, avenging the wrong to his kinsman Butler, used his cane to beat Sumner senseless on the Senate floor.

Rendered an invalid by his wounds, Sumner became a martyr in the North, his empty seat in the Senate a convenient symbol for Massachusetts Republicans in the 1856 presidential election campaign. John C. Frémont led their ticket to a statewide sweep, and Sumner was overwhelmingly reelected to the United States Senate in January, 1857.

For the next three years, Sumner made only rare appearances in the halls of Congress. Most of that time he spent in Europe, alternating between ineffectual treatments by physicians and extensive touring and social engagements. Not until June 4, 1860, did he feel well enough to deliver a substantial speech in the Senate. Entitled the "Barbarism of Slavery," it was his main contribution to Abraham Lincoln's successful presidential campaign, an effusion of vituperation against the slaveholders whom Sumner held responsible for his difficulties, both physical and emotional.

To the Southern threat of secession, Sumner retorted that there could be no compromise with slavery. For a time he hoped that the withdrawal of Southerners from Congress would make possible the acquisition by the United States of Canada. As for the cotton states, he was quite willing to let them depart. As his former friends and benefactors Senator William H. Seward of New York and Congressman Charles F. Adams of Massachusetts struggled along with others to construct a principled compromise designed to avert civil war, Sumner accused them of obliquity and labeled them Ishmaelites. He was willing to relinquish territory, he said, but he would never barter principle. He tried to prevent the appointment of Adams as Lincoln's minister to Great Britain and to undermine Seward's direction of United States foreign policy as secretary of state. Indeed, he worked covertly for the next two years to cause Seward's ouster from the cabinet in order to obtain the State Department for himself, but Lincoln greatly valued the services of the New Yorker and refused to give him up.

For the next eleven years, Sumner served as chairman of the Senate Foreign Relations Committee. He believed that his should be the decisive voice on United States foreign policy. Using spies in the State

Department such as the eccentric Adam Gurowski, denouncing Seward to foreign diplomats and journalists in Washington, and criticizing him to highly placed correspondents abroad, Sumner worked surreptitiously to appease the antidemocratic governments of European nations. His object was to avoid foreign complications, but his methods actually exacerbated them.

An example of this was the *Trent* affair. When the British government, in December, 1861, sent an ultimatum requiring the release of four Confederate envoys seized by a federal naval captain from a British mail steamer, the *Trent*, Sumner pleaded with President Lincoln to hold out for international arbitration of the question, an approach which would probably have brought Great Britain and France into the Civil War on the side of the slave states. Lincoln, following Seward's counsel, instead authorized the release of the captives.

Trying to rouse support in Massachusetts during 1862 for his reelection to a third term in the Senate, Sumner continually pressed the President to proclaim the entire abolition of slavery. Lincoln, trying to hold the border slave states in the Union, insisted that the object of the war was to restore the Union, not to free the slaves. Nevertheless, in February, 1862, Sumner publicly propounded the doctrine of state suicide, asserting that the seceding states had forfeited their sovereignty within the Union and must become conquered provinces. It was past time, he declared, for the confiscation of Southern property, especially of slaves, by the federal military authorities. When Lincoln issued his preliminary emancipation proclamation in September, Sumner claimed that the president was finally following his lead.

In the Senate during the last two years of the Civil War, Sumner was increasingly isolated even from the other radicals of his own party. In relentless pursuit of freedom and equal rights for black Americans, he regularly castigated rather than attempted to cajole his colleagues, and despite being cultivated assiduously by both the president and Mrs. Lincoln, he regularly criticized the chief executive in his conversations and correspondence for being lethargic, disorganized, and ineffectual. He refused to support Lincoln for renomination in 1864 and only reluctantly campaigned for him against General George B. McClellan, the Democratic nominee, as the least of two evils.

Because of his alienation from most of the other senators, Sumner played a minor role in constructing the apparatus of postwar reconstruction, including the passage of the Thirteenth, Fourteenth, and Fifteenth amendments to the Constitution. He was kept off the Joint Committee on Reconstruction and was barred from the committee set up to supervise the Freedman's Bureau and the enforcement of civil rights legislation in the South. He continually exasperated his fellow radicals by carping at their efforts but rarely suggesting practical alternatives. As always, he stressed principles, not means.

In October, 1866, four months after the death of his mother, Sumner married Alice Mason Hooper, the widowed daughter-in-law of a Massachusetts congressman. The senator was fifty-five; his new wife was still in her twenties. The marriage soon foundered. Mrs. Sumner sought younger male companionship and humiliated her husband by flaunting her liaison. Eight months after the wedding, the couple separated, and the senator never spoke to his wife again. In 1873, he divorced her.

Almost from the start of Andrew Johnson's presidency, Sumner excoriated him as a disgrace to the office. By early 1868, the Massachusetts senator was a determined exponent of impeachment, accusing Johnson of treason against the United States. When the effort to remove the chief executive from office fell short by a single vote in the Senate, Sumner bitterly denounced those who cast ballots against Johnson's deposition. Soon thereafter, he began campaigning for Ulysses S. Grant for president, in the process successfully seeking his own reelection to a fourth term.

While Johnson was still president, Sumner supported ratification of the Alaska purchase treaty negotiated by Secretary of State Seward. His opposition would have been fatal to that project, as it was to Seward's treaties to annex the Danish West Indies (later known as the Virgin Islands) and to purchase territory in the Dominican Republic for an American naval base. Sumner's committee also rejected the Johnson-Clarendon convention with Great Britain, negotiated on Seward's instructions in an attempt to ease dangerous tensions growing out of the Fenian crisis and out of the refusal of the British government thus far to arbitrate American claims for damages incurred at the hands of Her Majesty's subjects during the Civil War. Sumner declared in a Senate speech on April 13, 1869, that because British aid to the Confederates had caused the war to be doubled in duration, the English owed the American people damages of two billion dollars.

For a while, Sumner was able to dictate United States foreign policy to Seward's successor, the inexperienced Hamilton Fish. As the senator with the longest continuous service, he even exercised influence, for the first time, over domestic legislation. This stopped, however, after he repeatedly blocked bills and appointments favored by Grant, culminating his obstructiveness by getting the Senate to kill a treaty to annex the Dominican Republic (the president's principal foreign policy objective). The angry chief executive retaliated by dismissing Sumner's friend John L. Motley as minister to England. When Sumner threatened a peaceful settlement of the Civil War Alabama claims by calling for the transfer of Canada to the United States as his price for support of an arbitration award, Fish and Grant were able to get him ousted as chairman of the Foreign Relations Committee.

On May 31, 1872, a vitriolic Sumner delivered a four-hour speech, "Republicanism Versus Grantism," charging the president with nepotism and corruption, hoping thereby to help block Grant's renomination for a second term. The Republican National Convention at Philadelphia nevertheless endorsed the president by acclamation. Sumner then backed Horace Greeley, the Democratic and liberal Republican candidate for the presidency. Grant's easy victory, accompanied by the rise of the venal Benjamin F. Butler to political supremacy in Massachusetts, signaled the nadir of Sumner's influence in his home state. His health declined rapidly. Facing an uphill battle for reelection in 1874, virtually isolated and widely ridiculed in the Senate, having through many years driven away most of his friends and political allies by egotistical outbursts against them, and worried about heavy debts incurred during buying binges, Sumner lived his final months as a solitary invalid, his attacks of angina pectoris increasing in frequency and intensity, until on March 11, 1874, his heart finally stopped.

Summary

Sumner served in the United States Senate for more than twenty-three years. Yet he was never a universally respected leader in that body, nor is his name attached to any portion of the landmark legislation of his epoch. Whether his party was in or out of power, his role was invariably that of obstructionist. For this he was well suited: His diligence in preparing elaborate, didactic assaults on the purposes and programs of others, his power of invective, and his uncompromising adherence to his own ideas brought him a strong following among reformers of the North, who admired his fidelity to principles of human rights and who were not subjected personally to his vehemence. The widely repeated story, the main author of which was Sumner himself, that he played a decisive role in keeping the United States from armed conflict with Great Britain and France during the Civil War is untrue. His greatest service to the nation was that of keeping relentless pressure on other politicians for almost a quarter of a century to include black Americans under the protection of the Bill of Rights.

Bibliography

Blue, Frederick J. *Charles Sumner and the Conscience of the North.* Arlington Heights, Ill.: Harlan Davidson, 1994.

Donald, David. *Charles Sumner and the Coming of the Civil War.* New York: Alfred A. Knopf, 1960. Based on extensive research, this is the most thorough treatment of Sumner's life prior to the inception of the Civil War. While Donald is appreciative of his subject, he is more objective than most earlier writers.

__________. *Charles Sumner and the Rights of Man.* New York: Alfred A. Knopf, 1970. The fullest account available of Sumner's career during the period of the Civil War and Reconstruction, this is the concluding volume of Donald's highly praised modern biography.

Nason, Elias. *The Life and Times of Charles Sumner.* Boston: B. B. Russell, 1874. A biography rushed out with little time for serious research or reflection.

Pierce, Edward L. *Memoir and Letters of Charles Sumner.* 4 vols. Boston: Roberts Brothers, 1877-1893. Typically Victorian, this study comprises extracts from documents held together with uncritical commentary and reminiscences of the subject by people disposed to speak only well of him.

Ruchames, Louis. "Charles Sumner and American Historiography." *Journal of Negro History* 38 (1953): 139-160. Here is found the assessment that all of Sumner's biographers before Donald were uncritical and superficial.

Schurz, Carl. *Charles Sumner: An Essay.* Edited by Arthur Reed Hogue. Urbana: University of Illinois Press, 1951. This long eulogy of Sumner by a younger contemporary should be read skeptically but with appreciation of some shrewd insights.

Storey, Moorfield. *Charles Sumner*. Boston: Houghton Mifflin Co., 1900. A brief laudatory account in the famous "American Statesman" series. Though biased and not always factually reliable, it is probably the best introduction to Sumner's life available.

Sumner, Charles. *Charles Sumner: His Complete Works*. Boston: Lee and Shepard, 1900. This is a collection of speeches carefully edited in later years by their author. To obtain a closer approximation of what Sumner actually said, a careful researcher will consult contemporary newspapers, the *Congressional Globe*, and, if possible, Sumner's manuscripts.

__________. *The Selected Letters of Charles Sumner*. Edited by Beverly Wilson Palmer. Boston: Northeastern University Press, 1990.

Norman B. Ferris

ROBERT A. TAFT

Born: September 8, 1889; Cincinnati, Ohio
Died: July 31, 1953; New York, New York

A third-generation member of one of America's most enduring political dynasties, Taft entered the United States Senate from Ohio in 1939 and there achieved a position of leadership as a spokesman for conservative Republicanism.

Early Life

Robert Alphonso Taft was born September 8, 1889, the first of three children of William Howard and Helen Herron Taft. Robert's father, then a superior court judge in Ohio, became President of the United States in 1909; his paternal grandfather, Alphonso Taft, a successful lawyer, had served the Grant Administration as both secretary of war and attorney general prior to ending his years of public service with ministerial appointments to Austria-Hungary and Russia during the 1880's.

Robert Taft's youth was one of privilege; his first ten years were mainly spent in fashionable neighborhoods in Cincinnati or in Washington, D.C., while his father served as United States solicitor general from 1890 to 1892. In 1900, William Taft accepted an assignment in Manila as a commissioner and in 1901 became the first civilian governor of the recently acquired Territory of the Philippines. His family accompanied him.

From 1903 to 1906, Robert attended the Taft School, founded and run by his uncle Horace, in Watertown, Connecticut. The curriculum stressed academic rigor in the traditional subjects and the duty of young men of good family to take part in public service. At school, Robert excelled in academics. Nearly six feet in height and 170 pounds by the time he was graduated, he tried several sports with his customary earnestness but performed only passably.

In 1906, Robert Taft entered Yale, as family tradition dictated. In his junior year, his father became President of the United States, but by then, Robert, reserved and dignified, was immersed in his habits of diligent study and seemed little affected by his father's eminence. He had been first in his class at Taft, attained the same position at Yale, and finished first at Harvard Law School, still another step in the career progression that was expected of him and that he followed without question.

Life's Work

In 1913, upon completion of his studies at Harvard, Taft was offered a clerkship with Supreme Court Justice Oliver Wendell Holmes. He declined it to join a prestigious Cincinnati law firm. Taft's workload allowed him ample time to take part in civic life: legal-aid work, charitable fund-raising, and support for a home-rule charter for Cincinnati. In October, 1914, he married Martha Bowers, sister of a Yale classmate. The Tafts had four sons.

Taft reluctantly came to favor American entry into World War I. He volunteered for military service only to be rejected because of poor eyesight. In July, 1917, he joined the Food Administration as one of the wartime agency's four assistant counsels. The work was tedious but satisfying compared with what he had been doing in Cincinnati, and for Taft personally, these years of public service seem to have brought about a new independence from his father's guidance of his career. Loyal to Herbert Hoover, the head of the Food Administration, Taft went with him to administer the Paris office of the American Relief Administration organized at the end of the war. While he was proud of his role in helping to bring relief to some 200 million people in war-ravaged Europe, Taft, like Hoover himself, soured on the diplomatic intrigues that were still part of the European scene. Taft did give his support to the League of Nations, albeit coolly, and he was not then or in the future the single-minded isolationist critics would later label him. Still, he came to regard European leaders as selfish and would always be wary when issues concerning American involvement in world affairs arose. He believed that international law rather than collective security could best be used to preserve peace.

In 1919, Taft returned home to establish a law practice, which his younger brother Charles soon joined. Their specialty was corporate law, much of the firm's business coming from their uncle Charles Taft, long a man of affairs in Cincinnati. In 1920, Robert Taft was elected to the Ohio assembly. He soon gained the respect of his peers for his expertise in tax problems and compiled a good record on civil liberties, supporting them even when it meant opposing the interests of the Ku Klux Klan, then a force in Ohio politics. In his participation in municipal reform in Cincinnati and in his service in the state assembly, Taft demonstrated his belief in party loyalty. Perhaps recalling how Republican factionalism had marred his father's administration, he remained a steadfast Republican even when various issues in Ohio, especially those concerning reform in Cincinnati, caused some to bolt the party.

Although his father, now Chief Justice of the United States, tried to interest him in running for the governorship of Ohio in 1926, Robert Taft showed no inclination to do so. In his six years in Columbus, he had come to enjoy legislative work but preferred to return home to Cincinnati and his law firm, known since 1924 as Taft, Stettinius, and Hollister. His practice boomed, and Taft represented many of Cincinnati's leading corporations, became a director of several, and took part in various protracted negotiations that involved streetcar service and Cincinnati's crying need for a union terminal to accommodate its large rail traffic. Taft handled these cases with a deftness that won praise from all sides. Other than his law practice, his chief interests were in raising money for the Taft School and for the arts in Cincinnati. His principal recreations were golf, fishing, and taking care of the affairs of the farm on which he and his family resided.

In 1930, Taft won election to the state senate, hoping to achieve tax reform in Ohio. An intangible property tax was enacted, but other measures he wanted, such as county zoning and planning commissions, gained insufficient support. Taft, at heart an efficiency-minded Progressive, found his political goals unappealing to others during a time when nationwide depression brought new demands for welfare and slum-clearance programs. Taft was by no means against all legislative action in these areas, and during his earlier stay in Columbus had shown moderation on several questions involving labor, but the priority he normally placed on a balanced budget and efficiency in government made him seem callously insensitive to human needs. A strong supporter of Hoover in 1932, he lost his own bid for reelection in that year of Democratic triumph. It was the only election he ever lost.

By the middle of the 1930's, Taft was ready to take an increased role in national Republican politics. He championed Republican presidential candidate Alf Landon in 1936 and was rumored to be a possible running mate for Landon. Two years later, Taft was elected to the United States Senate.

He quickly earned the respect of Senate colleagues for the care with which he studied legislative issues and, from the start of his tenure in Washington, served on such important committees as Education and Labor, Appropriations, and Banking and Currency. During his first campaign for the Senate, he accepted important New Deal programs dealing with unemployment insurance and old-age pensions, but he never was comfortable with the New Deal's approach to government. Both from philosophy and his own experience, especially with the Food Administration, which had been involved in a host of complex and often disliked regulatory decisions, he opposed big government. He regarded the New Deal as seriously flawed in its careless administration, wasteful spending, and excessive interference with private enterprise. The forcefulness and intelligence with which he expressed his opinions quickly made him a prominent figure in the Republican Party.

As early as 1940, Taft was considered a possible presidential candidate. He was eager to enter the race and had assets as a campaigner: energy, ability to organize, and thorough knowledge of the issues. His chances were diminished, however, with the German conquest in the spring of 1940 of France and the Low Countries, for his previous insistence that Germany posed no threat to the United States now seemed shortsighted to many. He had other liabilities. Not only did he dislike mingling with a crowd, but also he was an uninspiring speaker. His talks were heavy with facts and often boring. Fortunately, his wife enjoyed campaigning on his behalf and brought to his campaigns an affability with the public that he lacked. She was, as Taft's most informed biographer states, the most helpful political wife since Jessie Benton Frémont nearly a century before. Republican Party leaders and the press, however, had already stereotyped Taft as a boring personality in an era increasingly dominated by charismatic politicians. Wendell Willkie, an internationalist and a more appealing candidate, gained the Republican nomination.

In the Senate, however, Taft became increasingly successful. He was reelected by a narrow margin in 1944 and, as a leader of a bipartisan conservative bloc in Congress, became one of the most powerful senators in modern American history. He was anathema to liberal Democrats because of his status among conservatives of both major parties. Because he spoke about public issues in forthright, often abrasive terms, he was easy to deride as an isolationist and a reactionary. In practice, his thought was more complex. He is perhaps best remembered for cosponsoring the Taft-Hartley Act of 1947, which to liberals and union spokesmen seemed a retrograde step in labor law. It did not, however, stifle unionism, as was feared by its opponents at the time; on many occasions since, Taft-Hartley's "cooling-off period" has been invoked when major strikes have been threatened. As he had in Ohio, Taft did work for some reformist measures—modest federal aid to education and public housing and federal grants to the states for improved health care. Fellow conservatives and liberals alike seemed puzzled by his support of such proposals, but in Taft's thinking the bills were consistent with his own conservative philosophy that all Americans deserved a fair start and that opportunity must be open to all.

In foreign affairs Taft also showed flexibility. Prior to Pearl Harbor, he had opposed Lend-Lease and other measures designed to aid Great Britain, but subsequently he supported American entry into the United Nations. With the emergence of the Cold War, he voted against American entry into the North Atlantic Treaty Organization (NATO), but once the United States had joined, he believed that American commitments to the alliance should be upheld. Like numerous other conservatives, he displayed more enthusiasm for American involvement in Asia; he derided the Truman Administration for "losing" China to Communism and called for a stronger American effort during the Korean conflict. To an extent his views had changed since his pre-World War II advocacy of noninvolvement, but basically he held that while the United States should oppose the expansion of Communism, American power had its limits and the United States should be wary of excessive commitments in distant areas of the world. Such views made him seem conservative in the early years of the Cold War. Ironically, they would make him a hero to some members of the succeeding generation's New Left, soured on America's interventionism in Vietnam and other Third World locations.

Disappointed by his failure to win the GOP presidential nomination in both 1940 and 1948, Taft was determined to make a strong effort in 1952. Taft and his supporters lashed out not only at the Truman Administration but also at his Republican rivals. Ordinarily a staunch supporter of civil liberties, he did not seek to curb the smear tactics of fellow Republican senator Joseph McCarthy of Wisconsin, who attributed setbacks in foreign affairs to Communist infiltration of the American government. Without regard for due process, McCarthy, and others who followed his lead, accused and brought ruin to many innocent people in government, the media, and in education. Taft seems to have hoped for the then-influential McCarthy's endorsement in 1952 and on several occasions seconded McCarthy's sweeping accusations. He did not, however, get McCarthy's backing. Neither did political newcomer Dwight D. Eisenhower, who had emerged as the chief obstacle to Taft's hopes. Prominent Republicans from the delegate-rich states of the East regarded the colorless Taft as a loser and backed the popular Eisenhower, who won the nomination on the first ballot.

The recriminations of the preconvention period had left Taft and Eisenhower at odds, but party figures attempted to reconcile the two. The effort worked, in part because Taft and Eisenhower were not that distant on domestic issues. Taft campaigned energetically for Eisenhower, and the two became friends and occasional golfing companions. Although Taft believed that he too could have won the election, he accepted Ike's triumph and became a strong backer of the new administration. Realizing that he would be too old to run again for president in 1960, Taft mellowed in his public appearances and praised Eisenhower, providing advice and able support in the Senate, where he secured the post of majority leader. He was determined to help make the first Republican administration in twenty years a success. Early in 1953, however, he was found to be suffering from a severe form of cancer. It spread rapidly, and he died in a New York City hospital.

Summary

Robert Taft spent more than three decades in public life. He achieved leadership positions in his party in Cincinnati, in the Ohio assembly, and in the United States Senate. He was recognized as "Mr. Republican," widely quoted on both domestic and international issues. He was never as extreme as his rhetoric or that of his more vocal disciples made him appear. Yet the perception of him as a reactionary on domestic issues and as an isolationist made him unappealing as a presidential candidate to influential Republicans who wanted to back a winner.

Inevitably measured against his political contemporaries such as Eisenhower and Franklin D. Roosevelt, he was found wanting in the personal flair that helped give them their widespread national following. He never received the nomination he sought so avidly. Taft's greatest distinction was therefore won in the legislative branch, where his diligent work habits and informed opinions won respect. He was one of the twentieth century's genuine masters of the legislative process.

Bibliography

Alexander, Holmes Moss. *The Famous Five*. New York: Bookmailer, 1958. This is a book of sketches on the first five former senators inducted into the Senate's own hall of fame. Provides an introduction to Taft's career.

Ambrose, Stephen E. *Eisenhower*. 2 vols. New York: Simon and Schuster, 1983-1984. Valuable for its portrayal of the man whose candidacy kept Taft from getting the 1952 presidential nomination he coveted. Eisenhower was the only Republican to hold the presidency while Taft was in the Senate.

Harnsberger, Caroline Thomas. *A Man of Courage: Robert A. Taft*. New York: Wilcox and Follett Co., 1952. A laudatory popular biography of Taft. The author asks if Taft is qualified for the presidency and repeatedly answers yes. What he lacks in charisma, she argues, he more than makes up for in "integrity and courage."

Kirk, Russell, and James McClellan. *The Political Principles of Robert A. Taft*. New York: Fleet Press Corporation, 1967. Provides a brief and convenient guide to Taft's public career and a more extended discussion of his political principles.

Merry, Robert W. "The Last Stand of Senator Robert Taft, Republicans' Guiding Voice." *Congressional Quarterly Weekly Report* 53 (March 18, 1995): 791-794.

Patterson, James T. *Mr. Republican: A Biography of Robert A. Taft*. Boston: Houghton Mifflin Co., 1972. Authorized by the Taft family but written by an outstanding academic historian. Detailed and judicious, it is a model of political biography and shows no effort by the late senator's family to censor the author's judgments. Provides an extensive bibliography.

Pringle, Henry F. *The Life and Times of William Howard Taft*. 2 vols. New

York: Farrar and Rinehart, 1939. The most thorough biography of Taft's father, authorized by Robert Taft himself.

Robbins, Jhan, and June Robbins. *Eight Weeks to Live: The Last Chapter in the Life of Senator Robert A. Taft*. Garden City, N.Y.: Doubleday and Co., 1954. The title of this twenty-three-page booklet makes the topic of this partial biography clear.

Robbins, Phyllis. *Robert A. Taft: Boy and Man*. Cambridge, Mass.: Dresser, Chapman and Grimes, 1963. Laudatory but helpful in that fully half the volume deals with Taft's youth.

Taft, Robert A. *A Foreign Policy for Americans*. Garden City, N.Y.: Doubleday and Co., 1951. One of two books that contain Taft's own writings, it provides a guide to the senator's outlook on international affairs.

Taft, Robert A., and T. V. Smith. *Foundations of Democracy: A Series of Debates*. New York: Alfred A. Knopf, 1939. This helpful volume makes available the series of radio debates Taft conducted with T. V. Smith, a Democratic congressman from Illinois.

White, William S. *The Taft Story*. New York: Harper and Brothers, 1954. Written by a reporter for *The New York Times* who knew Taft, this book deals primarily with Taft's career in the Senate.

Lloyd J. Graybar

William Howard Taft

Born: September 15, 1857; Cincinnati, Ohio
Died: March 8, 1930; Washington, D.C.

After serving as the twenty-seventh president of the United States, Taft finally achieved his personal goal and found both his greatest happiness and his greatest success as chief justice of the United States.

Early Life

William Howard Taft was born September 15, 1857, the oldest son of Alphonso Taft and his second wife, Louise Torrey Taft. The Tafts were remarkably close; they all took a lively interest in Taft's career, and his brother Charles provided the financial subsidy which made Taft's public service possible. His father had served as secretary of war and as attorney general in the cabinet of President Ulysses S. Grant. Alphonso failed to win election as the Republican candidate for governor of Ohio but under President Chester A. Arthur was minister to Vienna and St. Petersburg.

The Puritan heritage of the Taft family emphasized hard work and the value of an education. Young Taft accepted these family values and, like his brothers, was a good student. He was graduated second in his class at Yale in 1878. He returned to Cincinnati to attend law school and in 1880 was appointed assistant prosecutor of Hamilton County (in which Cincinnati was situated). Not until 1913 did Taft leave the public service which he so enjoyed and for which he was so well-suited by temperament.

Taft was always large, and eventually fat. With his fair hair, blue eyes, and walrus mustache, the six-foot, three-hundred-pound Taft was a fine figure of a man. He was always good-natured and thoughtful, with an infectious chuckle which remained throughout his life as one of his most endearing characteristics. Though he described himself as lazy and a procrastinator, Taft was capable of prodigious effort and was always conscientious. Though he was a Unitarian, Taft was tolerant of the faiths of others. Like his father and most members of his social class, Taft was a staunch Republican, and he never deviated from a strong party loyalty and a belief that only the Republicans could keep

William Howard Taft *(Library of Congress)*

the nation moving securely forward.

In 1885, Taft was appointed assistant county solicitor, a fact not nearly as important to Taft as the fact that he had fallen in love. In 1886, he married Nellie (Helen) Herron, an attorney's daughter of unusual intelligence, ambition, and strong convictions—qualities that Taft found admirable in a woman. After a European honeymoon, they built a home in Cincinnati. The following year, Taft was appointed judge of the superior court and in 1888 was elected to a full term. Already his judicial career had led Taft to cast his eyes and his hopes to the United States Supreme Court, a hope encouraged by his appointment as solicitor general in 1890 and to the federal circuit court in 1892. Taft's family, meanwhile, had grown to include a son, Robert (later to become a distinguished United States senator), a daughter, Helen, and six years later, their last son, Charles (later mayor of Cincinnati).

As a judge, Taft venerated the law and considered adherence to it a prerequisite for national stability. Though some of his decisions seemed antilabor, Taft was sympathetic to the workers and upheld their right to organize and to strike. He took a strong stand against the trusts, a position that drew him closer to one of his Washington friends, Theodore Roosevelt.

Life's Work

In 1900, Taft was called to Washington, D.C., where President William McKinley urged him to take on the responsibility of chairman of the Philippine Commission, assuring him that it would not endanger his chances of elevation to the Supreme Court. Taft had originally opposed the United States' acquisition of the Philippines, but once it was an American possession, Taft saw it as his duty to guide the Philippines toward eventual self-government. With the encouragement of his beloved Nellie, Taft accepted the chairmanship and set sail for Manila.

Taft was well-suited to his task; he was patient, tolerant, affectionate, and stubborn when necessary (which it often was as he clashed with military governor General Arthur MacArthur). Taft came to love and respect the native population of the Philippines. His judicial mind and basic impartiality made him effective in his position, so much so that in 1901 he was sworn in as civilian governor of the island. The capture of Emilio Aguinaldo, leader of the native insurgents, and his oath of allegiance to the American government made Taft's job easier. Taft particularly concerned himself with organizing municipal government, establishing an honest judiciary, and finding sources of adequate revenue for the Philippines.

Taft was distressed by news of the death of President McKinley but rejoiced at the elevation of his dear friend Roosevelt to the presidency. Taft suffered from overwork and the debilitating climate and briefly returned to the United States after two operations. He next traveled to Rome to settle the ongoing dispute over land that had once belonged to the Spanish friars but that the native insurgents claimed as captured lands. Once again he brought order out of chaos and obtained a settlement satisfactory to both sides before returning to the Philippines. Taft was deeply committed to the Philippines and the development of a stable government there. On two separate occasions he declined appointment to the Supreme Court. For Taft, duty came always first, and he believed that his major responsibility at that time was in the Philippines. At last, however, President Roosevelt laid greater claim to Taft's abilities, and in 1903, he was named secretary of war in Roosevelt's cabinet. Roosevelt valued Taft's legal mind and often used him to act as president pro tempore while he was away. Taft's service in the Philippines lent great prestige to the 1904 campaign. As secretary of war, Taft traveled widely—again to the Philippines, to Japan, to Mexico, to Cuba, and to the Panama Canal. He briefly acted as provisional governor of Cuba in 1906 and used his influence to reestablish local government under new election laws. Again Taft was offered appointment to the Supreme Court, and again he declined, this time in order to pursue the presidency itself. He seemed more and more likely to be the party's choice to succeed Roosevelt (who had earlier announced that he would not be a candidate). He was indeed nominated and, with vigorous support from Roosevelt, was elected in 1908. He prepared to complete the work of reform begun by Roosevelt.

Taft and Roosevelt, however, differed in political experience, in style of government, and, most important, in their interpretation of the Constitution. Roosevelt had always believed that he and the government could do anything not specifically forbidden; Taft, with his legal background, was a strict constructionist who believed that he and the government ought to act only in those areas specifically authorized by the Constitution. Although Taft was as genuine a reformer as Roosevelt, his more limited view of presidential activism made him appear to his contemporaries as far more conservative than he really was.

In the area of foreign policy, Taft followed dollar diplomacy both in Asia and in Latin America. He supported Japan rather than China in the Pacific and stood aside while Mexico endured a series of revolutionary upheavals. Taft was devoted to the idea of peace and supported arbitration treaties among the nations as an alternative to war.

In his four years as president, Taft gained more than adequate Progressive credentials. He brought antitrust suits against ninety corporations, compared with only fifty-four in the nearly eight years of Roosevelt's administration. Taft, however, had none of Roosevelt's political skill, nor was he able to use the press to publicize his accomplishments. In an era in which support for Progressive reform still ran strong, Taft was seldom credited for what he did. Taft's administration was responsible for the establishment of a postal savings bank, a tax on corporate income, further regulation of the railroads, the creation of a budget surplus, civil service reform, the establishment of a children's bureau, and the admission of New Mexico and Arizona as states.

All these accomplishments, however, were overshadowed by major crises, or blunders, which together alienated Taft from Roosevelt and lost him much of the Progressive support necessary for successful reelection. The first crisis occurred when reformist congressional insurgents determined to reduce the extensive powers of Speaker of the House Joseph Cannon. Though largely in sympathy with this purpose, Taft remained aloof from the fight, believing in the separation of the executive and legislative branches of government. His private letters reveal his support for reform, but he was publicly identified with the conservative leadership. The second crisis occurred over the issue of tariff reform (a politically divisive issue which Roosevelt had avoided for eight years). Again, although Taft supported reform, the measure that he supported did not go far enough to satisfy Progressive reformers. The mixed rates of the heavily amended Payne-Aldrich Tariff Act were unwisely supported by Taft in such glowing terms that, once again, he alienated reformers who had hoped for more.

Specifically alienating not only Progressive reformers but also Roosevelt were Taft's actions in the Ballinger-Pinchot controversy and the United States Steel case. Interior Secretary Richard Ballinger was heavily criticized by Roosevelt's protégé Gifford Pinchot (who served under Ballinger), who accused Ballinger of corruption and misuse of federal lands in connection with territory in Alaska that had been set aside for government use but was later released for sale to the public. Pinchot's criticism continued publicly after Ballinger was exonerated of any wrongdoing, and Taft had no alternative but to fire him for insubordination. Roosevelt saw this as a personal affront. Similarly,

Roosevelt viewed as a personal attack Taft's antitrust suit against the United States Steel Corporation for an earlier purchase of another steel company. Taft was unaware that in the economic crisis of 1907 Roosevelt had approved the purchase and given his word that there would be no government antitrust suit.

By 1912, Roosevelt had decided to challenge Taft for the Republican nomination, and Taft prepared to fight him for it, convinced that Roosevelt had become so radical that he was a danger to the nation. Taft controlled the party machinery and was renominated by the Republicans. Roosevelt turned to the Progressive Party and became their nominee. The bitter split between these two men made it all the easier for Democratic nominee Woodrow Wilson to be elected president. Taft ran a poor third, carrying only the states of Utah and Vermont. Taft was a gracious loser, and in his remaining months in office, he regained much of the personal popularity that he had enjoyed when he was first elected president.

When he left the White House, Taft accepted a position as a law professor at Yale University. In addition to his teaching responsibilities, he traveled widely and gave many speeches and wrote numerous articles to supplement his income. He also chaired the Lincoln Memorial Commission. By 1916, he had become reconciled with Roosevelt (in public at least) and ardently supported Hughes in opposition to Wilson, who by now was bitterly disliked by both Taft and Roosevelt.

When war broke out, Taft was eager to preserve neutrality but rallied to the nation's support after America entered the war in 1917. He supported the League of Nations as a logical successor to the League to Enforce Peace, which Taft had chaired in 1915. During the war, Taft was joint chairman (with Frank P. Walsh) of the National War Labor Board and its successor, the War Labor Conference Board. Once again, his judicial mind was a great asset as was his realistic approach to the needs of labor.

Taft rejoiced in the election of Republican Warren Harding as president in 1920. His lifelong ambition was at last fulfilled when he was appointed chief justice of the United States in 1921. Taft was a hardworking member of the Court, finally damaging his health by overwork. His tendency toward conservatism had grown more pronounced, especially in the areas of social legislation. Taft's radiant warmth and sincere desire for harmony did much to improve the efficiency of a court often divided on the issues. Taft was especially close to Oliver Wendell Holmes and relied on the intelligence of Louis Brandeis, in spite of their great differences on social issues.

The Court, under Taft, faced a heavy work load, primarily as a result of cases carried over from the war years, cases arising under the income tax laws, and cases involving Prohibition. Taft remained a conservative but was surprisingly sympathetic to labor. He consistently supported the right of labor to organize, to bargain, and to strike, but accorded labor no special privileges. He also supported a minimum wage for women and children. Taft supported a fairly broad interpretation of federal power to regulate business in the public interest, especially in cases under the Interstate Commerce Act. He was concerned as well over the general disrespect for the law engendered by the disregard of the Prohibition laws. As chief justice, Taft worked to preserve the harmony of the Court, seldom dissenting from the majority decision.

Taft was awarded an honorary degree from Oxford University in 1922, and he and his wife enjoyed the associations with royalty which the trip to England involved. He maintained a good Republican's interest in politics and privately supported the election of both Calvin Coolidge and Herbert Hoover. Gradually, however, Taft's health failed, and he resigned from the Supreme Court in February, 1930. He died on March 8, 1930, and was buried in Arlington Cemetery.

Summary

William Howard Taft was a monumental man whose imprint on America was felt in many ways. He was a superb administrator of the Philippines, where his genuine affection for the people did much to assuage their dislike for a colonial overlord. He served well as secretary of war and was a valuable asset to Roosevelt's administration. As president, however, his weaknesses were more apparent. His judicial mind and temperament were ill-suited to the turbulent world of politics, particularly in the era of Progressive reform in which he governed. The public was never aware of Taft's concern and support for reform, and Taft never perceived the importance of public opinion or the value of publicity. He was inclined to let his accomplishments speak for themselves; thus, it has been posterity which has most accurately valued his contributions.

Bibliography

Anderson, Donald F. *William Howard Taft: A Conservative's Conception of the Presidency*. Ithaca, N.Y.: Cornell University Press, 1973. This is a well-written, well-focused book covering only the presidential years and emphasizing Taft as a conservative. Excellent analysis of Taft's weaknesses, but less on his strengths.

Butt, Archibald W. *Taft and Roosevelt: The Intimate Letters of Archie Butt*. Garden City, N.Y.: Doubleday, Doran and Co., 1930. The lively correspondence of a man who worked closely and intimately as a military aide to both Roosevelt and Taft.

Coletta, Paolo E. *The Presidency of William Howard Taft*. Lawrence: University Press of Kansas, 1973. An issue-oriented account of Taft's presidential years with a fair balance of both his strengths and his weaknesses.

Collin, Richard H. "Symbiosis Versus Hegemony: New Directions in the Foreign Relations Historiography of Theodore Roosevelt and William Howard Taft." *Diplomatic History* 19, no. 3 (Summer, 1995): 473-498.

Duffy, Herbert Smith. *William Howard Taft*. New York: Minton, Balch, 1930. A memorial biography of the recently deceased president. Biased; lacks an evaluation of Taft's role in American political life.

Manners, William. *TR and Will: A Friendship That Split the Republican Party*. New York: Harcourt, Brace and World, 1969. A scholarly approach to the theme of Archie Butt's letters and an acknowledgment that Roosevelt and Taft are best understood in contrast with each other rather than studied alone.

Mason, Alpheus Thomas. *William Howard Taft: Chief Justice*. New York: Simon and Schuster, 1965. As the title suggests, this book focuses on Taft on the Supreme Court with little mention of his presidential years.

Minger, Ralph E. *William Howard Taft and United States Foreign Policy: The Apprenticeship Years, 1900-1908*. Urbana: University of Illinois Press, 1975. A study of Taft as secretary of war and governor of the Philippines and the development of his opinions on the broad questions of foreign policy.

Post, Robert C. "Chief Justice William Howard Taft and the Concept of Federalism." *Constitutional Commentary* 9, no. 2 (Summer, 1992): 199-222.

Pringle, Henry F. The Life and Times of William Howard Taft. New York: Farrar and Rinehart, 1939. Reprint. Hamden, Conn.: Archon Books, 1964. Of the many books written about Taft, this massive, two-volume biography is the best, an indispensable beginning for any study of Taft. Splendidly written, it evokes not only the accomplishments but also the spirit of the man.

Carlanna L. Hendrick

Zachary Taylor

Born: November 24, 1784; Orange County, Virginia
Died: July 9, 1850; Washington, D.C.

Climaxing a military career of nearly forty years with major victories in the Mexican War, Taylor used his popularity as a war hero to win office as twelfth president of the United States.

Early Life

Zachary Taylor was born November 24, 1784, at Montebello, a kinsman's country home in Orange County, Virginia. He was the third of eight children born to Richard and Sarah Dabney Strother Taylor, both members of prominent Virginia families. Richard Taylor was a lieutenant colonel in a Virginia regiment during the American Revolution; his father, also named Zachary Taylor, was a wealthy planter and surveyor general of Virginia.

During 1769 and 1770, Richard Taylor surveyed land in central Kentucky and around the Falls of the Ohio at the modern city of Louisville. In the spring of 1785, shortly after Zachary's birth, Richard Taylor moved his family to Jefferson County, Kentucky, where he carved out a farm known as Springfield, near Louisville. As a youth, Zachary studied under Kean O'Hara, who would become one of Kentucky's leading early nineteenth century educators, and Elisha Ayer, an itinerant Connecticut teacher. He also assisted his father with farm work.

In 1806, possessing a youthful passion for a military career, Taylor got a brief taste of army life as a volunteer in the Kentuckian militia. His long career as an officer did not commence until June, 1808, however, when he received a commission as first lieutenant in the United States Army from Secretary of War Henry Dearborn. Appointed to the Seventh Infantry Regiment, he spent several months on recruiting duty in Kentucky, followed by temporary command of Fort Pickering, near modern Memphis, Tennessee, before reporting to General James Wilkinson at New Orleans in June, 1809. A short time later, he contracted yellow fever and returned to Louisville to recover. While at home, he met Margaret Mackall Smith, whom he married on

June 21, 1810. They had six children, four of whom lived to maturity. Their daughter Sarah Knox Taylor was the first wife of Confederate president Jefferson Davis. Richard Taylor, their only son, became a lieutenant general in the Confederate army.

After his recovery and marriage, Taylor was promoted to captain and assigned to General William Henry Harrison, territorial governor of Indiana. In April, 1812, just before the War of 1812, Captain Taylor assumed command of Fort Harrison, near Terre Haute, which he successfully defended against an attack by some four hundred Indians the following September. Promoted to the rank of brevet major, he commanded several frontier posts during the second war with England.

Zachary Taylor *(Library of Congress)*

In early 1815, Taylor won promotion to the full rank of major, but when the army was disbanded, he was reduced to his prewar rank of captain. Deciding to pursue private business, he declined reassignment, resigned his commission, and returned to his family's Kentucky farm.

Now thirty years old, Taylor epitomized neither the country gentleman nor the military hero. Five feet, eight inches in height, he was muscular and broad-shouldered with disproportionately long arms. He had a full-shaped head with an oval face, a wide, somewhat slanting brow, and prominent cheekbones. His long nose and hazel eyes gave him an eaglelike appearance.

Life's Work

Zachary Taylor was devoted to the soil, but his passion for military service was even stronger. Thus, in 1816, when President James Madison offered to reinstate him at his previous rank of major, Taylor accepted. His initial assignment was command of Fort Howard, near Green Bay, Wisconsin, where he remained for two years. After a furlough in Kentucky, he received a promotion to lieutenant colonel in 1819 and was assigned to the Fourth Infantry at New Orleans. A series of commands and special assignments followed over the next twelve years. In 1822, he built Fort Jesup, Louisiana, and the following year, he served as commandant of Baton Rouge. In 1824, he was appointed superintendent general of the recruiting service at Cincinnati and Louisville and served until 1826, when he reported to Washington, D.C., to serve on a board chaired by General Winfield Scott to study militia organization. In May, 1828, Taylor assumed command of Fort Snelling, in the unorganized Minnesota territory. Fourteen months later, he took command of Fort Crawford at Prairie du Chien in the Michigan Territory, now part of Wisconsin. There he remained until mid-1830.

In April, 1832, Taylor was promoted to colonel. Meanwhile, the Black Hawk War had erupted in Illinois. Colonel Taylor, on leave in Kentucky after recovering from an illness, sped to Galena, Illinois, and in May took charge of the First Infantry Regiment, under command of General Henry Atkinson. Three months later, Taylor participated in the decisive Battle of Bad Axe on the Mississippi River, north of Prairie du Chien. Black Hawk escaped the battlefield but was captured in late

August. Taylor received custody of the defeated war chief and turned him over to Second Lieutenant Jefferson Davis, who escorted Black Hawk to Jefferson Barracks, Missouri.

With the end of the Black Hawk War, Taylor resumed command of Fort Crawford, where he remained until November, 1836. During this duty, he demonstrated a strong interest in the education of both white and Indian children and attempted to control the harsh practices of whiskey merchants and fur traders in their dealings with the tribes in the region. Upon relinquishing his command at Fort Crawford, the colonel reported to Jefferson Barracks and took charge of the right wing of the army's Western Department under General Edmund P. Gaines. In this capacity, Taylor exercised military authority over the entire Northwest.

His new command lasted less than eight months. In July, 1837, Taylor received instructions to take elements of the First Infantry from Forts Snelling and Crawford to Tampa Bay, Florida, where General Thomas S. Jesup was bogged down in the Second Seminole War. While the colonel was en route, Jesup violated a temporary truce and captured Seminole leader Osceola and about two hundred of his followers—but hundreds more waited deep in the Everglades.

Taylor and his troops arrived in Florida in the fall, and the colonel took command in the field. In early December, 1837, after weeks of preparation, Taylor left Fort Gardiner with a force of more than one thousand regular and volunteer troops. Pursuing the Seminoles into the vicinity of Lake Okeechobee, Taylor made contact with a large force on Christmas Day. In a fierce battle that cost the lives of several of his top officers, Taylor routed the Seminoles and drove them from the field. The victory won for Taylor a promotion to brevet brigadier general, and a short time later, he replaced General Jesup as commander of the Florida theater.

General Taylor remained in Florida for two more years before assuming command at Baton Rouge. The following year, Taylor succeeded General Matthew Arbuckle as commander of the Second Department, Western Division, headquartered at Fort Smith, Arkansas. There, he remained until May, 1844, when he returned to Fort Jesup to assume command of the First Department. In June, 1845, after the United States annexed Texas, he received orders to move his troops to Corpus Christi, on the Nueces River, to protect the new state in case of attack by Mexico. The following January, President James K. Polk ordered Taylor to move to the Rio Grande, occupying territory whose possession was a source of dispute. In late March, Taylor established a position opposite the Mexican town of Matamoros. A month later, several American soldiers were killed in a skirmish with Mexican troops. On May 13, 1846, Congress declared war on Mexico.

Taylor, however, did not wait for the declaration of war. On May 8, he engaged and defeated a much larger Mexican force at Palo Alto. The next day, he defeated the Mexicans again at Resaca de la Palma. As a result, Polk promoted him to major general and gave him command of the Army of the Rio Grande. More victories followed as he captured Monterrey in September and crushed a force under General Antonio Lopez de Santa Anna at Buena Vista in February, 1847.

With the end of the Mexican War, Taylor returned to the United States, receiving a hero's welcome at New Orleans in December, 1847. A short time later, he retired to his home in Baton Rouge and began tending to the affairs of Cypress Grove, the Mississippi plantation he had acquired a few years earlier. His retirement was brief. In 1848, the Whig Party, starved for victory, nominated the military hero for president and secured his election over Democrat Lewis Cass and Free-Soiler Martin Van Buren.

Although a slaveholder, President Taylor was a staunch Unionist. Faced with the volatile issue of slavery in the territories acquired from Mexico, he supported California's admission as a free state in 1849 and the organization of New Mexico and Utah without consideration of the slavery issue. When Congress convened in January, 1850, Senator Henry Clay proposed a series of compromise resolutions designed to defuse these and related issues, including a Texas-New Mexico border dispute, the fugitive slave question, and the future of the slave trade in Washington, D.C. While Congress debated the Compromise of 1850, delegates from nine Southern states met in Nashville in June to consider the defense of Southern rights and their section's future within the Union. Moderate voices prevailed, but more radical "Fire-eaters" raised the specter of secession. Taylor, however, continued to resist any compromise that would promote the expansion of slavery and promised to meet disunionist threats with force.

The political deadlock remained on July 4, when Taylor attended a ceremony related to construction of the Washington Monument. He became overheated and, according to tradition, tried to cool off by consuming large quantities of cherries and iced milk. That evening he contracted gastroenteritis, from which he died on July 9.

Summary

In many respects, Zachary Taylor symbolized both the aspirations and the anxieties of the American people during the mid-nineteenth century. In a period pervaded by the spirit of Manifest Destiny, his victories in the Mexican War contributed to the nation's acquisition of a vast new territory, including the future states of California, New Mexico, Arizona, Nevada, and Utah. Only four days before his death, President Taylor signed the Clayton-Bulwer Treaty with England, the first diplomatic step toward construction of the Panama Canal.

As president, however, the victor of Buena Vista had to deal with the practical consequences of Manifest Destiny. As both a Unionist and a plantation owner with more than one hundred slaves, he embodied the conflicting social and economic forces which confronted the nation during the decade before the Civil War, especially citizens of the border states and Upper South. In Taylor's case, Unionist sentiments formed during four decades in the nation's military service triumphed over his own economic interests. During the decade that followed his death, however, a growing number of his fellow Southerners resolved the conflict between slavery and Union in the opposite direction. When the election of Abraham Lincoln as president in 1860 convinced many Southerners that they no longer could protect their "peculiar institution" within the Union, they chose secession. They elected as their president Zachary Taylor's friend and former son-in-law, Jefferson Davis.

Bibliography

Bauer, K. Jack. *Zachary Taylor: Soldier, Planter, Statesman of the Old Southwest*. Baton Rouge: Louisiana State University Press, 1985. This well-researched, well-written volume is the first account of Taylor's life to appear since 1951. Particularly useful for the general reader, Bauer's work gives a balanced view of Taylor's early life, military career, and brief presidency.

DeVoto, Bernard A. *The Year of Decision, 1846*. Boston: Little, Brown and Co., 1943. Taylor fares poorly in this spectacular, almost theatrical saga of America's westward march. From the Mexican War to the Mormon emigration to Utah, DeVoto captures the profound national emotions that undergirded Manifest Destiny.

Hamilton, Holman. *Zachary Taylor: Soldier of the Republic.* Indianapolis: Bobbs-Merrill Co., 1941. Volume 1 of Hamilton's magisterial biography, this remains the best single book on Taylor's early life and military career. Thoroughly researched and highly readable, it is sympathetic yet balanced, especially in regard to Taylor's dealings with his military and political rivals.

__________. *Zachary Taylor: Soldier in the White House.* Indianapolis: Bobbs-Merrill Co., 1951. A worthy companion to the preceding volume, this book explores the brief but important tenure of the nation's last slaveholding president. Thoroughly researched, it demonstrates that Taylor was a much more active president than is commonly believed.

Potter, David M. *The Impending Crisis, 1848-1861.* Completed and edited by Don E. Fehrenbacher. New York: Harper and Row, Publishers, 1976. Taylor is one of the many important figures who appear in this excellent narrative of the political events leading from the Mexican War to the outbreak of the Civil War. An outstanding contextual volume, it synthesizes the vast literature dealing with the complex issues of slavery, expansionism, and sectional politics.

Singletary, Otis A. *The Mexican War.* Chicago: University of Chicago Press, 1960. This concise treatment of the war which climaxed American continental expansion is both historically sound and quite readable. Its emphasis is on military events and political intrigues at the expense of diplomatic relations between the United States and Mexico.

Smith, Elbert B. *The Presidencies of Zachary Taylor & Millard Fillmore.* Lawrence: University Press of Kansas, 1988.

Weinberg, Albert K. *Manifest Destiny: A Study of Nationalist Expansionism in American History.* Baltimore: The John Hopkins University Press, 1935. Zachary Taylor's name does not appear in this analytical study of American expansion from the Louisiana Purchase to the Spanish-American War, but the book is essential to understanding the policy motives behind the military ventures in which he participated.

Carl E. Kramer

NORMAN THOMAS

Born: November 20, 1884; Marion, Ohio
Died: December 19, 1968; Huntington, New York

Often called "the conscience of America," Thomas ran six times for president on the Socialist Party ticket and became one of the country's greatest critic-reformers.

Early Life

Norman Mattoon Thomas was born November 20, 1884, in Marion, Ohio, the home of Warren Gamaliel Harding, where he earned pocket money by delivering the *Marion Star*. He was the eldest of six children sired by the Reverend Welling Thomas, a Presbyterian minister whose father, also a Presbyterian minister, had been born in Wales. Norman's mother, Emma Mattoon, was also the child of a Presbyterian clergyman. The Thomas household was Republican in politics, devout in religion, and conservative in conduct, opposed to dancing, cardplaying, and Sunday merrymaking. Emma Thomas was acknowledged by the family as its dominant force, emphasizing a keen sense of personal and social responsibility that her firstborn practiced all of his life.

After his 1905 graduation from Princeton University as valedictorian of his class, Thomas took his first full-time job as a social worker at New York City's Spring Street Presbyterian Church and Settlement House, located in a poverty-stricken area. In 1907, he became assistant to the pastor of Christ Church in Manhattan. There he met Frances Violet Stewart, active in Christian social service and born into a moderately wealthy family of financiers. They were married September 1, 1910, and led a notably happy marital life, in their turn having six children and fifteen grandchildren.

From 1910 to 1911, Thomas attended the heterodox Union Theological Seminary. There he was most impressed by the writings of Walter Rauschenbusch, one of the leading figures of the Social Gospel movement, who argued that the ethical precepts of Jesus did not harmonize with the selfish materialism of a capitalist society. Thirty years later, Thomas wrote, "Insofar as any one man . . . made me a Socialist, it was probably Walter Rauschenbusch." Ordained in 1911, Thomas became pastor of the East Harlem Presbyterian Church and chairman of the American Parish, a federation of Presbyterian churches and social agencies located in immigrant neighborhoods. In 1912, he declared, "The Christian Church faces no more burning question than the problem of making brotherhood real."

Life's Work

The agonies of World War I crystallized Norman Thomas' social radicalism. He came to consider the war an immoral conflict between competing imperial powers, and in January, 1917, joined the Fellowship of Reconciliation, a religious pacifist group with a commitment to drastic social reform. Thomas came to regard resistance to the war as a clear choice of individual conscience over the dictates of an amoral state. His militant pacifism led him to support Morris Hillquit, the Socialist candidate, who ran on an antiwar platform in the 1917 New York City mayoralty race.

Thomas joined another pacifist, Roger Baldwin, in the 1917 establishment of the Civil Liberties Union, later renamed the American Civil Liberties Union. In the spring of 1918, he resigned from his church and the parish, aware that his radicalism was jeopardizing these institutions' chances for outside financial assistance. In October, 1918, he applied for membership in the American Socialist Party; he was motivated, he recalled later, by "grotesque inequalities, conspicuous waste, gross exploitation, and unnecessary poverty all around me."

The Party was led by three talented men: Victor Berger, Morris Hillquit, and Eugene V. Debs. The first two were its theoreticians and tacticians, but it was the populist, pragmatic Debs (1855-1926) who became American Socialism's greatest leader until Thomas' ascendancy. Debs grounded his convictions on emotional rather than philosophic premises: He had an evangelical devotion to social justice, a generous and sensitive temperament, sincerity, warmth, and an intuitive understanding of popular opinion.

In the 1920 election, Debs received 920,000 votes, but they were largely a tribute to his courage for having chosen imprisonment (from 1918 to 1921) to dramatize his pacifism; membership in the Socialist Party was down that year, from a 1912 peak of 108,000 to twenty-seven thousand. During the 1920's several conditions combined to keep the American Socialist Party's numbers and influence low: a dominant mood among the electorate of economic conservatism and intense nativism; hostility to organized labor by all three branches of government; a number of failed strikes; and the 1919-1920 "Red scare" mass arrests of radicals and labor leaders by the Department of Justice under Attorney General A. Mitchell Palmer. When Senator Robert M. La Follette campaigned for the presidency in 1924, he refused to run solely as the Socialist candidate, preferring to call himself a Progressive. Nevertheless, the Socialist Party energetically supported his campaign; 855,000 of La Follette's 3,800,000 votes were cast on Socialist levers.

Norman Thomas began his long career of seeking public office in 1924, running as a New York gubernatorial candidate on both the Socialist and Progressive tickets. Ironically, he had risen to Socialist leadership at a time when many people were leaving the Party. More ironically, the income his wife inherited from her conservative father enabled him to crusade for his causes on a full-time basis. He admitted that in this instance, "the critic of capitalism was its beneficiary."

By the mid-1920's, Thomas was the consensual choice to succeed Eugene V. Debs—who had never regained his health after his three-year imprisonment, and who died in 1926—as the leader of American Socialism. In 1928, he was chosen the party's presidential candidate—the first of six such nominations; he received 267,000 votes. In 1932 he was to poll 885,000; in 1936, 187,000; in 1940, 100,000; in 1944, 80,000; in 1948, 140,000.

Thomas attracted the deep affection and admiration of many people, often including ideological opponents. His physical appearance was impressive: He stood over six feet two, had strongly marked patrician features, vibrant blue eyes, well-bred manners, and an air of genteel self-confidence. Although a man of dignity, he could communicate warmth and cordiality to a wide range of people. His physical energy was phenomenal until his late seventies, when failing eyesight and crippling arthritis began to plague him. Since he had no hobbies, he focused his unflagging pace on not only campaigning, but also on writing sixteen books and scores of pamphlets, maintaining an enormous correspondence, attending countless conventions and committee meetings, and delivering thousands of speeches. Perhaps his only flaw as a leader was his remoteness—in contrast to Debs—from the rough-and-tumble realities of the American political panorama. He was by temperament an educator, moralist, and intellectual rather than a pragmatic accommodator of conflicting interests. Since he had no solid prospect of winning public office, he could afford to maintain an incorruptible integrity and the noblest of principles.

Thomas' virtuosity as a public speaker was his outstanding leadership asset. He was a masterful humorist, firing quick barbs at his targets. In 1932 he asked his listeners not to fix on Herbert Hoover as the person solely responsible for their economic suffering, since "such a little man could not have made so big a Depression" As for Harry S Truman, he "proves the old adage that any man can become President of the United States." Perhaps the best-known Thomas anecdote recounts a meeting he had with President Franklin D. Roosevelt in 1935. When Thomas complained to FDR about a particular New Deal measure, the president retorted, "Norman, I'm a damn sight better politician than you." Responded Thomas, "Certainly, Mr. President, you're on that side of the desk and I'm on this."

In 1932, with the country deeply mired in the Great Depression and capitalism seriously shaken, the Socialist Party hoped for a presidential vote of more than two million. The Socialist platform anticipated New Deal programs on many issues, demanding Federal appropriations for public works, reforestation, and slum clearance, increased public housing, a six-hour day and five-day working week, old-age pensions, health and maternity insurance, improved workmen's compensation and accident insurance, adequate minimum wage laws, and a compulsory system of unemployment compensation with adequate benefits derived from both government and employer contributions.

Contrary to Socialist expectations, the combined popular vote for all minority party candidates in 1932 barely exceeded one million, and Roosevelt embarked on an ambitious program to save capitalism by implementing a vast amount of social welfare legislation. Norman Thomas consistently chided the New Deal for what he regarded as its lack of any consistent underlying philosophy, for its opportunistic, helter-skelter improvisation and experimentation. This very pragmatism and daring, however, endeared FDR to the majority of the electorate—much to Thomas' frustration. In his *The Politics of Upheaval* (1979), the historian Arthur Schlesinger, Jr., considers that in the 1930's Thomas'

> essential contribution . . . was to keep moral issues alive at a moment when the central emphasis was on meeting economic emergencies. At his best, Thomas gave moving expression to an ethical urgency badly needed in politics. . . .

The 1930's witnessed an increasingly dangerous world situation, with Adolf Hitler's Germany, Benito Mussolini's Italy, and, late in the decade, Francisco Franco's Spain threatening the peace. Under the guise of opposing Fascism, communists in both Europe and the United States wooed liberals and radicals to form a united, "popular front." Norman Thomas temporarily flirted with the notion of such international solidarity in his 1934 book, *The Choice Before Us*. A 1937 trip he took to Europe, however, during which he witnessed Communist attempts to control Spain's Loyalist government through shabby betrayals and observed Stalin's purge trials of his former comrades, reaffirmed Thomas' mistrust of totalitarian Communism and his conviction of its basic incompatibility with democratic Socialism. The Moscow-Berlin Pact of August, 1939, outraged him as "a piece of infamy." Thomas made certain that, from 1939 on, the United States Socialist Party would vigorously oppose Communism, even when the Soviet Union was America's ally during World War II.

In the late 1930's and early 1940's Thomas' lifelong pacifist sentiments were in agonizing conflict with his detestation of Fascism and strong sympathy for the Spanish Republicans locked in civil warfare with Franco's Falangists. Thomas tried to solve this dilemma by backing aid for the Spanish government while opposing direct United States intervention on behalf of Great Britain and France after World War II had erupted in September, 1939. By late 1941, the Socialist Party's noninterventionist foreign policy, combined with Thomas' often acerbic criticism of the New Deal's socioeconomic program, had alienated many former members and well-wishers. Even though the Party fielded presidential tickets through 1956, it was never to recover its health from these losses. By the 1944 presidential campaign, Thomas' insistence on maintaining the fullest measure of civil liberties even amid a world war, and his opposition to the Allied demand on Germany and Japan for unconditional surrender had cost him much of his previous popularity: His vote total proved the lowest of his six national appeals.

In the 1948 presidential election, Thomas' main target was former vice president Henry Wallace, who had left the Democratic Party to run as an antimilitarist, radical candidate for president on the Progressive ticket. Thomas became convinced that the Progressive Party was controlled by communists, with Wallace serving as a naïve front man capable of such self-damning errors as describing the Soviet Union as a "directed democracy." When Thomas received less than 100,000 votes despite a spirited campaign, he became convinced of the futility of Socialist attempts to attract nationwide electoral support, and renounced further office seeking. In 1952 and 1956, the Party ran a Pennsylvania state legislator, Darlington Hoopes, for the presidency. He received twenty thousand votes in 1952, two thousand in 1956; no Socialist has since sought the presidency.

With his buoyant energy and sparkling mind, Thomas remained dynamically active through the 1950's and early 1960's. He resigned from various official posts in the Socialist Party in 1955, at the age of seventy-one, but remained its most magnetic advocate. The major party candidate to whom Thomas was most sympathetic during this period was Adlai Stevenson, with whom he shared a Princeton background, good breeding, and eloquent speech making. The American statesman with whom he disagreed most vehemently was John Foster Dulles, Eisenhower's secretary of state, also a fellow Princetonian as well as fellow Presbyterian. Thomas scorned Dulles' appeasement of demagogic Senator Joseph McCarthy; the bellicosity of his opposition to mainland China; his dismissal of Eleanor Roosevelt from the United States delegation to the United Nations; and his discharge of liberals and Socialists, no matter how talented, from foreign service posts.

Norman Thomas remained a morally consistent critic-commentator on American politics to the end of his fife. He voted for John Kennedy in 1960 and Lyndon Johnson in 1964, but with little enthusiasm for either candidate. In the former year, his favorite was an old friend, Hubert Humphrey, who lost the Democratic nomination to Kennedy. The Bay of Pigs fiasco shocked Thomas into an outraged telegram of protest, and thereafter he remained lukewarm through Kennedy's one thousand White House days, favoring the president's graceful style and careful separation of state from church, but worried about the moderate, cautious nature of Kennedy's liberalism. He voted for Johnson mainly to vote against the right-wing Barry Goldwater.

Though plagued by arthritic legs and a minor heart ailment,

Thomas maintained a strenuous lecturing, debating, and writing schedule in the early 1960's, keeping in the fast lane of what his friends called the "Thomas Track Meet." The only debating opponent who succeeded in spoiling his usually good temper was William Buckley, Jr., whom he regarded as a cold-blooded imperialist and self-righteous reactionary. Thomas' preferred activity during his last years was spending several consecutive days as guest in residence on a college or university campus, not only lecturing but also making himself available as casual participant in bull sessions with students and faculty. On lecture platforms he would sometimes limp slowly to the podium, leaning on his cane, then address his audience with the opening line, "Creeping Socialism!"

By his eightieth birthday in late 1964 he was cast in the role of Grand Old Man, admired and loved for his integrity, dignity, intelligence, and wit, given standing ovations at his appearances. When he returned to his birthplace for a birthday tribute, the local paper printed one letter critical of Thomas' opposition to American military involvement in Vietnam. He was relieved: "I feel better not to be too respectable." In 1966, he shocked his oldest grandson, a pastor, by permitting *Playboy* to interview him at considerable length. Thomas expressed a frequent regret of his old age: that he had seen the American working class becoming increasingly middle-class in its materialism; this "dilution of labor's down-the-line militancy has been one of the greatest disappointments in my life." In 1965, ophthalmologists diagnosed his retinal arteriosclerosis; by 1966 he was legally blind, bent by his arthritis, and in pain much of the time. He never complained, however, and his voice retained its booming roar. He finished dictating his twenty-first book, *The Choices*, four weeks before his death in a nursing home a month after his eighty-fourth birthday.

Summary

Norman Thomas devoted a long, honorable life to urging a largely uninterested American public to share his vision of democratic Socialism as a solution to social inequities and injustices. He served as a goad and gadfly in the Socratic tradition of appealing to his country's good sense and conscience. Some of the social welfare and civil rights legislation he sought was enacted into law during the administrations of Franklin Roosevelt and Lyndon Johnson—with Thomas given no or scant credit for having championed it. His great hope of building a strong Socialist movement in the United States was never realized, and he left his party, under circumstances beyond his control, weaker at his death than when he had joined it in young manhood.

Yet Norman Thomas' life can justly be called an extraordinary success story. He was a patrician moralist who maintained an unswerving passion for social justice, devotion to civil liberties, sympathy for the poor, deprived, and handicapped, hatred of war's wasteful slaughter, and faith in the ultimate wisdom of a free people. Profoundly reasonable and fair in temperament, he found expression for his evolving views first in humanitarian Christianity, then in a muted, non-Marxist Socialism. The personal esteem he gained was extraordinary: Thomas became not simply an adornment to hundreds of liberal and left-democratic causes but also an admirable member of the pantheon of great American dissenters that includes Henry Clay, Daniel Webster, Eugene V. Debs, Robert M. La Follette, and Martin Luther King, Jr.

Bibliography

Bell, Daniel. *Socialism and American Life*. 2 vols. Princeton, N.J.: Princeton University Press, 1952. An incisive, lucidly written historical and sociological analysis, particularly useful for describing the background and development of marxist socialism in the United States.

Duram, James C. *Norman Thomas*. Boston: Twayne Publishers, 1974. A concise study of Thomas' books and pamphlets, with comprehensive notes and references.

__________. "Norman Thomas as Presidential Conscience." *Presidential Studies Quarterly* 20, no. 3 (Summer, 1990): 581-590.

Harrington, Michael. Review of two Thomas biographies in *The Reporter* 25 (November 9, 1961): 64-66. A leading young socialist whom Thomas befriended portrays him as a representative of the American Protestant drive for social justice and moral improvement.

Rosenberg, Bernard. "The Example of Norman Thomas." *Dissent* 11 (Fall, 1964): 415-422. A review of two Thomas biographies. Rosenberg cogently analyzes Thomas' place in contemporary American society and urges fulfillment of Thomas' vision of a better world.

Seidler, Murray B. *Norman Thomas: Respectable Rebel*. Syracuse, N.Y.: Syracuse University Press, 1967. The most scholarly biographical-critical study to date, it focuses on Thomas' successes and failures as leader of the Socialist Party.

Swanberg, W. A. *Norman Thomas: The Last Idealist*. New York: Charles Scribner's Sons, 1976. A vivid, well-written biography that emphasizes the warmth and courage of Thomas' character, has a multitude of illustrative photographs, but often gets so immersed in details that it loses sight of the larger ideological terrain.

Gerhard Brand

HARRY S TRUMAN

Born: May 8, 1884; Lamar, Missouri
Died: December 26, 1972; Kansas City, Missouri

As president of the United States from 1945 to 1953, Truman defended and institutionalized the New Deal reform program of Franklin D. Roosevelt and established the doctrine of containment that guided American policymakers in the Cold War era.

Early Life

Harry S Truman, whose career enhanced Missouri's reputation for producing tough and stubborn individuals, was born in the southwestern part of that state on May 8, 1884, but grew up in rural Jackson County, in and around Independence. His parents, John Anderson and Martha Ellen Truman, were prominent, well-connected citizens of the area, and Harry looked back on his childhood years as happy, secure ones. He was captivated by the world of books, however, which revealed to him that there was a bigger, more rewarding realm within his reach. Success in that realm could be attained, he believed, by strictly adhering to the work ethic taught by his parents and by developing his ability to manipulate people by learning what motivated and pleased them. His parents also taught him a Victorian set of moral absolutes, a tendency to see the world in black and white terms, that later influenced his decision making.

When he was graduated from high school in 1901, his father's "entangled" finances prevented young Truman from going to college. He held several unsatisfying jobs in the next few years and then farmed until 1917, when he served in the army during World War I. After a small business firm he had opened in Kansas City failed in 1922, Truman, whose restless ambition had always left him with an edge of frustration, finally found the career that brought him fulfillment. He entered county politics with the backing of Thomas J. Pendergast, the "boss" of the Kansas City Democratic Party machine.

In 1934, after great success in local politics, Truman, with Pendergast's support, won election to the United States Senate. He strongly supported Franklin D. Roosevelt's New Deal program and then gained

Harry S Truman *(Library of Congress)*

national recognition during World War II as head of a committee investigating defense contracts and mobilization bottlenecks.

In 1944, a number of Democratic Party leaders plotted to remove liberal Henry A. Wallace as vice president. Truman surfaced as one of the few prominent individuals acceptable to these bosses and to all the wings of the party. Roosevelt and the convention concurred, and the ticket won the 1944 election.

Life's Work

President Roosevelt's death on April 12, 1945, gave Truman an opportunity to join the heroes who had enlivened his bookish world. The public initially responded favorably to the plainspoken Missourian, and the honeymoon continued as World War II ended, with Germany surrendering on May 7, 1945, and Japan on August 14. The end of the war brought reconversion problems, however, that would have challenged a political magician such as Roosevelt. They overwhelmed Truman. While searching for a chimerical formula that would allow him to please business, labor, consumers, and citizens hungry for scarce meat, Truman stumbled from policy to policy, convincing people that he was a bewildered throttlebottom.

Amid this turmoil, the beleaguered president formulated his domestic program. Operating within the reform legacy of the New Deal, he revealed to Congress on September 6, 1945, what later became the Fair Deal. His legislative requests included legislation requiring the government to maintain full employment, improved unemployment compensation benefits and minimum wages, major housing reforms, assistance to small business, and continued farm price supports. Later additions to the Fair Deal slate included national compulsory health insurance, federal ownership of atomic energy resources and development, aid to education, and civil rights legislation for blacks. Congressional response was disappointing. It gave Truman the watered-down Employment Act and created the Atomic Energy Commission under civilian control. Through executive orders, Truman forbade discrimination against blacks in the civil service and began to desegregate the armed forces. In his second term, Congress passed a housing act.

Perhaps his greatest reform contribution came when the Republicans won both houses of Congress in 1946 and set out to destroy much of the New Deal reform legacy. This allowed Truman to assume his most effective role: defender of the common man from the forces of reaction. He continued this role in the 1948 election, and further protected the New Deal by his upset victory over Republican New York Governor Thomas E. Dewey. No major New Deal program fell before the conservative onslaught, although the Taft-Hartley Act placed some restrictions on labor.

In foreign policy, Truman left a more perilous legacy. By 1947, the Cold War had started. Soviet leaders believed that since the birth of the

Communist government in 1917, Western capitalist nations had been intent on destroying it. Soviet Premier Joseph Stalin intended to use his nation's great military strength, which had destroyed German dictator Adolf Hitler's armies, to build a buffer zone against these hostile Western powers. He hoped to work cooperatively with the West and cautiously refrained from meddling in areas the Western powers considered vital, but caution also compelled him to establish his nation's own sphere of dominance in Eastern Europe.

Truman was poorly suited to deal with the complexities of this situation. He had never been much interested in foreign affairs, and he held a black-and-white view of the world. He quickly came to two conclusions on which he based policy toward the Soviet Union: that Soviet leaders were breaking all of their wartime agreements, making future negotiations senseless, and that the only thing the Russians understood was force. Once committed to these propositions, he ignored all evidence to the contrary. He believed that he could use American military and economic power to coerce the Soviets into compliance with Washington's demands. The test explosion of the first atomic bomb in July, 1945, and use of the weapon against a collapsing Japan on August 6 and August 9 added to his confidence. He later claimed that his actions saved lives by eliminating the necessity of invading the Japanese mainland. The highest American military leaders believed that the bombing was unnecessary, however, especially since the Soviet Union's declaration of war on Japan, which took place on August 8, would, they believed, shock Japan into surrender. Truman dropped the bombs to force Japan to surrender and to intimidate the Soviet Union into accommodation with the United States.

By acting on the assumption that Russians only understood force, Truman convinced Stalin that the West was still intent on the Soviet Union's destruction. When Moscow countered what it viewed as a threat by, for example, tightening its control over Poland and other Eastern European nations, it confirmed Washington's belief that the Soviet Union intended world conquest. The cycle of suspicion and fear spiraled toward the Cold War, with each side taking defensive actions that appeared to be offensive threats to the other.

In 1947, Truman initialed the containment policy that became the fundamental American Cold War strategy. Abandoning serious negotiation, the United States moved to encircle the Soviet bloc, hoping such pressure would cause it to change, to mellow, internally. Over the next few years, one containment action followed another: the Truman Doctrine that promised support for free people facing totalitarian pressures, the Marshall Plan, the Berlin Airlift, and the North Atlantic Treaty Organization. Truman's decisions to fight the Korean War, to finance the French war in Vietnam, to rearm the United States and its Western European allies, and to incorporate West Germany and Japan into the anti-Soviet bloc further raised the containment barrier.

Domestic and foreign problems increasingly merged during Truman's second term, and together they unraveled the popularity he had gained during his 1948 election campaign. China had long been torn by civil war, and in 1949 it "fell" to Mao Tse-tung's Communists. Republican fury made Truman vulnerable to the bizarre charge of being soft on Communism and indifferent to growing fear of internal subversion. In 1946, Truman himself had initiated a loyalty program designed to eliminate Communists from government and had fed fear of subversion by using extreme anti-Communist rhetoric crafted to build public support for containment. Red hysteria, led by demagogues such as Senator Joseph R. McCarthy of Wisconsin, surged in 1950. Although Truman had been partly responsible for McCarthyism, it turned on his administration and undermined his ability to govern.

Truman confronted what he regarded as the greatest challenge of his presidency on June 24, 1950, when the army of North Korea swept across the thirty-eighth parallel into South Korea, an American ally. Truman interpreted this as a Soviet-directed attack on the West, a test of Western resolve. He ordered General Douglas MacArthur, commander of American forces in the Far East, to dispatch American troops to Korea. In September, 1950, MacArthur's forces, operating under the authority of the United Nations, first halted and then pushed the North Koreans back in disarray.

As the North Koreans retreated, Truman faced another major decision. Should he push them back across the thirty-eighth parallel and then halt, content with achieving the original war aim, or should the forces of the United Nations cross the parallel, destroy the North Korean army, and unify Korea? He chose the latter course, and MacArthur drove north toward the Chinese border. In November, 1950, after American leaders ignored China's clear warnings, 300,000 Chinese "volunteers" intervened, shattering the offensive and forcing the longest retreat in United States history. In 1951, the battlefront stabilized near the thirty-eighth parallel, but peace did not come until 1953, during Dwight D. Eisenhower's presidency.

By early 1951, public support for the war had eroded. Then, on April 11, 1951, after a number of public disagreements with MacArthur, Truman recalled the general, who was perhaps the American people's most admired military hero. This action, during an increasingly unpopular war, coupled with the growing force of McCarthyite attacks on the Administration, almost destroyed Truman's ability to govern. He had already decided not to run for reelection in 1952 and supported Adlai Stevenson for the nomination. Republican candidate Dwight D. Eisenhower, promising to clean up the "mess in Washington," easily defeated Stevenson.

Summary

On January 20, 1953, Truman returned to Independence, Missouri, where he lived until his death on December 26, 1972. In retirement, Truman had the satisfaction of seeing many of his Fair Deal proposals take effect, including social security and housing expansion, government health-care programs, and civil rights legislation. Truman also watched his popularity rise to folk-hero status among the general public. Scholars concurred with this evaluation. In 1981, American historians ranked him as the nation's eighth greatest president, and one prominent Truman biographer predicted that he would take his place behind Abraham Lincoln as America's second most beloved president.

These admiring historians believed Truman's greatness rested on his foreign policy. Under his leadership, the United States committed itself to playing a continuing role in international affairs. His administration devised the containment strategy, which served as the foreign policy foundation for his successors in office, and established barriers, such as NATO, against the inundation of the "Free World" by aggressive Communism.

Other historians, however, questioned the wisdom of his policy. The Vietnam War compelled many scholars to reexamine the American past generally, and they often focused on the Cold War period specifically. These revisionists believed that either through an arrogant attempt to impose the American system on the world or through ignorance of Soviet desires and needs and overreaction to Stalin's cautious policy, the United States provoked the Cold War and initiated the dangerous tension that imperiled civilization. Many revisionists concluded that under Truman the United States began to build a national security state that led it to meddle in the affairs of other nations, while civil liberties eroded at home. This globalism diverted resources to military adventures, while American cities decayed and social problems mounted.

Thus, while many of the tumultuous conflicts that dominated the newspaper front pages during the Truman years later seemed petty and were largely forgotten, the man from Independence remained even after his death the center of controversy revolving around issues central to modern history.

Bibliography

Cumings, Bruce. *The Origins of the Korean War: Liberation and the Emergence of Separate Regimes, 1945-1947*. Princeton, N.J.: Princeton University Press, 1981. Excellent first volume in a projected two-volume study of the background of the Korean War. The roots of the war lay in 1945 and 1946, Cumings argues, when the United States undermined the democratic movements that were attempting to carry out needed reforms in South Korea.

Ferrell, Robert H. *Harry S. Truman: A Life*. Columbia: University of Missouri Press, 1994.

Gaddis, John L. *Strategies of Containment: A Critical Appraisal of Postwar American National Security Policy*. New York: Oxford University Press, 1982. A rich and provocative study of containment theory, arguing that the United States since 1947 has alternated between the limited containment theory of George Kennan and the more global conception of United States interests that Truman accepted in 1950 and afterward.

Hamby, Alonzo L. *Beyond the New Deal: Harry S. Truman and American Liberalism*. New York: Columbia University Press, 1973. Traces the tumultuous relationship between Truman and the liberals in the confusing years following Roosevelt's death.

__________. *Man of the People: A Life of Harry S. Truman*. New York: Oxford University Press, 1995.

McCullough, David G. *Truman*. New York: Simon & Schuster, 1992.

Miller, Richard L. *Truman: The Rise to Power*. New York: McGraw-Hill Book Co., 1986. The best available study on Truman's prepresidential years. This is the starting place for an understanding of Truman.

Paterson, Thomas G. *On Every Front: The Making of the Cold War*. New York: W. W. Norton and Co., 1979. A short analytical survey of relations between the United States and the Soviet Union.

Pemberton, William E. *Bureaucratic Politics: Executive Reorganization During the Truman Administration*. Columbia: University of Missouri Press, 1980. A study of Truman's administrative reform program, the most extensive reorganization program in United States history.

Sherwin, Martin J. *A World Destroyed: The Atomic Bomb and the Grand Alliance*. New York: Alfred A. Knopf, 1975. Sherwin does not believe that the atomic bombs were dropped on Japan merely to frighten the Soviet Union, as some charge, but argues that possession of the bomb influenced United States policy toward Moscow. He also believes use of the bomb was probably unnecessary to bring peace.

Truman, Harry S. *Year of Decisions*. Garden City, N.Y.: Doubleday and Co., 1955.

__________. *Years of Trial and Hope*. Garden City, N.Y.: Doubleday and Co., 1956. Truman's memoirs are a detailed description of his actions and policies, often quoting extensively from key documents. While an excellent source, they should be supplemented by additional reading.

Yeargin, Daniel H. *Shattered Peace: The Origins of the Cold War and the National Security State*. Boston: Houghton Mifflin Co., 1977. One of the best studies of the origins of the Cold War. It focuses on the ideology of United States decision makers.

William Pemberton

William Marcy Tweed

Born: April 3, 1823; New York City
Died: April 12, 1878; New York City

William Marcy "Boss" Tweed's name is synonymous with corruption and dishonesty in urban government. Through the power waged by Tweed's Tammany Hall political machine, New York City and its citizens were systematically bilked of millions of dollars in taxes meant for civic projects. Tweed was eventually brought down by his own greed and the combined efforts of a reform coalition of prominent citizens, ordinary people, The New York Times, *and political cartoonist Thomas Nast.*

Early Life

William Marcy Tweed was born April 3, 1823, in lower Manhattan, New York City, the son of Richard and Eliza Tweed. Tweed's great-grandfather, a blacksmith, had emigrated to America from Scotland around 1750. His father was a maker of chairs, and William left school at eleven to apprentice in that trade. At thirteen, he apprenticed with a saddler, leaving to spend a brief stint at a private school in New Jersey to learn bookkeeping. He became a junior clerk at a New York mercantile firm before advancing to a position as head bookkeeper at the small brush manufactory in which his father had invested. At nineteen, he became an officer in the company, and at twenty-one, he married Mary Jane Skaden, the daughter of the factory's principal investor.

The young Tweed, an energetic, powerfully built, ruddy-faced, jovial man, six feet tall and a robust three hundred pounds, may have found the business of making brushes a dull undertaking, for he soon discovered an outlet much more to his liking: volunteer firefighting. By 1850, he had become foreman of a company he had helped to organize, the celebrated Americus No. 611. He was then twenty-seven years old. In the latter half of the nineteenth century in America, volunteer firefighting organizations were one of the ways for ambitious young men to get ahead in politics. Powerful "Big 611," easily identified by the Bengal tiger symbol painted on the company's fire engine, propelled its leader into the public eye; he was soon running for the position of alderman in his home ward under the auspices of the

Democratic Party. He lost by a small margin, but he won his next race easily owing to a split in the Whig vote engendered by a third candidate—a friend of Tweed who was persuaded to do him a favor. The year was 1852, and Tweed was learning how to succeed in politics.

Life's Work

He was learning fast and from the best—the New York City Common Council was widely and cynically known at that time as The Forty Thieves—and the brush factory was soon abandoned for more lucrative pastures. He was an urban political animal, in his element in city politics, a truth realized when he served for two unmemorable years (1853-1855) in the U.S. House of Representatives in Washington, D.C., something he would not repeat again. From then on, he would stick to running for the state senate and city aldermanic positions. In 1856, however, he lost his next race for alderman. Undaunted, and now drawn into the Tammany faction with Peter B. Sweeny and Richard B. Connolly in opposition to Mayor Fernando Wood, he was picked to be head of a new, bipartisan, popularly elected board of supervisors formed to check election fraud. It became, instead, another opportunity for graft and corruption.

Other appointed and elected offices beckoned in quick succession, and Tweed became commissioner of schools, deputy street commissioner, a New York state senator (1867-1871), and chairman of the New York state finance committee. On the Tammany Hall front, he was elected sachem in 1857 and by 1859 was clearly the most influential man in the organization. (He appropriated the Bengal tiger from the volunteer fire company to stand as a symbol of the society, alongside the head of Tammany, a Native American.) He dominated the 1860 state Democratic convention and was thus able to secure several choice spots for his friends and allies. Owing to his influence, Sweeny was elected district attorney in 1857 and Connolly county clerk; George G. Barnard was elected to the office of recorder and later to the New York State Supreme Court. Another crony, A. Oakley Hall, succeeded Sweeny as district attorney in 1860. Although Tweed himself was defeated in a run for the office of sheriff in 1861, the election was not a total loss, as his enemy Fernando Wood was also defeated in the mayoral race.

Undeterred by his lack of legal expertise, Tweed had himself certified by his friend Barnard as a lawyer, and he further enriched his coffers by opening a law office in 1860. He extorted large payoffs for his services from companies desirous of doing business with New York such as the Erie Railroad. In 1864, he bought control of the New York Printing Company, which shortly thereafter became the official printer for the city; other businesses were also coerced into having to deal with the company. His next acquisition, the manufacturing Stationers' Company, was a way for him to sell supplies to the city at graft-inflated prices. The greatest boondoggle of all, the new county courthouse (later to be known as the Tweed Courthouse), was built with stone and marble from a Massachusetts quarry owned by Tweed. The courthouse, expected to cost half a million dollars, wound up costing the city's taxpayers approximately $13 million, most of it winding up in Tweed's capacious pockets.

Now a millionaire as well as a sachem of Tammany Hall, Tweed began to move in much more exalted circles. In 1867, he bought a large residence uptown in Murray Hill, off Fifth Avenue. He was now hobnobbing with neighbors such as the banker J. P. Morgan. He became a partner of the notorious financier/robber barons Jay Gould and James Fisk and became a director of several important utility companies and financial institutions. Gould and Fisk paid him off handsomely, in stock and a board directorship, for enabling them to get the Erie Classification Bill through the state legislature in order to legalize fraudulent railroad stock issued by their firm.

By the time Tweed secured the post of grand sachem of Tammany Hall in 1868, his power in New York was absolute. The "Tweed Ring," a confederation of like-minded crooks and ward heelers with whom "Boss" Tweed surrounded himself, were the rulers of all they surveyed. The ebullient Tweed shared his ill-gotten gains with his ring, increasing the proportion of their graft intake from 50 percent of all bills rendered to the city in 1869 to an astounding 85 percent shortly thereafter. Proceeds were divided by Tweed, the city comptroller, the county chairman, and the mayor. They also had a separate fund used exclusively for bribery.

Tweed moved into an even larger house on 43rd Street and Fifth Avenue and maintained a stable and carriage house an 40th Street. By the early 1870's, he had been named to the boards of the Harlem Gas Company, the Brooklyn Bridge Company, and the Third Avenue Railway Company and was president of the Guardian Savings Bank. He also organized the Tenth National Bank to control city monies and his ever-increasing personal fortune.

Incredibly, a number of New York City's respected leaders were duped for a long period as to Tweed's criminal character. The city charter of 1870, which further cemented the Tweed Ring's hold on New York, was actually supported by honest and upstanding luminaries such as philanthropist Peter Cooper and newspaper publisher Horace Greeley. Retribution, however, was on its way. The talented Austrian-born political cartoonist Thomas Nast launched the first volley against the Tweed Ring in 1869 with a series of caricatures that ran in *Harper's Weekly*—among them the memorable "Let Us Prey," which depicted Tweed and his cronies as fat vultures feeding off the city. The Tammany Tiger became a familiar symbol in Nast's drawings; he did not let up his barrage until 1872. In the fall of 1870, *The New York Times* ran an editorial concerning the massive cost overruns on the county courthouse. Some months later, in the spring of 1871, whistleblowers within the Tammany organization supplied hard proofs of widespread swindling and corruption to George Jones, publisher of *The New York Times*. Though the Tweed Ring attempted to bribe the newspaper so that the story would not see print, it appeared in July of that year; soon thereafter, an indignant group of citizens met at the Cooper Union to form a committee to take back their city. Democratic state chairman Samuel Jones Tilden filed an affidavit citing Tweed and his ring's misdeeds, and the affidavit became the basis of a civil suit for recovery of the city's money.

Despite this notoriety, the serious threat of imminent arrest, and his summary expulsion from the Tammany Society, Tweed was reelected to the state Senate. By December, 1871, however, his astonishing luck had run out, and he was arrested in a criminal action. (Others in his ring, taking no chances, had already fled abroad.) It took two trials to convict Tweed; in late 1873, he was fined $12,750 and sentenced to twelve years in prison. He nevertheless managed to get his sentence reduced on appeals to one year and paid only $250 in fines. He was rearrested in early 1875 in a civil action brought by New York state to recover $6 million of what had been stolen. Unable to secure the $3 million in bail set by the state, he escaped from his prison cell later that year, fleeing first to Florida, then Cuba, and from there to Spain. A

Nast cartoon printed in *Harper's Weekly* on July 1, 1876, led to his arrest in Spain, and he was returned to the United States in the late fall of that year. The warrant issued in New York for his arrest described him thus at the end of his career:

> [F]ifty-five years of age, about five-feet eleven inches high, will weigh about two hundred and eighty pounds, very portly, ruddy complexion, has rather large, coarse, prominent features and large prominent nose; rather small blue or grey eyes, grey hair, from originally auburn color, head nearly bald on top from forehead back to crown, and bare part of ruddy color; head projecting toward the crown. His beard may be removed or dyed, and he may wear a wig or be otherwise disguised. . . .

Unable to pay the judgment that had been levied against him in the civil action, in which he was convicted in absentia of 204 out of 240 counts, he was confined to jail. His subsequent lengthy and detailed testimony confessing his guilt, an attempt to be pardoned for his crimes, did not work. He died of pneumonia in the Ludlow Street prison on April 12, 1878. At his side was his manservant, who had opted to accompany him to jail; everyone else, including his family, had long since deserted him.

Summary

William Marcy Tweed has come to stand for all that is bad in American urban politics. He helped to spawn a particularly grotesque breed of individual—the bloated, powerful political boss—whose like has appeared again and again on the local and national scene; few such successors, however, have even begun to approach the phenomenal levels of graft achieved by the Tweed Ring and its leader. In the twentieth century, Mayor Richard Daley of Chicago and Carmine De Sapio of New York City were old-time political bosses in the spirit—if not the intense corruption—of Boss Tweed. Modern historians estimate that the Tweed Ring stole betweeen $30 million and $200 million from the city of New York, but a final, definitive figure will probably never be known.

The tragedy of William Marcy Tweed, though, was that he had tremendous leadership and organizational skills, which, combined with a genial personality, could have served him well and long if he had chosen to follow an honest career in government. He did have good instincts when it came to running a municipal government, and some of what he did was positive and humanitarian. He was responsible for the widening of Broadway and for the preservation of the Central Park site that became the Metropolitan Museum of Art; he helped new immigrants to the city—at a time when they were disdained and overlooked by most New Yorkers—by seeing to it that they had food, clothing, and shelter. He helped set up the Manhattan Eye and Ear Hospital, opened orphanages, almshouses, and public baths, sought funding for parochial schools, and worked to increase state aid to private charities. He also was behind the effort to obtain a greater degree of home rule for New York City. Although it has been argued that these public services were mere sops granted to the poor in an attempt to gain even more political power, some scholars do not agree with such an assessment.

The scope of the corruption, fraud, and graft of Tweed and the Tweed Ring, however, remains unparalleled in urban government, and their unrestrained feeding at the public trough is what history most vividly remembers. For his years of systematically cheating the city and manipulating public trust, Tweed has continued to be vilified as one of the nineteenth century's most reprehensible men. On his death, New York City mayor Smith Ely refused to fly the City Hall flag at half-staff; that verdict still stands.

Bibliography

Allen, Oliver E. *The Tiger: The Rise and Fall of Tammany Hall.* Reading, Mass.: Addison-Wesley, 1993. A look at the times and political machine that spawned Boss Tweed.

Bales, William A. *Tiger in the Streets.* New York: Dodd, Mead, 1962. A straightforward account of Tweed's life and career.

Callow, Alexander B., Jr. *The Tweed Ring.* New York: Oxford University Press, 1966. Detailed, thoroughly documented history of Tweed and the men he handpicked to defraud the city of New York.

Hershkowitz, Lao. *Tweed's New York: Another Look.* Garden City, N.Y.: Doubleday, 1977. A reevaluation of Tweed's impact on New York City.

Mandelbaum, Seymour J. *Boss Tweed's New York.* New York: J. Wiley, 1965. Gives credit to Tweed for exerting strong leadership at a time of chaos and change in the growing metropolis of New York City.

Werner, Morris R. *Tammany Hall.* Garden City, N.Y.: Doubleday, Doran,

1928. Sets Tweed against the background of the Democratic political machine.

Zink, Harold. *City Bosses in the United States: A Study of Twenty Municipal Bosses*. Durham, N.C.: Duke University Press, 1930. Excellent chapter on Tweed, with good references.

Jo Manning

JOHN TYLER

Born: March 29, 1790; Greenway, Charles City County, Virginia
Died: January 18, 1862; Richmond, Virginia

Upon the death of President William Henry Harrison, Tyler became the first vice president to succeed to the presidency following the death of a chief executive. Tyler established the precedent that in such circumstances the new president holds the office in both fact and name.

Early Life

John Tyler was born on March 29, 1790, near Richmond, Virginia. His father was a distinguished Virginian who served as governor, as speaker of the state House of Delegates, and as a judge. Tyler was reared in an atmosphere of aristocratic privilege and refinement and imbued with a sense of responsibility and commitment to public service. He attended the College of William and Mary and excelled academically, while his interest in political theory and practice grew. He shared the strict constructionist Jeffersonian Republican views of his father, under whom he began to read law at the age of seventeen. Tyler was admitted to the Virginia bar in 1809, and at the age of twenty-one, he was elected to the Virginia House of Delegates. After brief military service in the War of 1812, Tyler returned to civilian life as a public servant. His striking physical appearance was a considerable political asset. He was six feet tall, slender, with a high forehead, aquiline nose, fair complexion, brilliant eyes, and a ready smile.

Life's Work

Tyler first achieved national office with his election to the United States House of Representatives in 1816. As a congressman, Tyler was dedicated to the principles of his family and section. He was a strict constructionist in his view of the Constitution and favored limitation of the powers of the federal government. These views led Tyler to oppose nationally financed internal improvements projects because they might extend the power of the federal government. He opposed creation of the first Bank of the United States for the same reason, as well as on constitutional grounds. While Tyler was consistent in his

John Tyler *(Library of Congress)*

opposition to the slave trade, he nevertheless voted against the Missouri Compromise in 1820, believing that the "peculiar institution" would perish for lack of suitable geographical areas for its expansion. Tyler was defeated in a United States Senate race in 1820 and retired briefly from politics to serve as chancellor of the College of William and Mary. He was elected governor of Virginia in 1825, won a seat in the United States Senate in 1827, and began to move toward national prominence.

Tyler supported William H. Crawford for the presidency in 1824 and was elected to the Senate as an anti-Jacksonian. As the Republican Party split into factions and began the process of dividing into National Republicans and Democratic Republicans, Tyler was offended by the rising tide of mass politics that came to be known as "Jacksonian Democracy." While the aristocratic Virginian was very cordial and effective when dealing with members of his own class, the common folk and their heroes made him uncomfortable. Tyler was especially critical of what he termed the barking of newspapers and the brawling of demagogues. Nevertheless, in 1828, the Virginia senator supported Jackson's successful presidential bid as the candidate of the Democratic Republicans. While Tyler agreed with Jackson's views on some matters, he was repulsed by what he perceived as the new president's authoritarianism, and soon his principles caused Tyler to split from the Tennessean and the Democratic Party.

Even when Tyler agreed with the president's positions on key issues, he often disapproved of his methods. Prime examples were nullification and the bank. Nullification became an issue during Jackson's presidency because of two developments affecting the South. The first was the tariff: In 1828, Congress passed a high protective tariff which Southern planters, dependent on an export economy, strongly opposed. Tyler was among the Southern senators who spoke and voted against this "Tariff of Abominations." The second development was the unification of the Northeast and Northwest into a national political force, relegating the South to minority status among the sections. Southern extremists were beginning to talk about separation from the Union in order to rescue the South from the tyranny of the majority. Vice President John C. Calhoun understood and empathized with the growing fear and frustration of the South yet wanted desperately to preserve the Union. Calhoun developed the theory of Nullification as a means of protecting the interests of the minority section within the Union.

Nullification and the tariff were linked when South Carolina threatened to declare the tariff null and void within its borders if it was not repealed by Congress. Despite an effort by Congress to avoid confrontation by passing a new compromise tariff, Calhoun decided the time had come to test his doctrine, and South Carolina began the process of Nullification. President Jackson issued an extremely strong proclamation rejecting South Carolina's constitutional position and threatened personally to lead a military force into the state to enforce the tariff and the will of the federal government. Congress passed the Force Act authorizing the president to use force to ensure that federal laws were obeyed. Tyler found himself in a troubling and ambiguous situation. On one hand, he shared South Carolina's opposition to high tariffs, but on the other, he did not accept the doctrine of Nullification. He also considered, however, Jackson's Nullification proclamation to be a violation of the Constitution, and he was the only senator to vote against the Force Act. Furthermore, Tyler objected to the forcefulness of Jackson's reaction to South Carolina's challenge.

The bank question created similar contradictions and ambivalence. Tyler opposed the attempt to recharter the Bank of the United States on economic and constitutional grounds. When President Jackson attempted to destroy the bank, however, by removing the government's deposits from its coffers, Tyler was among the senators supporting resolutions condemning Jackson's actions. When the Virginia legislature ordered him to recant and vote for a motion to expunge the resolutions, Tyler resigned from the Senate and left the Democratic Party.

The Virginian now found himself drifting into uncharted political territory. He was among those Southerners who were moving toward the new Whig Party, which was emerging in opposition to the executive tyranny of "King Andrew." Yet Tyler was somewhat out of step with his new political companions. His political and constitutional views were not consistent with those of most other Whigs. Tyler had left Jackson and the Democrats largely as a result of methodology rather than constitutional differences. He had remained true to his original views and philosophy, while the Whig Party seemed a loose coalition of diverse groups with room for considerable philosophical latitude. Nevertheless, although he was defeated in a Senate election in 1839, Tyler was nominated for the vice presidency on the Harrison ticket the following year as the Whigs attempted to win the votes of other former Southern Democrats.

By now the Virginia politician who featured in one of the most famous campaign slogans in American political history had matured into a dignified and appealing figure. He continued to be somewhat distant in dealing with the masses and was sometimes accused of vanity, but most considered him friendly and considerate. He was unfailingly good-humored and patient and scrupulously honest. Even Tyler's political enemies found him difficult to dislike, and they respected his ability as a campaigner, for he had become a polished and effective orator. Tyler was nominated not because of his character or abilities, however, but because he appealed to disaffected Southern Democrats. Ironically, within a few short months the entire political structure was in turmoil, and Tyler was thrust onto center stage.

The Harrison and Tyler ticket won the election of 1840 easily, but within a month of his inauguration, Old Tippecanoe was dead. Supposedly, the dying chief executive's last words were a request that his vice president carry out the true principles of government. Ironically, the leaders of the Whig Party were soon to learn that Tyler did not share their concept of what constituted those true principles. Their chagrin and apparent amazement upon learning about the Virginian's views were somewhat surprising, for throughout his long political career, Tyler had demonstrated a philosophical and constitutional consistency that is unusual among politicians.

The marriage of Harrison and Tyler was strictly one of convenience. The Virginian had scarcely known, and was not favorably impressed by, Old Tippecanoe. The Whigs, however, expected that the actual leadership in a Harrison Administration would emanate from Congress, and Tyler was a close friend of Senator Henry Clay of Kentucky. Clay probably believed that Tyler would support the Whig programs that the Kentuckian planned to introduce in Congress, including plans for a new national bank. Tyler's oratory in the presidential campaign was sufficiently vague to provide substance for such a view, but within a few months, Clay would be a bitter political enemy, attacking the Virginian as a traitor to the Whig Party.

The first question faced by Tyler and the nation was fundamental: What was his status upon Harrison's death? Was he president in fact or only in name? Whether he was simply to attempt to carry out Harrison's views and programs or operate just as though he had been elected to the office was unclear. This was the first time that a vice president had ascended to the presidency upon the death of a chief executive, and the Constitution is rather vague concerning the succession. It says simply that if the president is removed from office, dies, resigns, or is unable to discharge his duties, the office will devolve on the vice president. This phrase could imply that the vice president inherits the office itself or, equally plausible, that the vice president simply performs the duties of the office. Tyler, usually the strict constructionist, interpreted the Constitution very broadly and claimed all the rights and privileges of the presidency. There was some contemporary criticism of his position, but the practice has been accepted and followed since that time.

Tyler retained the Harrison Cabinet members, reinforcing the impression that he would follow in the dead president's footsteps. Clay and the Whig leadership quickly and confidently submitted their legislative program, which called for a higher tariff and the creation of a new Bank of the United States. Congress enacted legislation for both the bank and the tariff, but the Whigs soon discovered that they had misread the situation. Tyler vetoed both measures with language that was highly reminiscent of Andrew Jackson. Some Whigs angrily charged that Tyler was a traitor, others that he was jealous of Clay. In actuality, Tyler was neither. He was simply acting in accord with the strict constructionist, agrarian views which he had absorbed from his father and had held since his youth. He stood his ground in the face of tremendous pressure, which included recriminations from Clay, blandishments from majoritarian Whigs, and a rock-throwing mob that attacked the White House.

Tyler argued that the legislation creating the new bank was unconstitutional and that the proposed institution posed the threat of an economic monopoly. He suggested a modified "exchequer" system as a compromise, but the Whig leaders forged ahead and again attempted to created a new bank, this time thinly disguised as a "fiscal corporation." Tyler vetoed that too, and the situation deteriorated into open warfare between the Whig president and his party. Tyler also struck down Clay's distribution program and other Whig legislation, and the Kentuckian resigned from the Senate in frustration and disgust.

Clay's resignation was followed by that of most of Tyler's cabinet members. The president replaced them with men of his own stripe, former Democrats who shared his views. There were public demonstrations against Tyler, he was burned in effigy, and in January, 1843, the Whigs brought impeachment charges against the man they now called "His Accidency." He was not convicted, but the Whigs formally expelled him from the party, as it disintegrated into shambles.

Tyler was now a man without a party, but he continued to perform his duties in accordance with his principles and in apparent good humor. During his presidency, he signed the Pre-emption Act, which made land more accessible and stimulated settlement in the Northwest, he helped end the Seminole War, and he was involved in the resolution of the Canadian boundary dispute with Great Britain. By 1844, he hoped for election to the presidency as an independent candidate but failed to generate significant support. Tyler then withdrew from the race and endorsed the Democrat, James K. Polk of Tennessee, who ran and won on an expansionist platform. During his last days in the presidency, the Virginian signed measures annexing Texas and admitting Florida to statehood.

John Tyler retired to his James River plantation in Virginia, a man without a party. He continued to be interested in public affairs and his graciousness, character, and obvious goodwill won the affection of his neighbors. He became an honored citizen and was an influential Southern leader as sectional turmoil increased during the 1850's. Tyler remained loyal to the Union and attempted to promote compromise on sectional issues but finally voted in favor of secession as a delegate to the Virginia secession convention. He served in the provisional Congress of the Confederacy and was elected to the Confederate House of Representatives but died in January, 1862, before taking his seat. He was buried in Richmond.

Summary

John Tyler was the first vice president to inherit the presidency upon the death of a chief executive, the first president to face impeachment charges, and the only one to be officially expelled from his party. He is remembered today primarily as a historical footnote, but he deserves better. He was a man of great integrity and considerable ability who remained steadfast in his views and true to his principles. Despite the turmoil of his presidency he achieved some positive accomplishments and significantly shaped the theory of vice presidential succession under the United States Constitution.

Bibliography

Chitwood, Oliver Perry. *John Tyler: Champion of the Old South.* New York: D. Appleton-Century Co., 1939. Though dated, this book remains the standard biography of Tyler.

Fraser, Hugh Russell. *Democracy in the Making: The Jackson-Tyler Era*. Indianapolis: Bobbs-Merrill Co., 1938. A dated but useful account.

Gunderson, Robert G. *The Log-Cabin Campaign*. Lexington: University of Kentucky Press, 1957. This work discusses Tyler's role in the 1840 presidential campaign.

Howe, Daniel Walker. *The Political Culture of the American Whigs*. Chicago: University of Chicago Press, 1980. Howe analyzes the anti-Jackson movement which helped to create the Whig Party.

Lambert, Oscar Doane. *Presidential Politics in the United States, 1841-1844*. Durham, N.C.: Duke University Press, 1936. This is a dated but useful treatment.

Morgan, Robert J. *A Whig Embattled: The Presidency Under John Tyler*. Lincoln: University of Nebraska Press, 1954. Morgan's work focuses on Tyler's presidency.

Peterson, Norma Lois. *The Presidencies of William Henry Harrison and John Tyler*. Lawrence: University Press of Kansas, 1989.

Seager, Robert. *And Tyler Too*. New York: McGraw-Hill Book Co., 1963. This is a joint biography of Tyler and his second wife, Julia Gardiner Tyler.

James E. Fickle

MARTIN VAN BUREN

Born: December 5, 1782; Kinderhook, New York
Died: July 24, 1862; Kinderhook, New York

Van Buren played a central role in the development of the modern party system. As president from 1837 to 1841, he kept the peace, eased sectional tensions over slavery, and formally separated the Treasury from private banks.

Early Life

An early example of a self-made man, Martin Van Buren began his career in Kinderhook, a small village on the post road to New York City about twenty miles south of Albany. There, on December 5, 1782, he was born into the family of Abraham and Hannah Van Buren, both of respectable if undistinguished Dutch stock, going back to early Colonial days. After an apparently happy childhood, the young Van Buren ended formal schooling at fourteen and spent the next seven years in law offices, first at Kinderhook and then in New York. Admitted to the bar in 1803, he began practice in his home village, soon moved to Hudson, and, in 1816, settled in Albany, where he continued practice for twelve more years. Each move marked a new level of success in the law and could be measured by the growing respect of his fellows and by an income, derived largely from small clients, which laid the basis for an estate later estimated at $200,000. In 1807, he married a childhood playmate and distant cousin, Hannah Hoes, and sired four sons—Abraham, John, Martin, and Smith Thompson—before Hannah's death in 1819. There were later flirtations and rumors of a second marriage, but Van Buren remained a widower.

Politics as well as the law engaged the ambitious Van Buren and opened a career leading from the state senate in 1812 to the White House twenty-five years later. Time spent in his father's tavern—a gathering place for Republicans in the exciting decade of the 1790's—had sparked his interest and had begun to draw out an uncommon aptitude which was to make him one of the first and best politicians in the nation's history. Foes ascribed his success to the arts of management and intrigue, calling him the Little Magician. Such epithets as "sly fox" and "noncommittalism" were also associated with his name. Friends, by contrast, appreciated his uncanny ability to "read men," to fathom the motives of opponents and conciliate the interests of followers. Moving into the political arena once dominated by upper class gentlemen, Van Buren cultivated the needed qualities of prudence, compromise, and self-control. Elements of style also signaled the ambitions of a lower-class person in the period of transition to a

Martin Van Buren *(Library of Congress)*

more democratic society and found symbolic expression in the care which the young legal apprentice gave to his wardrobe. On borrowed funds, he replaced his simple Republican attire with the knee breeches, buckled shoes, and tricornered hat of his Federalist mentor. Along with fine clothes would come a taste for good wine, suavity of manners, and great conversational gifts.

Personal appearance enhanced his style and image. Crowned with curly hair of sandy red and graced with ease of movement, the young Van Buren commanded attention in spite of his thin and smallish five-foot, six-inch frame. In later years, he gained a large amount of weight and lost most of his hair, but thick sideburns of reddish gray framed an imposing brow. Lending further distinction to his countenance were big, blue, penetrating eyes and the ever-present trace of a smile, suggesting benign contentment to some and calculating guile to others. Here was a man, one bemused Virginia aristocrat observed, who might row to his object with muffled oars.

Life's Work

Van Buren's career in public office was a mix of personal ambition and a statesman's sensitivity to the needs of a rapidly changing society. In 1812, he began an eight-year tenure in the state senate, and for four of those years he also held the office of attorney general. The first part of his senate service was distinguished by unswerving support of the War of 1812 at a time when Federalists voiced bitter opposition; by the end of the war he attracted national attention with his proposal for conscripting troops. In 1817, he gave belated but indispensable support for digging the Erie Canal, a project closely linked to his political foe, DeWitt Clinton. At the same time, Van Buren opposed most applications for new bank charters, for he wished to moderate the forces of change which were transforming an agrarian society into one featuring manufacture, commerce, and the spirit of enterprise. He also played a central role in the state convention which made the old state constitution of 1777 more conformable to the new democratic age. More offices were opened to the elective principle, and the number of adult, white male voters was more than doubled.

It was also during his senate years that Van Buren and his associates developed a disciplined party organization along modern lines. Nurtured by spoils and animated with an ethic of loyalty to the will of the majority expressed in caucuses and conventions, the party apparatus reached out from Albany to all parts of the state. Techniques of mass appeal and a style of campaigning not unlike religious revivals generated excitement and drew the people into the political process. While rank-and-file party workers were attracted to spoils, "new men" such as Van Buren saw the party as a means of access to the power of government once reserved for the elite. Through its democratic organization and appeal, Van Buren and his party were normally able to outmatch the old style of elite politics followed by Clinton and, by the mid-1820's, gained control of the state.

Supported by his party, Van Buren won election to the United States Senate in 1821 and remained in that post for the next seven years. His reputation had preceded him to the Senate, where he soon enjoyed great influence and claimed the chair of the Judiciary Committee. A central concern was to revive two-party competition, which had ended, with the rapid decline of the Federalists, in the so-called "era of good feelings." Van Buren saw it as an era of bad feelings: Political conflict did not cease but turned inward, shattering the unity of the Republican Party into personal and sectional factions. The Missouri Controversy was one result; another was the disputed election of 1824, resolved at last by the House of Representatives in favor of John Quincy Adams—a neo-Federalist in Van Buren's eyes. Van Buren then assumed leadership of the opposition to the new administration with the object of reestablishing the political base of the old Republican Party which had reposed in Virginia and New York. To attract Southern support, he spoke out for states' rights against the idea of strong national government advocated by Adams. Working closely with others, he fashioned a North-South coalition behind Andrew Jackson in 1828, and he pictured the presidential contest with Adams as a rerun of the old battles between Republicans and Federalists. To aid the cause, Van Buren ran for governor of New York and, as he hoped, his election contributed to Jackson's triumph. After three months at Albany, Van Buren resigned as governor and joined Jackson in Washington.

During Jackson's presidency, from 1829 to 1837, Van Buren served in turn as secretary of state, minister to England, and vice president. At the State Department, he gained by treaty the long-standing goal of opening trade with the British West Indies. His tenure as minister in

1831-1832 was cut short when political foes in the Senate refused to confirm his recess appointment. Happily for his career, however, the Senate action created a backlash of sentiment which enabled Jackson to choose him, through the party's first national convention, as vice president for the second term. In whatever position he held, Van Buren enjoyed great influence with Jackson. Except for the issue of internal improvements, he had little impact on the formulation of specific policies. His influence was of a more general kind, namely, that of helping shape Jackson's perception of the presidency in party terms. All earlier presidents, no matter how partisan their actions, had identified with the eighteenth century ideal of a "patriotic chief" above party. Yet Jackson set a new pattern by acting both as a president of the party and a president of the whole country. With Jackson's support, Van Buren received the party's nomination for president and, thanks to the divided state of the Whig Party, he won the election of 1836.

During his own presidency, from 1837 to 1841, Van Buren addressed three key matters. First, as a party president, he worked to contain sectional tensions over slavery. He enlisted the support of Northern Democrats to sustain the House "gag" on abolitionist petitions and to complete Jackson's timetable for removing Indians from the Old Southwest. In return for this support, he prevailed on Southern Democrats to surrender for the time their desire for bringing slaveholding Texas into the Union. Second, Van Buren kept the peace with Great Britain. The aid many Americans gave to the rebels in Canada created great tensions, but the president held firmly to the policy that citizens violating Canada's neutrality could expect no protection from the government. An even greater crisis arose over the disputed boundary with New Brunswick, leading by early 1839 to an impending confrontation between British forces and the Maine state militia. With bipartisan support, the president restrained further movements by the militia and worked out a truce arrangement with the British minister in Washington. The treaty resolving the boundary dispute came in the following administration, but Van Buren rightly claimed a "peace with honor."

At great political cost, finally, Van Buren pushed through Congress his central domestic measure for an independent Treasury. As his basic response to the Panic of 1837, it would separate Treasury operations from all private banks. Jackson had severed the connection with the national bank and deposited government revenues in selected state banks. Unhappily, these funds added to the momentum of other forces which, by 1835, generated a speculative mania and then the collapse two years later. Van Buren's plan would have the Treasury keep and disburse its own funds and use only specie or government paper, but no bank notes, in all its operations. The effect on the general currency of the country would be deflationary to some degree, yet the clear need of a depressed economy would seem to be for some degree of currency inflation. While fully aware of this fact, Van Buren held to the view that, over the long term, a deflationary policy would assure a sound recovery and work against any future cycle of boom and bust. Whig foes, by contrast, skillfully exploited the short-term need for some form of currency inflation, rightly sensing its popularity in a nation increasingly committed to enterprise. The Whigs also put their political house in order as they looked to the election of 1840. Ending their earlier divisions, they nominated a military hero of sorts, General William Henry Harrison, and conducted a "log cabin" campaign that utilized to the fullest extent those techniques of mass appeal which Democrats had developed earlier. As a result, Van Buren was soundly defeated in his bid for reelection.

Van Buren was never able to avenge his stunning defeat. Principled opposition to the issue of Texas annexation four years later denied him the party nomination, which went instead to James K. Polk. For a number of reasons—among them a sense of betrayal by his party and a genuine concern for its increasingly pro-Southern tilt—he agreed to stand as the candidate of the Free-Soil Party in 1848 on a platform of opposing the spread of slavery. Within two years, however, he returned to his old party. Even though it remained strongly pro-Southern throughout the 1850's, he still believed that its states' rights doctrine and its appeal in both sections made it indispensable for preserving the Union. After the Civil War broke out, he supported President Abraham Lincoln, but before his death in July, 1862, it was clear that the war was in the process of transforming the federative Union of states into a more consolidated nation.

Summary

Historians for the next half century generally tended to echo the epithets fashioned by Van Buren's foes and to underrate the Little

Magician's contribution to the nation's history. His idea of disciplined party organization, two-party competition, and a party presidency survived the Civil War and helped shape political life ever since. As president, he served the nation well by keeping peace with Great Britain at a time when war might have brought disaster to the young country. To his credit, some other depression president might have welcomed war as a diversion from domestic problems. Van Buren also merits good marks for his courage and consistency on the issue of an independent Treasury, for many expected him to follow a more popular course. His central measure also lasted a long time. Repealed by triumphant Whigs in 1841 and then restored by President Polk, the independent Treasury measure remained in operation until the Federal Reserve System was established. It did not end the cycle of boom and bust—as the panics of 1857, 1873, and 1893 show—but it is doubtful if any other plan would have worked much better in a country so fully committed to free enterprise. Along with his modest but real acts of statesmanship, in sum, Van Buren should also be remembered as an authentic expression of the American Dream, a genuine example of the self-made man.

Bibliography

Alexander, Holmes. *The American Talleyrand: The Career and Contemporaries of Martin Van Buren*. New York: Harper and Brothers, 1935. The most hostile biography of Van Buren. It elaborates Whig charges against the spoilsman politician, opportunist, and schemer but is lively and well written.

Cole, Donald B. *Martin Van Buren and the American Political System*. Princeton, N.J.: Princeton University Press, 1984. The best of the biographies. Thorough, balanced in assessment, and well researched, it does an especially good job placing Van Buren in the context of economic and political development.

Curtis, James C. *The Fox at Bay: Martin Van Buren and the Presidency, 1837-1841*. Lexington: University Press of Kentucky, 1970. The first full-length work on the presidential years. Light on analysis of the economic background but good on the intraparty politics in Van Buren's party.

Lynch, Denis Tilden. *An Epoch and a Man: Martin Van Buren and His Times*. New York: Horace Liveright, 1929. Dated but the most balanced of the older biographies. Contains much useful material on the personal life of Van Buren but fails to put his public career in context.

Morrison, Michael A. "Martin Van Buren, The Democracy, and the Partisan Politics of Texas Annexation." *Journal of Southern History* 61, no. 4 (November, 1995): 695-723.

Niven, John. *Martin Van Buren: The Romantic Age of American Politics*. New York: Oxford University Press, 1983. The first biography on Van Buren in nearly fifty years. Well written, good on his private life, and good in synthesizing works which assess him in a favorable light. Too brief, however, on the presidential years.

Remini, Robert V. *Martin Van Buren and the Making of the Democratic Party*. New York: Columbia University Press, 1959. The best single volume on Van Buren's work in party organization. If he is pictured as a "politician," Van Buren is also pictured as a Jeffersonian ideologue and man of principle.

Shepard, Edward M. *Martin Van Buren*. Boston: Houghton Mifflin Co., 1889. Part of the "American Statesman" series and the most sympathetic of the older biographies. It shares the Whig judgment against spoils but praises Van Buren for his Jeffersonian ideals and hard-money policy.

Wilson, Major L. *The Presidency of Martin Van Buren*. Lawrence: University Press of Kansas, 1984. Part of the Kansas presidential series. Thorough on the economic background of the Panic of 1837, the currency implications of the independent Treasury, and the party debate leading to Whig victory in 1840.

Major L. Wilson

George C. Wallace

Born: August 25, 1919; Clio, Alabama

A four-time governor of Alabama and twice a candidate for the presidency, Wallace during the 1960's became a leading spokesman for continued segregation and southern conservativism.

Early Life

George Corley Wallace was born on August 25, 1919, in Clio, Alabama. The Wallace family had been among the earliest settlers in Barbour County, where George spent his youth. His father was a farmer known for his quick temper and his passion for local politics. His mother, who came from a cosmopolitan neighborhood outside Birmingham, stoically accepted life in rural Alabama. Despite his family's relative poverty, George had a comfortable boyhood. The oldest of three boys and a girl, he was private and introspective, yet he was a good student and popular among his classmates. Throughout his youth, athletics played an important part in George's life. In high school, he quarterbacked his school football team and was runner-up in the state Golden Gloves boxing competition.

Politics was part of Wallace's life from an early age. One of his first memories was of watching local officials count votes; at seven, he helped his father hand out campaign material. Two years later, his grandfather was elected Barbour County probate judge after a campaign managed by George's father. Wallace later described the election as among his most exciting boyhood experiences. By his teen years, he was campaigning for candidates in state elections. Because of his political interests, he was encouraged to compete for an appointment as a page for the Alabama state senate. He was one of four winners, and he spent the summer of 1935 working in the state senate. Upon completion of his appointment, Wallace decided that he would one day like to serve as governor of Alabama.

During these early years, Wallace's political philosophy began to take shape. Most important in the molding process was his father. Blaming northern industrial interests for the problems of the agrarian South, the elder Wallace bemoaned federal regulations that, he contended, limited the South's ability to educate its people and to prosper. In reaction, he embraced the basic tenets of southern populism, including the principle of rigid segregation. During the early Depression years, he became an outspoken Roosevelt Democrat; at the same time, he vehemently opposed any federal intrusion into state or local matters. Young George accepted most of his father's political positions.

George Wallace *(Archive Photos)*

Upon graduation from Barbour County High School in 1937, Wallace enrolled in the pre-law program at the University of Alabama. Because his family could not afford to help with any of his academic expenses, he found several part-time jobs and began working his way through college. Two months into his freshman year, his father, who had suffered from chronic health problems for years, died. George immediately returned home and proposed withdrawing from the university to run the family farm. Yet his mother, who had always encouraged George's education, implored him to return to school, which he did. Two years later, he moved to advanced law studies, and he was graduated with a law degree in 1942.

The following October, Wallace was inducted into the Army Air Corps as an aviation cadet. Disenchanted with the training regimen, however, George requested reassignment. He spent the rest of his military service as a flight engineer and became part of a crew that flew numerous missions over Japan during the last weeks of World War II. While still an aviation cadet, he married sixteen-year-old Lurleen Burns.

Life's Work

Upon his discharge from the Air Corps in December, 1945, Wallace, his young wife, and their new daughter returned to Alabama, where George began his political career in earnest. Among his first stops was the office of Governor Chauncey Sparks. He had met Sparks, who was also from Barbour County, during his days as a legislative page and had actively campaigned for him. The governor personally saw to it that Wallace was appointed as assistant attorney general; however, both men understood that the position was temporary and that George would soon pursue elective office. Two months after his appointment, Wallace took an unpaid leave of absence to run for the state legislature. Riding a wave of resurgent southern populism and aided by boundless energy on the campaign trail, he won election—making him, at twenty-seven, the state's youngest legislator.

Wallace served two terms in the state legislature. During those eight years, he spoke repeatedly about the need to raise Alabama's standard of living, one of the lowest in the nation. Among his more important initiatives was a call for the creation of a group of state-operated technical and vocational schools. He also became a champion of local government by introducing legislation designed to generate a bond issue that would help Alabama cities attract industry without sacrificing local control. Among his standard themes was a call to southern pride. Like his father, he warned about a northern post-Civil War legislative assault on the South. He advised southerners to remain vigilant and resist federal policies that might alter tradition. The federal policies he condemned most often involved civil rights issues.

While establishing himself as a capable and energetic legislator, Wallace also began to establish a base for his own statewide political organization. Among those he courted were former governor Sparks and current governor James "Big Jim" Folsom. Like Wallace, both generally took a progressive stand on economic issues. Both had also fought the "big mules" of Alabama politics—the local cliques of bankers, industrialists, and plantation owners who collectively had controlled much of the state's political structure for decades. In preparing his organization, Wallace also won support from several prominent businessmen and a few influential newspaper reporters.

Wallace first attracted national attention during the 1948 Democratic National Convention. Selected as an alternate delegate from Alabama, he got his chance to participate when a portion of the state's delegation walked out of the convention in reaction to the party's civil rights platform plank. Rather than join the "Dixiecrat" rebellion, he chose to stay and vehemently protest the plank as well as Harry Truman's presidential nomination. The episode enhanced Wallace's stature within Alabama and brought him national recognition. Eight years later, as he prepared to run for governor, Wallace again actively opposed his party's civil rights position. This time, key leaders from southern delegations chose him as their spokesman to the platform committee. With the help of several powerful southern Democrats, he was able to dilute the language of the plank, making it merely an ambiguous pledge to end discrimination.

In 1952, Wallace was elected judge of the Third Circuit of Alabama, a district that included Barbour County. During the election, he established a style that would characterize his future campaigns. Aggressive and confrontational, he encouraged polarization of his voters by appealing to their fears and prejudices. Generally considered a congenial and fair judge, Wallace in 1958 became known as the "fighting judge" during a showdown with federal authorities. As part of an investigation into discrimination against black voters, Wallace was ordered by the U.S. Civil Rights Commission to make available voter-registration books. He refused, claiming that the rights of Alabamians were being intruded upon by the federal government. Threatened with contempt charges and concerned about an approaching gubernatorial election, however, he eventually acceded to the commission's demands.

Wallace was defeated in the 1958 gubernatorial election, but he won the office four years later. Though economic issues constituted an important part of his platform, a resolute opposition to federally required integration of Alabama schools became his primary plank. In June, 1963, less than a year after becoming governor, he lived up to his pledge to "stand in the schoolhouse door" when he personally attempted to block the enrollment of African American students at the University of Alabama; he yielded only after he was challenged by National Guard troops. The confrontation brought a flood of media coverage and much notoriety to Wallace. Similar episodes at Tuskegee, Birmingham, Huntsville, and Mobile further established him as the nation's leading segregationist.

Rendered ineligible from running for reelection by his state's constitution, Wallace maneuvered the 1966 Democratic gubernatorial nomination to his wife Lurleen. Though she took a more active role as governor than most expected, there was little doubt that George continued to direct Alabama government. In 1968, two years into her term, however, Lurleen died from cancer. Despite the loss, Wallace maintained his grip on the state and was elected governor in 1970, 1974, and in 1982.

During his years as governor, Wallace steadfastly embraced several issues. Education, particularly at the postsecondary level, was always part of his agenda. Throughout his political career, he also advocated improving business conditions within the state. Likewise, road construction and the quality of state's health-care facilities, especially in regard to the elderly and mentally disabled, were themes he regularly addressed. Yet segregation continued to be the issue most identified with him; from his earliest days in the state legislature, he defended the practice. When segregationist laws throughout the South were challenged in the 1960's, Wallace reacted aggressively against civil rights leaders and federally mandated integration. Only during his last term as governor did he begin to acknowledge that his earlier stance was wrong.

Wallace's political aspirations were not limited to Alabama. In 1964, despite being a lifelong Democrat, he considered becoming Republican Barry Goldwater's vice-presidential running mate. Four years later, Wallace captured forty-six electoral votes while running for the presidency as the candidate of the American Independent Party. He would run again in 1972 Democratic primaries. It was at a campaign stop in Laurel, Maryland, in May, 1972, that Wallace was shot five times in an assassination attempt. The attack left him paralyzed below the waist.

Although he remained a political force to be reckoned with, Wallace's influence nationally eroded after the attack. In 1982, campaigning from a wheelchair, he won a fourth term as governor by publicly recanting much of his earlier segregationist rhetoric. Slowed by failing health and marital problems, he retired from politics five year later.

Summary

During the 1960's, George Wallace became the political voice of the traditional South. In many ways, his appeal recalled that of Populist candidates of the early twentieth century. Wallace advocated the interests of the small farmer, the blue-collar laborer, and the small business. At the heart of his appeal was a rejection of federal civil rights and school-integration policies. His fiery rhetoric and confrontational style aroused a grassroots conservatism throughout the South and elsewhere in the nation.

As a presidential candidate, Wallace tapped into a deep pool of voters who considered their interests to be underrepresented. In appealing to this constituency, he introduced several campaign themes that later became part of the conservative Republican agenda that carried Ronald Reagan into the White House. Among them was a call for massive tax reform, a pledge to support a school-prayer amendment to the constitution, an aggressive stance on law-and-order issues, and a promise to expand military programs. He also vowed to end federally required school busing. His appeals directly addressed an ever-deepening public distrust of the federal government and a concern about a disintegrating social order.

Biography

Black, Earl. *Southern Governors and Civil Rights: Racial Segregation as a*

Campaign Issue in the Second Reconstruction. Cambridge, Mass.: Harvard University Press, 1976. Provides a context for understanding Wallace's segregationist policies and identifies him as one of the most outspoken opponents of federal involvement in school integration.

Canfield, James Lewis. *A Chase of Third Party Activism: The George Wallace Campaign Workers and the American Independent Party*. Washington, D.C.: University Press of America, 1984. While the author's focus is on the campaign, he provides much information about Wallace and his political philosophy during the 1968 presidential election.

Carter, Daniel T. *The Politics of Rage: George Wallace, the Origins of the New Conservatism, and the Transformation of American Politics*. New York: Simon & Schuster, 1995. A biographical investigation of Wallace's influence upon the rise of conservatism in American politics. Combines scholarly analysis and an appealing style.

Lesher, Stephan. George Wallace: American Populist. New York: Addison-Wesley, 1993. A thorough biography of Wallace. The author suggests that his subject reflected traditional southern values in the context of the mid-twentieth century.

Taylor, Sandra Baxley. *Me 'n' George: A Story of George Corley Wallace and His Number One Crony, Oscar Harper*. Mobile, Ala.: Greenberry Publishing, 1988. Focuses on Wallace's early political years and his rise to governor.

Paul E. Doutrich

HENRY A. WALLACE

Born: October 7, 1888; Adair County, Iowa
Died: November 18, 1965; Danbury, Connecticut

Wallace was an outspoken critic of post-World War II American foreign policy. He was also one of the principal architects of American farm policy and an eloquent spokesman for some of the most important ideas of twentieth century American liberalism.

Early Life

Henry Agard Wallace was born on October 7, 1888, on a farm in Adair County, Iowa. His father, Henry Cantwell Wallace, was of Scotch-Irish origin; his mother, May Brodhead, was of English, Dutch, and French Huguenot background. Henry Agard's father, a farmer at the time of his birth, became, in 1893, a professor of agriculture at Iowa State College, his alma mater. Henry's paternal grandfather, "Uncle Henry" Wallace, a minister of the Gospel turned farmer and founder of the influential weekly newspaper *Wallace's Farmer* in 1895, was the greatest influence on young Henry Agard's intellectual development. Grandfather instilled in grandson a lively intellectual curiosity and a peculiar mixture of practicality and high idealism.

The young Wallace labored for many years in the shadow of his father and his grandfather, both well-known figures in rural journalism and in Iowa Republican politics; only after the two of them had died would he really begin to make his mark. Although Henry Agard's father was by no means wealthy, family circumstances were comfortable enough to permit Henry to attend Iowa State College, where he studied agricultural science. After he was graduated in 1910, Wallace conducted pioneering research in agricultural economics, producing the first charts of corn-hog ratios. He also continued his studies on the breeding of corn; the fruit of this research was the founding, in 1926, of a company for developing and selling hybrid corn seeds.

When Wallace's father, Henry Cantwell Wallace, became secretary of agriculture under Calvin Coolidge, Wallace became editor of *Wallace's Farmer*. As an editor, Wallace, a nominal Republican, became well-known during the 1920's for his relentless attacks on the ruling

Republican Party's alleged indifference to the problems facing the American farmer. In 1932, he strongly supported Franklin D. Roosevelt's successful campaign for the presidency against Republican incumbent Herbert Hoover. In that election, the traditionally Republican state of Iowa, hard hit by the fall in agricultural prices that accompanied the Great Depression, voted for Roosevelt. As a reward for his help, Wallace received a high position in the new administration. Not until 1936, however, would he formally join the Democratic Party.

Life's Work

When Wallace went to Washington, D.C., in March, 1933, at the age of forty-four, as Roosevelt's new secretary of agriculture, he was a most atypical cabinet member. About five feet, ten inches tall, he kept his weight to a trim 160 pounds through vigorous exercise. Although middle-aged, Wallace looked much younger; his boyish appearance was accentuated by his full head of still reddish-brown hair, which was often unkempt in appearance. He had gray eyes, a long, lantern-jawed face, a long nose, and a sensitive mouth. His voice was high-pitched, but he was often able to make up with his earnestness for any deficiencies of oratorical delivery. Wallace lacked the gift for small talk so prized at Washington social gatherings of the time. His strong religiosity, and his avoidance of smoking, drinking, or swearing, set him apart from many people in Washington political circles.

Wallace, despite his lack of previous experience in government, proved to be an effective administrator. He was aided by the large numbers of trained social scientists whom he brought with him into the department. Working together with such intellectuals not only enabled Wallace to carry out policy more efficiently but also seems to have speeded his transition from a mere spokesman for agrarian interests to a proponent of a broader liberal economic philosophy. The New Deal farm policy devised by Wallace, embodied in the somewhat hastily prepared Agricultural Adjustment Act of 1933, tried to restore farm prosperity by getting American farmers to cooperate in cutting back on agricultural production, thereby raising prices. As an emergency measure to further this goal, millions of pigs were slaughtered; this action, coupled with the practice of paying farmers to grow less, caused many to criticize the policy as wasteful.

The reduction of crop surpluses through production cutbacks, although at first the most important part of Wallace's program, was by no means Wallace's only contribution to agricultural policy. Through the rural electrification program, electric power was brought to many farm families who had never before enjoyed its blessings. In the latter half of the 1930's, Wallace won the enactment of his plan for the so-called ever-normal granary, in which the federal government would store the surpluses from good years to help in times of poor harvests. It was in the latter half of the decade, too, that emphasis began to be placed on encouraging farmers to practice techniques of soil conservation; dust storms of the era had shown how necessary such techniques were. The food stamp program was devised by Wallace's subordinate Milo Perkins in 1938 to rebut accusations of wastefulness aimed at New Deal farm policy. Stamps would be issued enabling the poor to receive surplus food, thus at once combating crop surpluses on the land and relieving hunger in the Depression-stricken cities.

Wallace came to realize that the problem of agricultural overproduction could be resolved only by tackling the problem of underconsumption, both at home and abroad. Although he had briefly supported high tariffs in the 1920's, he had come to oppose protectionism by 1930, criticizing the high Hawley-Smoot Tariff enacted in that year. Convinced that a mutual lowering of tariff barriers by the nations of the world was necessary both to open new markets for American agriculture and to increase the chances of lasting peace in the world, Agriculture Secretary Wallace staunchly supported the efforts of Secretary of State Cordell Hull to negotiate reciprocal trade treaties with various nations. To increase consumption at home, Wallace came to advocate social security, minimum wage legislation, and better conditions for workers.

In February, 1935, Wallace abruptly dismissed various key officials of the department who had aroused resentment among white Southern landowners by trying to improve conditions for Southern black sharecroppers. It was not until the latter half of the 1930's that a conscience-stricken Wallace made some effort to help tenants and sharecroppers displaced by farm production cutbacks. At Wallace's urging, the Resettlement Administration and, later on, the Farm Security Administration were set up to aid the poorer segments of the farming community.

Although Wallace's record as agricultural secretary had thus not been particularly radical, he had, by 1940, gained a reputation within the Democratic Party as an extreme liberal ideologue. This reputation arose from Wallace's ceaseless attempts, from 1933 onward, to articulate through books, pamphlets, and speeches a coherent philosophy of New Deal liberalism, and to defend this philosophy against its enemies in the uncompromisingly biblical rhetorical style inherited from his preacher grandfather. Wallace's words were more doctrinaire than his acts; nevertheless, he aroused such suspicion in conservative Democratic Party circles that it took Roosevelt's emphatic personal insistence to secure Wallace's nomination for vice president in 1940.

As vice president from 1941 to 1945, Wallace was neither as busy nor as blessed with success as he had been as agriculture secretary. As head of the Board of Economic Warfare from 1941 to 1943, Wallace quarreled so heatedly with conservative Secretary of Commerce Jesse Jones that President Roosevelt, determined to soft-pedal ideological New Dealism for the sake of wartime unity, felt compelled to relieve the Iowan of that position. Wallace had insisted on decent conditions for workers in Latin American lands that were producing for the American war effort; the State and Commerce departments regarded such insistence as an unwarranted interference in other countries' internal affairs.

Unsuccessful in the bureaucratic wars, Wallace put more time than ever before into playing the role of spokesman for New Deal liberalism, a philosophy that he wished to see expanded from the domestic to the international arena. During World War II, Wallace advocated, as prerequisites for a lasting peace, both the creation of a strong world organization and the raising of living standards in Asia and Latin America through massive American aid. For Wallace, material well-being was a necessity if democracy was to thrive; democratic government, in turn, was necessary for peace among nations. Wallace's advocacy of massive foreign aid was widely ridiculed at the time, but his advocacy of a world organization did pay off: on July 28, 1945, the United States Senate ratified the United Nations Charter.

In 1944, a presidential election year, Roosevelt, in the interests of party unity, dropped Wallace from the ticket and accepted as his vice presidential running mate the Democratic senator from Missouri, Harry S Truman. Appointed secretary of commerce by an ailing President Roosevelt in 1945, Wallace retained that position after Roosevelt's death in April of that year.

As secretary of commerce, Wallace championed the cause of government planning for full employment, and he stated this belief vigorously in the book *Sixty Million Jobs* (1945). The Full Employment Act of 1946, embodying Wallace's ideas in a somewhat watered-down form, established a Council of Economic Advisers to aid the Federal government in its pursuit of the goal of full employment.

By 1945, Wallace had come to symbolize, within the Democratic Party, the aspirations of liberal intellectuals, blacks, and trade union members, as distinguished from the interests of the Northern big-city machine bosses and Southern conservative political chieftains who had so long dominated the party. Wallace squandered this vast reservoir of support, however, by his disastrous decision to oppose President Harry S Truman on issues of foreign policy.

By September, 1946, Wallace was troubled by the friction between the United States and her wartime ally, the Soviet Union. On September 12, 1946, in a speech in Madison Square Garden, Wallace publicly criticized the notion that the United States should take a tough line toward Soviet Russia. President Truman, preoccupied by both foreign and domestic problems and unsure how to deal with the Soviets, had approved Wallace's speech beforehand without realizing the impact it might have. Faced with the indignation of Secretary of State James F. Byrnes, who saw Wallace as undercutting his own negotiations with the Soviets, Truman was forced, on September 20, to dismiss Wallace from office.

After his resignation, Wallace served for about a year as editor of the liberal periodical *The New Republic;* from there he continued to criticize Truman's foreign policy. Wallace strongly condemned the Truman Doctrine, proclaimed in March, 1947. Despite his general approval of American aid to foreign countries, Wallace also opposed Marshall Plan aid to war-ravaged Western Europe. Because the Soviet Union was excluded and because it was not under the auspices of the United Nations, Wallace argued that such a program would only make Soviet-American relations worse and endanger world peace.

In 1948, Wallace ran for president of the United States on a third-party ticket, that of the Progressive Party. In the course of his presidential campaign, Wallace resolutely refused to criticize Soviet foreign policy. The Communist coup in Czechoslovakia in February, toppling a genuinely democratic regime, and the Russian imposition of the

Berlin blockade in July both undermined the credibility of Wallace's approach to foreign policy, causing even liberal opinion to desert his candidacy. When the returns were counted in November, Truman had been reelected over his Republican opponent; Wallace had finished a poor fourth in the popular vote, slightly behind even Strom Thurmond, the candidate of the States' Rights Democratic (Dixiecrat) Party. The very elements to whom Wallace had hoped to appeal—liberal intellectuals, labor union members, black voters in the Northern states—had, by and large, resisted the Iowan's blandishments and remained loyal to Truman. Wallace's political career, ruined by his own lack of realism, was over.

In June, 1950, Wallace broke with the Progressive Party over the Korean War: He supported Truman's decision to send American troops to aid the South Koreans against the North Korean Communist invaders. Wallace had never really sympathized with Marxism as an ideology or with the authoritarian aspects of the Soviet system; his misguided defense of Soviet foreign policy had been inspired by a sincere love of peace, coupled with a serious misunderstanding of the true nature of Joseph Stalin's tyranny.

After 1950, Wallace devoted himself to nonpolitical pursuits, carrying out, at his country home just north of New York City, crossbreeding experiments on strawberries, chickens, and gladioli. On November 18, 1965, after prolonged suffering, he died of a degenerative disease of the nervous system.

Summary

Although Wallace was a failure as a politician, he did leave behind a considerable legacy in the world of ideas. Wallace, through his preachings as country editor and through his actions as agriculture secretary, popularized the notion of intervention by the federal government to stabilize prices; the wisdom and value of such intervention has been upheld by later administrations, including some conservative Republican ones. The food stamp program, dropped with the coming of World War II, was ultimately revived under the John F. Kennedy Administration, and was continued and expanded under succeeding administrations. The attempts made under the Kennedy and Lyndon B. Johnson administrations (1961-1969) to fine-tune the national economy were inspired by the kind of Keynesianism popularized by Wallace in the 1940's. The creation of the Peace Corps and the Agency for International Development under the Kennedy Administration, and the pursuit of international tariff reduction by both the Kennedy and Johnson administrations reflect the enduring influence of Wallace's ideas; the Iowan had long stressed the need for both freer trade and expanded foreign aid if world peace and American economic well-being were to be furthered.

Wallace is especially significant as an early critic of post-World War II American foreign policy. America's involvement in a costly and losing conflict in Vietnam, from 1961 through 1975, has caused some scholars to reassess Wallace's criticism, for which he was so vilified in his lifetime. Such reassessment by no means redeems Wallace from the charge of naïveté; until 1950 he was as blind to Stalin's faults as he was acutely aware of his own country's errors.

In Wallace's career, one sees the peculiar difficulties faced by an American meliorist liberal when he tries to apply the lessons derived from his domestic political experience to the far different environment of international relations; this particular dilemma has reappeared in different forms in the careers of later American liberal leaders.

Bibliography

Ezekiel, Mordecai. "Henry A. Wallace, Agricultural Economist." *Journal of Farm Economics* 48 (November, 1966): 789-802. A warmly favorable recollection of Wallace by an economist who was one of his principal advisers in the Department of Agriculture. Sets forth in considerable detail Wallace's scientific accomplishments and his intellectual legacy but passes over in one sentence Wallace's unsuccessful foray into third-party politics.

Hamby, Alonzo L. "Henry A. Wallace, the Liberals, and Soviet-American Relations." *Review of Politics* 30 (April, 1968): 153-169. Hamby shows that sympathy for Soviet Russia, a supposedly anti-Fascist power, had once been common to all liberal intellectuals; Wallace differed from the majority of them only in clinging to this viewpoint long after postwar realities had disillusioned others.

__________. "Sixty Million Jobs and the People's Revolution: The Liberals, the New Deal, and World War II." *Historian* 30 (August, 1968): 578-598. Hamby ably explains how Wallace became the leading spokesman of American liberalism during the war years. The author sees, as one motive for the shift of liberals such as Wallace toward Keynesianism, a fear that mass unemployment after the war might provide the seedbed for a strong American fascist movement.

Kelley, John L. "An Insurgent in the Truman Cabinet: Henry A. Wallace's Effort to Redirect Foreign Policy." *Missouri Historical Review* 77 (October, 1982): 64-93. Making full use of the recently opened diaries of President Truman and of Truman's press secretary, Charles G. Ross, Kelley provides a fresh look at the cabinet crisis that arose over Wallace's Madison Square Garden speech of September 12, 1946.

Kirkendall, Richard S. "Commentary on the Thought of Henry A. Wallace." *Agricultural History* 41 (April, 1967): 139-142. Sees Wallace as having evolved, during his years as secretary of agriculture, from a purely agrarian viewpoint to a broader liberal philosophy embracing urban as well as rural concerns. Asserts that the Iowan had lost the support of conservative farm organizations by 1940. Sees the influence of adviser Mordecai Ezekiel as of crucial importance in Wallace's turn toward Keynesianism.

Lord, Russell. *The Wallaces of Iowa*. Boston: Houghton Mifflin Co., 1947. This contemporary study of Wallace is extremely detailed on the New Deal period but rather skimpy thereafter; it does, however, provide valuable information on Wallace's early life and family background.

Markowitz, Norman D. *The Rise and Fall of the People's Century: Henry A. Wallace and American Liberalism, 1941-1948*. New York: Free Press, 1973. Markowitz offers a revisionist scholarly view of Wallace's view of Soviet-American relations as courageous and realistic; the Iowan's naïveté, the author believes, lay rather in thinking that capitalism could be transformed from within into a new type of society. Despite its somewhat questionable interpretation, Markowitz's book provides an excellent factual account of Wallace's activities during the Truman years, especially his dismissal from office in 1946 and his presidential bid of 1948.

Schapsmeier, Edward L., and Frederick H. Schapsmeier. *Henry A. Wallace of Iowa: The Agrarian Years, 1910-1940*. Ames: Iowa State University Press, 1969. Strongly sympathetic to Wallace. Although it provides many interesting factual details on Wallace's early years, it falls short as a work of analysis. Thus it fails to provide any satisfactory explanation of that peculiar mixture of idealism and pragmatism shown by Wallace during his years as secretary of agriculture.

Walker, J. Samuel. *Henry A. Wallace and American Foreign Policy*. Westport, Conn.: Greenwood Press, 1976. Walker traces Wallace's views on foreign policy from 1920 to the late 1940's; the material on the Iowan's early views on international trade is particularly interesting. Its treatment of Wallace's later political career, however, is flawed by the absence of a coherent argument.

White, Graham J. *Henry A. Wallace: His Search for a New World Order*. Chapel Hill: University of North Carolina Press, 1995.

Paul D. Mageli

George Washington

Born: February 11, 1732; Westmoreland County, Virginia
Died: December 14, 1799; Mount Vernon, Virginia

As commander in chief of the Continental army during the American Revolution, as president of the Constitutional Convention of 1787, and as first president of the United States, Washington was the principal architect of the nation's independence and its federal political system.

Early Life

Born on February 11 (February 22, New Style), 1732, into a family of middling standing among Virginia's planter elite, George Washington was the eldest son of his father's second marriage. A favorite of his half brother Lawrence Washington of Mount Vernon, young George capitalized on this brother's marriage into the prominent Fairfax family and the inheritance of Lawrence Washington's estate. Thus, despite his losing his father at age eleven and his being a low-priority heir to his father's lands, he was by his mid-twenties able to achieve greater prominence both in estate and position than his ancestors.

His connections allowed him to succeed Lawrence Washington as a major and adjutant of militia in 1752, and the following year he carried a message from Virginia's governor to the French forces encroaching on Virginia-claimed lands in the upper Ohio valley. In 1754, Lieutenant Colonel Washington surrendered a small Virginia detachment under his command to French forces in southwestern Pennsylvania. Thus began the French and Indian War (known as the Seven Years' War in Europe).

Washington's war record was solid but undistinguished, except for his well-recognized bravery during General Edward Braddock's defeat on the Monongahela River in 1756. Failing to receive the royal military commission he sought, he returned to Mount Vernon, engaged in modern farming techniques, expanded his land holdings, and, in 1759, married a wealthy widow, Martha Dandridge Custis. Their marriage was childless, but Washington adopted her two children.

George Washington (*Library of Congress*)

Life's Work

Elected to the Virginia House of Burgesses, Washington never achieved a reputation of outspokenness comparable to that of a Patrick Henry. A delegate to the First and Second Continental Congresses, Washington impressed his colleagues with his mastery of military affairs and was selected by them to serve as commander in chief of the newly formed Continental army in 1775. He took command of the mostly New England force shortly after its defeat at Breed's (Bunker) Hill and immediately sought to reform it into an effective fighting force. Containing the British forces inside Boston during the winter of 1775-1776, he forced them to evacuate the city the following spring. Action then moved to New York City, where he suffered defeats on Long and Manhattan islands and was eventually driven across the Hudson into and across New Jersey. His counterattacks at Trenton and Princeton during the winter of 1776-1777 revived American hopes and allowed his forces to winter in northern New Jersey.

The following year, he countered the two-pronged British invasion from Canada down the Lake Champlain-Hudson Valley route and from New York via sea against Philadelphia by sending General Horatio Gates with some of his regulars to join local units in combating the northern invasion and by leading the Pennsylvania campaign himself. In the latter area, Washington was soundly defeated by General Sir William Howe's forces but escaped to rebuild his army during the bitter winter at Valley Forge. General Gates won a remarkable victory at Saratoga which encouraged the French government to recognize the United States. The subsequent alliance with France allowed the Americans to continue their efforts and forced the British to concentrate their naval and military forces against an ever-widening war that eventually saw combat from the Indian Ocean to the Caribbean Sea.

The new international conflict caused the British to withdraw from Philadelphia to New York in 1778. When Washington sought to destroy their forces at Monmouth, New Jersey, the result was an indecisive battle which could have turned into a route had not the American commander personally rallied his troops. For the next three years, Washington headquartered his forces near West Point, New York, while combating some British raids and pinning the British forces in the New York City-Long Island vicinity. When the British developed a southern strategy to return Georgia and the Carolinas to the empire,

Washington countered by sending Generals Benjamin Lincoln and Horatio Gates to the region. The result was defeat for both officers at Charleston and Camden. In early 1781, Washington sent Nathanael Greene southward, and that officer was able to conduct an effective area defense that thwarted General Charles Lord Cornwallis' attempts to conquer the Carolinas. Exasperated, Cornwallis sought to cut off Greene's supply line and to draw him northward by invading Virginia. At this point, Washington coordinated with General Count Jean Baptiste de Rochambeau, commander of a French expeditionary force currently in Rhode Island, and through him Admiral Count François de Grasse, commander of the French West Indian fleet, to unite their forces against Cornwallis in Virginia. The resultant surrender of Cornwallis at Yorktown in October, 1781, effectively ended British attempts to reintegrate the United States into the Empire even though the treaty of peace would not be signed until 1783.

After Washington resigned his commission in 1783 (a remarkable event in itself, since most observers expected him to become another Oliver Cromwell), he maintained a high public profile during the next several years but did not seek major positions until 1787, when he became a delegate to the Constitutional Convention and presiding officer of that body. Although his position precluded his taking an active part in the deliberations, he played a significant behind-the-scenes role in the convention and, by lending his name to the final document, helped to ensure its eventual ratification.

During the convention and the ratification process, it was assumed that Washington would become the first chief executive of the new government. Elected president in 1789, he established precedents for the new office that are still followed today. Unlike modern presidents, who receive the privileges and prestige of the office, Washington lent his public reputation to the presidency and thereby enhanced its repute.

His government faced difficult tasks in the fields of administrative organization, foreign relations, and economic policy. Influencing each of these areas would be both the clash of personalities and the clash of political interests. Washington sought to resolve the issues without involving himself in the controversy. For the most part, except in the area of foreign policy, he was successful.

One of the most critical areas was the creation of an independent executive system, which was not fully developed in the Constitution. Here Washington prevailed over those desiring to use the Senate as sort of a privy council under the "advise and consent" clause, and those, such as Alexander Hamilton, desiring a parliamentary cabinet system with the major executive officers responsible to the Congress. Among Washington's other achievements were the creation of federal administrative agencies separate from those of the states; the introduction of orderly and stable relationships between officials based on law, instructions, and precedents; the maintenance of high standards of integrity, honesty, and competence; the recognition of claims of locality upon political appointments (often called "senatorial courtesy"); and the dominance of federal authority over individuals, demonstrated decisively in the suppression of the Whiskey Rebellion. Some of Washington's administrative policies, such as the use of the veto only in relation to constitutional questions, did not long survive his presidency. In the same vein, his use of the cabinet as a consultative body had a short life.

Other developments during his tenure can be attributed less to Washington's personal efforts than to the circumstances of the time or to the role of others. The creation of the judicial system was largely the responsibility of Roger Sherman, the Bill of Rights that of James Madison. The latter also formulated the first national revenue system. Alexander Hamilton created a financial system that funded the government debts, instituted a national central bank, and established a national mint and stable currency. Washington either actively endorsed or did not oppose (in itself an act of endorsement) these efforts.

In military affairs, Washington often used his secretary of war as a cipher and conduit in a field where he had considerable expertise. His greatest disappointment in this field was Congress' rejection of his proposals for a national military system; instead, it passed the Militia Act of 1792, which left the nation without any effective defense posture.

In foreign affairs he closely worked with Thomas Jefferson in his first administration and followed the often misguided instincts of Hamilton in the second. The Jay Treaty of 1795 was the most divisive event of his tenure and did far more to encourage partisan politics than did any other policy matter. Despite the political consequences of Washington's diplomacy, he is generally given appreciative accolades for his maintenance of neutrality in the Anglo-French struggle that drew most of the Western world into its vortex.

Washington undoubtedly believed that the greatest weakness of his administration was the development of partisan politics. Both the president's supporters and his opponents favored a consensual political environment which saw partisan activities as divisive of national solidarity and indicative of corruption and personal ambition. The main intent of Washington's farewell address was to warn against political parties.

His final legacy to the presidency was the decision not to run for reelection in 1796 and the consequent two-term tradition that continued until 1940. He established a precedent of turning the office over to a duly elected successor instead of waiting for either death or revolt to remove him from office. Washington did not believe that his presence in the office was indispensable, and he instinctively knew that the peaceful transfer of power to a duly elected successor constituted an important building block in erecting a stable nation.

His retirement from the presidency in 1797 did not remove him entirely from public service. When the Quasi War with France broke out in 1798, President John Adams called Washington back to command the army with the rank of lieutenant general. In this capacity he normally remained at Mount Vernon and delegated much of the running of the army to Major General Hamilton. He died after a short illness in late 1799.

Summary

No American figure has for so long dominated the national scene as has George Washington. For nearly twenty-five years, Washington remained the symbol of American nationhood, commanding its armies in a war for national independence, presiding over the convention that drafted its fundamental political charter, and transforming that charter's vague articles into political reality as the first chief magistrate of the Republic. As both general and president, he shaped the American military tradition with its subordination to civilian authority. As president, he established the contours of the American federal system and, even though he opposed its development, the party system. A far better statesman than general, he is probably better remembered for his military than for his political contributions to American history.

Bibliography

Alden, John R. *George Washington: A Biography*. Baton Rouge: Louisiana State University Press, 1984. The only high-quality one-volume study of the whole life available, and the best introduction to Washington's career.

Cunliffe, Marcus. *George Washington: Man and Monument*. Boston: Little, Brown and Co., 1958. The best brief introduction to the man's place in American history. Cunliffe contrasts Washington's life with his popular image.

DeConde, Alexander. *Entangling Alliance: Politics and Diplomacy Under George Washington*. Durham, N.C.: Duke University Press, 1958. The best introduction to Washington's foreign policy, which the book strongly endorses.

Ferling, John E. *The First of Men: A Life of George Washington*. Knoxville: University of Tennessee Press, 1988.

Flexner, James Thomas. *George Washington*. 4 vols. Boston: Little, Brown and Co., 1965-1972. The best of the multivolume biographies, with an especially good treatment of Washington's military career in the second volume.

Freeman, Douglas Southall. *George Washington*. 7 vols. New York: Charles Scribner's Sons, 1948-1957. John A. Carroll and Mary Wells Ashworth completed the final volume of this detailed, monumental, but nonanalytical study by a Pulitzer Prize-winning biographer.

Hofstadter, Richard. *The Idea of a Party System: The Rise of Legitimate Opposition in the United States*. Berkeley: University of California Press, 1969. Comprehensive analysis of the antiparty tradition of the early republic and of Washington's ambiguous place in early partisan politics.

Kammen, Michael. *A Season of Youth: The American Revolution in Historical Imagination*. New York: Oxford University Press, 1978. A thorough and imaginative reappraisal of the revolutionary theme and Washington's place in it.

Knollenberg, Bernard. *Washington and the Revolution*. New York: Macmillan Publishing Co., 1940. Solid appraisal of Washington's military career, but not as insightful as either Flexner or Weigley.

Lewis, Thomas A. *For King and Country: The Maturing of George Washington, 1748-1760*. New York: HarperCollins, 1993.

McDonald, Forrest. *The Presidency of George Washington*. Lawrence:

University Press of Kansas, 1974. Decidedly pro-Hamiltonian and anti-Jeffersonian, McDonald's study is a concise treatment of the presidential years that makes Washington more a symbol than a decisive figure.

Smith, Richard Norton. *Patriarch: George Washington and the New American Nation*. Boston: Houghton Mifflin, 1993.

Weems, Mason Locke. *The Life of Washington*. Edited by Marcus Cunliffe. Cambridge, Mass.: Harvard University Press, 1962. This reprinting of the 1809 edition of the book that did much to create the Washington myth contains an excellent introduction by Cunliffe.

Weigley, Russell F. *The American Way of War*. New York: Macmillan Publishing Co., 1973. Contains an excellent chapter on Washington's contributions to the American military tradition.

Wills, Garry. *Cincinnatus: George Washington and the Enlightenment*. Garden City, N.Y.: Doubleday and Co., 1984. A scholar-journalist's often deft insights into Washington's self-image and his popular image in the eighteenth and nineteenth centuries.

David Curtis Skaggs

DANIEL WEBSTER

Born: January 18, 1782; Salisbury, New Hampshire
Died: October 24, 1852; Marshfield, Massachusetts

The greatest orator of his time, Webster, more than any other individual, articulated a near-mystical devotion to the Union which would define Northern patriotism during the Civil War.

Early Life

Daniel Webster was born January 18, 1782, in Salisbury, New Hampshire. His father, Ebenezer, a veteran of the French and Indian War and of the American Revolution, was a tavern keeper, farmer, and local politician. Webster's mother, Abigail Eastman, was a second wife, who, like her predecessor, bore Ebenezer five children; Daniel was the youngest except for one girl. The teamsters who put up at his father's tavern nicknamed him "Black Dan" because of his dark complexion, jet-black hair, and black eyes.

Slight of stature for his age, although with an unusually large head, Daniel was often spared the heavier chores which his brothers and sisters shared on the farm. As a boy he cultivated his precocious mind and strongly emotional nature. Books were hard to come by, but he read everything he found and, blessed with almost total recall, remembered what he read. His father, with whom he had a close relationship, hoped Daniel would get the kind of education he had missed, and in May, 1796, enrolled him in the Phillips Academy in Exeter. Tile boy was shy and sensitive about his homespun clothing, clumsy cowhide boots, and awkward manners, but he made "tolerable progress" with his studies. Only in declamation was he unable to match his fellows; at the public exhibitions, despite careful preparation, he could never command sufficient resolution to rise from his seat and present his speeches.

In December, 1796, Webster returned to Salisbury without having completed his course. A brief period of country schoolteaching ended with an arrangement for him to study with a minister in the neighboring community of Boscawen, who had offered to prepare him for Dartmouth College. At Dartmouth, Webster pursued his studies with energy, was graduated near the top of his class, and was elected to Phi Beta Kappa. In contrast to his failure at Exeter, he was outstanding in his college literary society and developed a reputation as a public speaker. While only a junior, he was invited to deliver a Fourth of July address at Hanover.

Following graduation, Webster spent several years in rather desultory preparation for a legal career. He read law with a Salisbury attorney, taught in the academy in Fryeburg, Maine, and finally went to Boston, Massachusetts, in July, 1804, where he was accepted as a clerk in the law office of a leading New England Federalist, Christopher Gore. After completing his studies and being admitted to the bar in March, 1805, he began to practice law in Boscawen, where he could be near his family In September, 1807, his father having died the previous year, Webster moved to Portsmouth, New Hampshire, where he remained for nine very happy years. In May, 1808, he married Grace Fletcher, a clergyman's daughter. In August, 1816, he moved with his wife and two children to Boston, a rising metropolis.

Life's Work

Webster entered politics as a strict constructionist and an antinationlist. During two terms in the House of Representatives as a Federalist, 1813-1817, Webster opposed the War of 1812. Although he did not advocate secession, he kept up his obstructionist activities in Congress, while the Republican administration grew increasingly desperate. As a spokesman for the dominant merchants and shippers of New England, he vigorously opposed protective tariffs as probably unconstitutional and certainly inexpedient; in later years, as a protectionist, he was hard put to refute himself.

What national reputation Webster enjoyed prior to 1830 was largely derived from his appearances before the United States Supreme Court. He joined with Chief Justice John Marshall in giving a nationalistic, Hamiltonian interpretation to the Constitution. His skillful arguments in the *Dartmouth College* case (1819), *McCulloch v. Maryland* (1819), and *Gibbons v. Ogden* (1824) brought him recognition as the nation's leading constitutional lawyer.

In 1822, Webster won the Boston district seat in the House of Representatives. He shortly transcended his early sectionalism to become an outstanding nationalist, favoring a national bank, federal appropriations for internal improvements, and, reflecting New England's shift from commerce to manufacturing, a protective tariff. He became known as one of the chief exponents of the "cause of humanity" because of his advocacy of American support for Greek independence from the Ottoman Empire. In June, 1827, the Massachusetts legislature elected the ex-Federalist as a National Republican to the United States Senate. After the death of his wife, he was married in December, 1829, to Caroline Le Roy, the daughter of a wealthy New York merchant.

Webster's second reply to South Carolina senator Robert Y. Hayne, delivered in the Senate on January 26-27, 1830, answered Hayne's defense of John C. Calhoun's Nullification doctrine with a powerful defense of national sovereignty. It gave Webster a reputation as one of the leading statesmen of the nation. His new stature made Webster a potential presidential candidate, and thereafter the hope of reaching the White House was constantly in the back of his mind and influenced many of his actions.

Webster's support for President Andrew Jackson during the Nullification crisis of 1832-1833 brought rumors of a rapprochement between the two antagonists. Webster thought of uniting Jacksonians and Websterites in an anti-Nullification "Constitution and Union" Party that would secure his own election to the presidency in 1836. He made overtures to Jackson, only to be rebuffed, and had no choice but to join the emerging Whig Party and to seek the presidency through that organization. His candidacy for 1836 ended when most Northern Whigs and Anti-Masons supported General William Henry Harrison, a hero of the War of 1812. Webster received only the fourteen electoral votes of Massachusetts.

In the "log-cabin-hard cider" election of 1840, Webster campaigned for Harrison; and the victorious candidate made him secretary of state. The elderly Harrison died on April 4, 1841, only one month after his inauguration. Webster continued in office under Harrison's successor, John Tyler. His effort to settle the Northeastern boundary dispute with Great Britain was successfully concluded with the signing of the Webster-Ashburton Treaty of 1842. Webster's decision to remain in the Tyler Cabinet after all of his fellow Whigs had resigned severely strained his party ties and threatened his political future. Tyler's desire to annex Texas gave Webster the excuse he needed to give up his office in May, 1843.

Webster went back to the Senate in 1845. Mindful of the lasting harm that his opposition to the War of 1812 had done to his presidential ambitions, he reluctantly supported the Mexican War, but he never believed it to be justified. The election of 1848 brought him the usual fourth year frustration as the Whigs nominated General Zachary Taylor, the victor of Buena Vista, who was elected. Webster's Seventh of March speech in support of the Compromise of 1850 was his final effort to eliminate the slavery issue from national politics; it enraged New England antislavery men, who likened him to a fallen angel. Webster became, after Taylor's death in July, 1850, secretary of state in Millard Fillmore's administration. His presidential ambitions were again revived in 1852, but the Whigs nominated General Winfield Scott. Sick in mind and body, Webster repudiated Scott's candidacy and correctly prophesied the downfall of the Whig Party. He died at his farm, Marshfield, on October 24, 1852, murmuring, "I still live!" Reflecting no more than his mental confusion about experiencing death, these final words would later take on a much broader symbolic meaning to many people.

Summary

Webster was a highly flawed yet fascinating human being, the stuff of which legends are made. He drank and ate to excess, spent money recklessly, and was chronically dependent on powerful creditors such as the National Bank. Combined with his political ambition, these weaknesses in his character constituted the "Black Dan" alter ego of his patriotic, disinterested, "Godlike Daniel" self. The Democrats never tired of reminding the voters that the champion of the Constitution and the Union had been a partisan Federalist congressman during the War of 1812. A perennial presidential candidate after 1830, Webster had to transcend New England's regional interests, while continuing to serve them. Intoning hymns to the Union was an obvious solution, and Webster's high point was his great debate with Hayne. Generations of Northern schoolchildren would memorize his ringing appeal: "Liberty *and* Union, now and forever, one and inseparable!" Webster believed that the United States had a special destiny and that Americans had a unique character with which to fulfill it. The last hopes of mankind, he said at Bunker Hill in 1825, rested on the success of the Union, the American experiment in popular government. Webster was less successful in trying to get the federal government to adopt a policy of economic nationalism, helping business in an age of economic growth through high tariffs, bank charters, and transportation subsidies. In his various roles as constitutional lawyer, orator, politician, and diplomat, he strengthened the sense of American nationalism. President Abraham Lincoln would echo Webster's Union theme in his Civil War addresses, such as the one at Gettysburg on November 19, 1863.

Bibliography

Bartlett, Irving H. *Daniel Webster*. New York: W. W. Norton and Co., 1978. This gracefully written, psychologically insightful biography is an attempt to understand the Black Dan-Godlike Man paradox along with the enigmatic inner man behind the dual images.

Baxter, Maurice G. *Daniel Webster and the Supreme Court*. Amherst: University of Massachusetts Press, 1966. Webster exerted a particularly strong influence on the bench in its application of the commerce and contract clauses. Baxter's handling of Webster's legal career, and especially his many appearances before the Supreme Court, is masterful.

__________. *One and Inseparable: Daniel Webster and the Union*. Cambridge, Mass.: The Belknap Press of Harvard University Press, 1984. Benefiting from the Webster Papers project at Dartmouth College, this is the long-awaited full-scale scholarly biography. Webster is portrayed as an ardent patriot, an advocate of American nationality, and a champion of peace and Union—who was at the same time a self-promoting politician who changed his principles to meet the interests of his constituents and who was sometimes insensitive to the great moral issues of the day.

Brown, Norman D. *Daniel Webster and the Politics of Availability*. Athens: University of Georgia Press, 1969. An account of Webster's presidential ambitions during the years in which a second American party system of National Republican-Whig and Democratic parties emerged out of the superficial Republican unity of the so-called Era of Good Feelings. General Andrew Jackson's tremendous popular success influenced Whig strategists to pass over Webster in 1836, 1840, 1848, and 1852, in favor of military heroes for the presidency.

Current, Richard N. *Daniel Webster and the Rise of National Conservatism*. Boston: Little, Brown and Co., 1955. This excellent brief biography emphasizes Webster's advocacy of a national conservatism for the United States as his response to the needs of the business community. The elements of his political philosophy were an expansive but peaceful Americanism, self-discipline, Constitution worship, beneficent technology, the harmony of group interests, and power tied to property.

Dalzell, Robert F., Jr. *Daniel Webster and the Trial of American Nationalism: 1843-1852*. Boston: Houghton Mifflin Co., 1973. Dalzell explains better than any previous study Webster's actions during his tragic last years, when the pressures on him to confirm, modify, or abandon his nationalism were the greatest.

Nathans, Sydney. *Daniel Webster and Jacksonian Democracy*. Baltimore: The Johns Hopkins University Press, 1973. This study explores Webster's responses, as a man and as a type of political leader, to the organized, systematic, and continued party strife that took firm root in the era of Andrew Jackson.

Smith, Craig R. *Defender of the Union: The Oratory of Daniel Webster*. Foreword by Halford R. Ryan. New York: Greenwood Press, 1989.

Norman D. Brown

GEORGE WASHINGTON WILLIAMS

Born: October 16, 1849; Bedford Springs, Pennsylvania
Died: August 2, 1891; Blackpool, England

As the author of the first reliable history of black Americans and a prominent political spokesman and observer, Williams contributed to the development of African American identity and racial pride.

Early Life

George Washington Williams was born in Bedford Springs, Pennsylvania, on October 16, 1849. His father, a free black named Thomas Williams, is believed to have been the son of a white Virginia planter and a slave woman. Sometime during the 1840's, the elder Williams moved to Bedford Springs, where he met and married Ellen Rouse, a light-skinned local black woman. George was the second of five children born to the couple. His childhood was a difficult one, plagued by frequent moves, family instability, a scant education, and Thomas Williams' heavy drinking. Although the elder Williams eventually tempered his life-style enough to serve as the minister of a black church in Newcastle, Pennsylvania, George became incorrigible and was placed in a refuge house for delinquent juveniles. There, he discovered literature and religion, interests that were to permeate his adult life.

Drawn by a sense of adventure, Williams went off to fight in the Civil War at age fourteen. By falsifying his age and using an assumed name, he was able to enlist in a black Union army regiment in August, 1864. He saw action in the closing battles in Virginia, including the campaigns against Petersburg and Richmond. After the war, his unit was transferred to Texas, but he soon left it and joined the revolutionary forces that were fighting to overthrow Emperor Maximilian, an Austrian interloper on the Mexican throne. Shortly before Maximilian's capture and execution in 1867, Williams returned to the United States and reenlisted. He served for more than a year as a cavalry sergeant at military posts in Kansas and Indian Territory (modern Oklahoma) until discharged in 1868.

Although untrained and barely literate, Williams was licensed as a Baptist preacher shortly after his military career ended. In September,

1870, he enrolled at the Newton Theological Institution, a Baptist school and seminary near Boston, Massachusetts. Williams completed both his general studies and his theological training in an astonishingly brief four years and was recognized as a good student. In June, 1874, he was graduated from Newton, was ordained in the Baptist clergy, and married Sarah A. Sterrett. A prominent member of

George Washington Williams *(The Associated Publishers)*

Boston's black community during his Newton years, Williams was named pastor of the city's historic, black Twelfth Baptist Church in 1873. While in that position, he joined other black leaders in working for passage of a national civil rights bill, publicly voiced his concerns about the course of Reconstruction, and penned a history of the local congregation. When he resigned his pastorate in October, 1875, it was to pursue these two emerging interests—politics and history.

Life's Work

One month before resigning his Boston pastorate, Williams went with his wife and infant son to Washington, D.C., which had become a gathering place for many of the nation's black leaders. With their assistance, he soon inaugurated a new weekly newspaper called *The Commoner*, which he hoped would reach beyond the "chilling shadow of slavery" and become "a powerful agent for reorganizing the race." Although he believed that it would attract a national audience, few subscribed and he was unable to sustain it beyond eight issues. The brevity of his encounter with the national political scene merely heightened Williams' interest in politics.

In February, 1876, Williams was called to the pastorate of the Union Baptist Church in Cincinnati, Ohio. He quickly made his mark on the local black community as an energetic pastor, an articulate spokesman and imaginative leader in racial affairs, and a regular contributor to the *Commercial*—a leading local newspaper—on a variety of local and national issues. He also became active in local Republican Party circles, rapidly gaining control of the party machinery in the city's black precincts. Nominated as a candidate for the Ohio legislature in 1877, Williams proved a strong campaigner, but he was overwhelmingly defeated as many white voters openly refused to cast their ballot for a black man. After this taste of politics, he left the ministry and briefly published a newspaper called *The Southwestern Review* (1877-1878). When it folded, the peripatetic Williams embarked upon the study of law with Alphonso Taft, the father of President William Howard Taft and a politician of national prominence in his own right. He later attended lectures at the Cincinnati Law School.

Continuing to campaign extensively for Republican candidates, Williams proved to be particularly adept at "waving the bloody shirt"—linking the Democratic Party with the Confederacy, slavery, and responsibility for starting the Civil War. In 1879, he was again nominated as a candidate for the Ohio legislature. Despite widespread criticism, he campaigned hard, openly courted white support, and was narrowly elected. Williams distinguished himself as an active legislator, sponsoring several reform measures, including legislation to control the use of alcoholic beverages. On occasion he became the center of controversy, as when he called for a civil rights resolution after encountering racist treatment in Columbus restaurants, hotels, and newspapers. He also unsuccessfully sought the repeal of a state law prohibiting interracial marriages.

In 1881, Williams refused to seek a second term in the Ohio legislature. His announced reason was the desire to devote his time to historical research and writing. The centennial celebrations of American independence in 1876 had heightened his early interest in history. Moving to Columbus, he began work on a general history of African Americans. A diligent and thorough researcher, he succeeded in completing a massive, two-volume study of his race from its African origins through the end of Reconstruction. This work, entitled *History of the Negro Race in America from 1619 to 1880* (1883), established Williams as a capable historian and was well received by leading Eastern magazines and newspapers. The New York *Independent* called it "an epoch-making book."

Although sales of his first book were disappointing, Williams began work on a second, which was eventually published as *History of the Negro Troops in the War of the Rebellion, 1861-1865* (1888). The work proved to be much broader than the title, examining the role of black soldiers in the American Revolution, the War of 1812, the Haitian Revolution, and other conflicts. This work was widely heralded, but the subsequent appearance of Joseph T. Wilson's *Black Phalanx* (1888), another history of black participation in the Civil War, limited sales and publicity for the volume. Williams also researched a two-volume history of Reconstruction, but it was never published. He experimented with other literary forms, penning a play on the African slave trade and a novel on the subject of interracial marriage. Although the novel was rejected by numerous publishers, its first eight chapters were eventually published in the Indianapolis *World* (1888), a black newspaper.

Shortly after the publication of his *History*, Williams returned to Massachusetts to live. Although he practiced law and stumped the state for Republican candidates, he derived most of his income from lecturing on black history, Africa, and general literature. Delivering hundreds of lectures throughout the Northeast, he soon gained a reputation as an eloquent speaker, and the handsome, mustached Williams must have cut a striking figure for his audiences.

Williams maintained his interest in politics. On March 2, 1885, two days before leaving office, President Chester A. Arthur, a Republican, nominated him to serve as minister resident and consul general to

Haiti. Although the Senate immediately confirmed him, and he was sworn in, the incoming Democratic administration of President Grover Cleveland refused him the post. He challenged the action in federal court but was denied redress. He abandoned the effort in 1889 after the newly inaugurated Republican president, Benjamin Harrison, appointed black leader Frederick Douglass to the post.

Depressed by his inability to obtain a diplomatic position, Williams turned his attention to Africa. In 1884, he had written articles on African geography, and, in testimony before the Senate Committee on Foreign Relations, he had urged American recognition of the Congo Free State. In the years that followed, he visited Europe several times to attend conferences on the African slave trade and African missions. In 1889, he interviewed King Leopold II of Belgium about his efforts to bring commerce and Christianity to the Congo (modern Zaire). When S. S. McClure of the Associated Literary Press commissioned him to write a series of articles on the Congo, and railroad magnate Collis P. Huntington asked him to report on the progress of the Congo railway being built by the Belgians, he visited the African continent.

Although King Leopold attempted to discourage him, Williams sailed for Africa in January, 1890. He spent four months exploring the Congo from the mouth of the Congo River to its headwaters at Stanley Falls. The trip revealed the Belgians' inhuman exploitation of black Africans. Williams responded by publishing *An Open Letter to His Serene Majesty, Leopold II, King of the Belgians* (1890), which extensively criticized Belgian colonial policy in the Congo. After visiting Portuguese and British possessions in East Africa, Williams went to Egypt, where he contracted tuberculosis. By the spring of 1891, he had improved enough to return to England, where he intended to write a full report of the European colonial impact on Africa. Concerned for his health, he hurried to the coastal city of Blackpool, where he hoped that the Irish Sea air and the curative powers of a local spa would restore his health. They did not. Williams died of tuberculosis and pleurisy on August 2, 1891.

Summary

George Washington Williams contributed many "firsts" to the African American experience. He was one of only a few blacks outside the South to serve in a state legislature during the nineteenth century.

Representing Hamilton County, Ohio, he distinguished himself during a single term in the Ohio legislature.

Williams is best remembered for his contributions to the writing of African American history. His books were the first reliable studies of the black role in America's past. On the cutting edge of historical research, Williams gathered information from thousands of volumes, but also employed church minutes, school statistics, newspapers, and oral interviews in compiling his works. This took him on an extensive tour of Western military posts, where he interviewed numerous black veterans of the Civil War. Williams explored beyond the stereotypes and prejudices in his research on the war and thus reclaimed a place for blacks in the history of the American Revolution, the antislavery movement, and the Civil War. He also delved into African history and was among the first historians to provide a realistic portrayal of the African kingdoms of Benin, Dahomey, Yoruba, and Ashanti. The epic quality of his work brought it attention in major magazines and newspapers, which was highly unusual for black research at that time. In researching his history of black soldiers in the Civil War, Williams became one of the first students of that conflict to use the official records of the Union and Confederate armies. Although he eventually moved away from historical studies, he left his mark on future investigations of the African American experience. Twentieth century black leader W. E. B. Du Bois called Williams "the greatest historian of the race."

Williams was the first African American to investigate extensively European colonialism in Africa. His criticism at first stirred controversy in the United States and abroad, but later colonial observers substantiated his claims. As a result, the Congo Reform Association was founded in 1904 to crusade against conditions in the Congo Free State. In 1890, these accomplishments prompted readers of the *Indianapolis Freeman* to vote Williams one of the ten greatest African Americans in history.

Bibliography

Franklin, John Hope. *George Washington Williams: A Biography*. Chicago: University of Chicago Press, 1985. The only reliable biography of Williams, this well-documented and balanced study is based on years of extensive research in a wide variety of obscure sources.

_________. "Stalking George W. Williams." *American Visions* 4, no. 2 (April, 1989): 28-32.

Gerber, David A. *Black Ohio and the Color Line: 1860-1915*. Urbana: University of Illinois Press, 1976. This valuable, well-documented work provides a context for understanding Williams' Ohio years. It includes a lengthy discussion of black institutions, politics, and race relations in Ohio during the 1870's and 1880's.

Slade, Ruth. *King Leopold's Congo: Aspects of the Development of Race Relations in the Congo Independent State*. London: Oxford University Press, 1962. Examines King Leopold II's policies in the Congo Free State. It credits Williams as one of the first critics of colonialism to demonstrate that Belgian officials in the Congo violated international trading practices established by European diplomats.

Thorpe, Earl E. *Black Historians: A Critique*. New York: William Morrow and Co., 1971. A general overview of African American historians from 1836 to the present. It critically analyzes Williams' historical writings and compares him with Joseph T. Wilson and other black historians of his time.

U.S. News & World Report. "Tracking a Pioneer: Forgotten Case." 109 (September 17, 1990): 53.

Williams, George Washington. *History of the Negro Race in America from 1619 to 1880*. 2 vols. New York: G. P. Putnam's Sons, 1883. Reprint. New York: Arno Press, 1968. The best way to understand Williams' historical contribution is to pursue this massive, two-volume study of African Americans from colonial days through Reconstruction. It has been conveniently reprinted in a single volume by Arno Press and *The New York Times*.

Roy E. Finkenbine

James Wilson

Born: September 14, 1742; Carskerdo, Scotland
Died: August 21, 1798; Edenton, North Carolina

Wilson was a leader in the movement for American independence, one of the most important members of the Philadelphia Convention, which created the United States Constitution, and a powerful advocate in Pennsylvania for its ratification. He was renowned for his learning in law and political theory, and George Washington appointed him to the first United States Supreme Court.

Early Life

James Wilson was born September 14, 1742, on the small farm of his parents, William and Alison Wilson, north of Edinburgh, near St. Andrews, Scotland. The Wilsons were not indigent, but as more children arrived they were obliged to practice rigorously the thrift for which their countrymen are known. They were intensely religious people, deeply imbued with the stern theology of John Calvin. They were a literate people, who believed that all should have direct access to the word of God by reading the scriptures.

The young James Wilson showed an aptitude for learning, and it was decided that he should become a clergyman. There was always much reading aloud, mostly of religious books, at home, followed by discussions and debate. By the time he was fifteen, Wilson had studied Latin, Greek, mathematics, and science, and he was eager to continue his education. He walked the six miles to St. Andrews, where he entered a competitive examination for a university scholarship and won.

He completed four years of study at St. Andrews University, which had become part of the Scottish Enlightenment with its acceptance of the new ideas of Isaac Newton, John Locke, Frances Hutcheson, David Hume, and other great thinkers of the time. While this put him in touch with currents of learning which were shaping the Western world, it also shook some of the more severe dogmas of his early Calvinistic thought. He had undertaken a fifth year of study, of divinity, when the death of his father required that he instantly return home to help support his mother and his three younger brothers.

At this point, Wilson abandoned the idea of becoming a clergyman and instead served as a tutor in a nearby family. Bored and restless, he soon went to Edinburgh and there became an accountant. This, too, soon bored him, and he began to plan to go to America, where some of the family's relatives and friends had already settled. His mother hated the idea but finally gave her consent. Relatives and friends contributed what they could for the considerable expense of the move, and, with their support and blessing, in the fall of 1765, he sailed to a new world of opportunity, as so many of his countrymen already had done.

Life's Work

Wilson arrived in America with two precious assets, his St. Andrews University education and the driving ambition which had made him leave Scotland. He also had a letter of introduction to Richard Peters, an Anglican cleric who was also a trustee of the College of Philadelphia. Thus equipped, he secured an appointment as a tutor at that institution. By that time, Philadelphia had become the foremost American city. It already possessed many of the best features of urban life. It was cosmopolitan and prosperous, and it offered cultural, intellectual, and even political opportunities.

Wilson was quite alert to all of this, and to the fact that the truly successful young men were the lawyers who profited well from a litigious people. He was appreciated at the college, where he was even granted an honorary master's degree in May, 1766, as an acknowledgment of his impressive learning, but he was restless, as always, and ambitious to get on with more momentous work and better remuneration. He decided to study law. He managed to enter the office of John Dickinson as an apprentice by borrowing money for the fee. Dickinson was already a legal luminary and destined to be among the most famous of Philadelphia lawyers; he was also deeply involved in the momentous political events of the next twenty-five years.

Wilson was able to add to his excellent general education and his prolonged pondering of theological and philosophical problems a searching study of the nature and meaning of law. His concern ran far beyond the procedures, forms, and practices of litigation. He immersed himself in the history and development of government in Pennsylvania and in England. He read the great classics on law and on constitutions, including the recently published *Commentaries on the Laws of England* (1765-1769) of Sir William Blackstone. His natural intellectual curiosity and zest for scholarship made him thorough and accurate; his striving ambition led him to arrange and retain this learning, ready for practical application.

In less than a year, he began his own practice, starting in the small community of Reading, the seat of Berks County, fifty miles from Philadelphia. For a time he had little business, but he expanded his efforts by getting admitted to practice in the neighboring counties of Lancaster, Chester, and Cumberland. Within another year or two, he had a good number of clients, a modest but growing income, and an enviable reputation as a young man of great promise. He moved to Carlisle in the fall of 1770, but he was somewhat distracted from his law practice by falling in love with Rachel Bird, a local heiress who, she said, had decided never to marry. Wilson persisted, and at last she consented; they were married in November, 1771.

By the early 1770's, James Wilson was a tall, strong young man with a somewhat awkward manner. His ruddy face usually bore an alert expression of genuine interest in what others might be saying to him. He was, though, quite nearsighted, and his peering through thick glasses struck some people as a mannerism of aristocratic arrogance. He had only a hint of the Scottish burr of his youth, and his speaking was clear, accurate, and persuasive. He was widely praised for the excellence of his court presentations, and in time he had a considerable reputation as a public speaker. The leading elements of Carlisle society accepted Wilson as one of their own quickly and easily. Many of them were Scots, most were prosperous, and nearly all were deeply disturbed by the recent changes in England's policies regarding the American Colonies.

At the close of the French and Indian War in 1763, Parliament had begun to antagonize Americans through a new set of imperial policies. Wilson had arrived in America just as one of the most inflammatory measures, the Stamp Act (1763), had been enacted. It was denounced in America as taxation without representation, and there had even been intercolonial cooperation in the mounting resistance. It was repealed in 1766, but Parliament also issued a sweeping assertion of its total authority over the Colonies. John Dickinson, Wilson's legal mentor at that time, was greatly interested in the constitutional attack on Parliament's pretensions to power, and when new taxes came in 1767, Dickinson became famous as the foremost expositor of the American resistance, writing under the name, "The Pennsylvania Farmer." Wilson then decided that he, too, should write an essay explaining his own ideas as to why the British Parliament had no rightful authority over the American Colonies. He was advised by trusted friends that it was too extreme, that it would anger many powerful men; while he was considering what to do, the hated taxes (except for that on tea) were repealed, political tensions were eased, and Anglo-American relations, most people believed, would again be harmonious. The essay was put away for a time.

New provocations came, however, and by 1773 it was Boston which was in the center of things, with the destruction of cargoes of tea (the Boston Tea Party) followed by severe punishment in the form of Parliament's 1774 enactments, which closed the Boston port and instituted military government there. Parliament's actions caused an uproar throughout the Colonies. Mass meetings were held in many places, including Philadelphia and Carlisle. It was decided not only to express outrage against Parliament but also to hold a Provincial Convention in Philadelphia, consisting of delegates from all the counties of Pennsylvania, to take further action. Wilson became deeply involved; he was a delegate to the convention, and soon afterward, he revised his earlier essay and had it published.

The article received much attention, especially from the delegates who were now arriving in Philadelphia for the First Continental Congress. It was remarkable for its coherence, its unassailable argumentation, and, above all, its advanced notion of the nature of the British Empire. Wilson asserted that Parliament had no proper right to legislate for America, yet the Colonies were bound by loyalty to the crown as part of an imperial union of virtually autonomous units—a description of the very much later British Commonwealth of Nations. From this time onward, Wilson was widely regarded as a great thinker and leader in the American Revolution.

Wilson's services in that cause were many. He was a member of the Second Continental Congress, where he served on a number of important committees. When the question of American independence became unavoidable, Wilson, who really doubted the idea, nevertheless finally supported it and signed the Declaration of Independence. In Congress, he was especially concerned about the difficulty of financing the war, and he worked closely with his friend, Robert Morris, in creating the Bank of North America. He also was a strong advocate for the creation of a national domain out of the unsettled Western lands beyond the Appalachians, with a view to organizing new states there. By the end of the war, he was an ardent advocate of strengthening the central government, and he had become involved in a multiplicity of business affairs, many of them visionary schemes of land speculation.

Meanwhile, Wilson had been profoundly distressed at the course of the revolution in Pennsylvania. He thought that the new state constitution, widely regarded as a radical one, was a dreadful calamity, with its unicameral legislature, plural executive, loyalty oath for voters, subservient judiciary, and other novelties. His prominence in the bitter, persistent opposition to the constitution made him extremely unpopular with those in control of state affairs. In time they saw to it that he was no longer one of the state's delegates to Congress. His ever closer association with Robert Morris and others of the wealthy merchant-lawyer class in Philadelphia made him the target of many rumors of profiteering and corruption—so much so that, at one point, his house was besieged by a large, armed, angry mob. Several men were killed before relief arrived to lift the "siege of Ft. Wilson."

After the war, Wilson's business affairs became even more complex and uncertain; he seemed always to be plagued with cash shortages and debt. Luckily, the political climate gradually became more congenial for him. Opposition to Pennsylvania's 1776 constitution grew, and the move to overcome the defects of the Articles of Confederation and build an effective national government got under way. This provided Wilson with the occasion of his greatest contribution to the new nation.

By 1787, Wilson had long since moved to Philadelphia; he was no longer a frontier lawyer, for he had gained entrance into the upper reaches of Eastern society, an eager participant in their great economic and political plans as well as their social life. As a member of the Philadelphia Convention which drew up the United States Constitution, he was second in importance only to James Madison. He was perhaps the clearest expositor of the notion of dual sovereignty—the idea that the national government must be supreme in some matters, while states remained in control of others. He consistently urged that government must be based on popular participation, and he, along with Madison and a few others, managed at least to get one house of Congress elected directly by the voters. He tried in vain to ensure popular election of the president; he finally proposed the complex electoral college formula, which he thought better than having Congress choose the president, as so many wished. He thought it imperative to have strong executive power; he also argued that an independent judiciary was indispensable. He was extremely influential in the discussions of many of the most crucial features of the new United States Constitution.

Wilson was also a central figure in Pennsylvania's quick action to ratify the Constitution. The Federalists, as the Constitution's supporters were being called, now controlled the state government there, and they quickly managed to arrange a ratifying convention, to be held in November, 1787. There Wilson was their principal resource person and main speaker. Within three weeks, the convention voted to ratify (December 12, 1787). Only Delaware had acted faster, ratifying five days before.

Pennsylvania Federalists, continuing in firm control, had one more major item on their agenda: replacing the 1776 constitution. Soon the Assembly agreed to a new constitutional convention, and Wilson was again hard at work. Few had despised the old constitution as Wilson had, and few had suffered as much abuse as a result. Now he had the great satisfaction of leading a congenial convention, dominated by those who thought as he did, in drafting a document which provided for a bicameral legislature, strong executive power, and an independent judiciary. He was the principal architect of Pennsylvania's constitution of 1790.

Wilson wanted very much to be appointed the first chief justice of the United States; he even wrote an unfortunate letter to George Washington suggesting this, and it received a stiff, noncommittal reply. He was appointed as an associate justice, a substantial consolation prize. His next triumph was of a different sort. He gave a series of lectures on law at the College of Philadelphia (later the University of Pennsylvania), in which he advocated the establishment of a distinctly American system of jurisprudence. The opening lecture (December, 1790) was attended by President Washington, some members of Congress, and many other dignitaries. Wilson stressed the close connection between law and liberty. All citizens of a free society, he said, must know something of the nature and elements of law, in order to preserve their freedom. Wilson had become the premier theorist of American law.

The last years of Wilson's life were ones of disappointment and calamity. Of the modest number of cases that reached the Supreme Court in the 1790's, only a few offered an opportunity for the enunciation of significant constitutional ideas. In the most important one, *Chisholm v. Georgia* (1793), Wilson was an important participant in the decision to permit citizens to sue states, but that bold exercise in constitutional interpretation was extremely unpopular, and it was soon overturned by the adoption of the Eleventh Amendment. Along with his colleagues on the Court, however, he managed to maintain the idea of an independent judiciary, and they also assumed the right to review the constitutionality of state and federal laws.

Wilson's private business affairs occupied increasing amounts of his energy and his time. He had long been eager to acquire Western land, and now he became involved in one grand speculative project after another. None succeeded. Wilson's financial losses were ever larger, and he was unable to repay loans and other debts when due. He was jailed twice by creditors, released at last on bail provided by borrowed money. Finally he fled to the home of his friend and colleague, Justice James Iredell of North Carolina, suffering severe mental stress and occasional derangement. After further illness, he died in Edenton, North Carolina, on August 21, 1798.

Summary

Wilson was an important figure among those who launched the American Revolution. Trained in the law, seriously concerned about ideas of constitutional liberty, he rapidly came to the fore as a powerful advocate of American rights. This gained for him a place in various revolutionary committees, conventions, and other bodies where he brought energy, time, and talent to the cause of American independence. More than independence was needed, however, and Wilson knew it: The new country had to be governed, governed better than any other. It was in devising new arrangements of governing power that his greatest work was done.

His ideas for the new government of Pennsylvania were not popular for some years, though ultimately they did prevail when he assumed a leading role in drafting that state's second constitution in 1790. His greatest service was in the Philadelphia Convention (1787), where he found sympathetic colleagues in the great work of drawing up a national constitution. He was a powerful advocate of strong executive power, but he believed that the executive should be chosen as directly as possible by the people. His idea of an independent national judiciary, possessed of the power to resolve questions of constitutional meaning, was one of his boldest ones. His notion of a federal union easily embraced the concurrent exercise of power by both the state and the national government, but his insistence on national supremacy in most major matters, such as foreign policy, war and peace, and regulation of trade, marked him as one of the most farsighted and prophetic of the nation's founders.

The quality of his thinking continues to impress scholars and analysts of political theory and jurisprudence. His intellectual resources were extensive, and the logic of his discourses made them persuasive in his day. On the other hand, it was not his style to be succinct, and the scope of his thought was broad; these elements of his writings limited his influence with later generations, as did the severe decline in his prestige during his later years.

Certain of his personal qualities were the undoing of his reputation. He became importunate in his eagerness for fame and wealth, taking chances in one imprudent venture after another. He did not have that expansive personal charm which would create close friends who would be concerned that he received his due as a great patriot and a masterly architect of government in America. Nevertheless, his work endures, and the existing nation is, in many important respects, the one he sought.

Bibliography

Brunhouse, Robert L. *Counterrevolution in Pennsylvania: 1776-1790.* Harrisburg: Pennsylvania Historical and Museums Commission, 1942. Standard account of a movement of great importance in Wilson's life. He was especially outspoken and perhaps tactless in denouncing the constitution of 1776, and the story of its being replaced is one in which he was a central figure. Scholarly and reliable on this bitter battle.

Pascal, Jean-Marc. *The Political Ideas of James Wilson, 1742-1798.* New York: Garland Pub., 1991.

Rossiter, Clinton L. *1787: The Grand Convention.* New York: Macmillan, Publishing Co., 1966. Well-balanced portrayal of the episode wherein Wilson's most important work occurred. Rossiter's organization of ideas, along with his readable prose, make this a book which one is likely to find interesting as well as reliable. Includes a brief account of the ratification of the United States Constitution and the first few years of its use.

Seed, Geoffrey. *James Wilson*. Millwood, N.Y.: Kraus International, 1978. Very perceptive study of Wilson's political ideas. The author's intent is to make Wilson's place secure among the first rank of the Founding Fathers, and he argues the case well. Especially detailed analysis of Wilson's contributions to the United States Constitution.

Selsam, John Paul. *The Pennsylvania Constitution of 1776*. Philadelphia: University of Pennsylvania Press, 1936. Basic story of the "radical" constitution produced by the revolution in Pennsylvania. The closest approach to democracy in the American Revolution occurred in Pennsylvania, where the new charter broadened the right to vote and rendered government especially responsible to the people. A central paradox of Wilson's thought—his insistence on popular participation in government, but his loathing of this constitution—can be better understood after consulting this work.

Smith, Charles Page. *James Wilson: Founding Father, 1742-1798*. Chapel Hill: University of North Carolina Press, 1956. Only book-length biography of Wilson. Though in places needed sources of information do not exist, the author provides plausible probabilities. Readable, with sensitivity and well-balanced judgments of the man.

Tinkom, Harry M. *The Republicans and Federalists in Pennsylvania: 1790-1801*. Harrisburg: Pennsylvania Historical and Museum Commission, 1950. Partisan controversies became strident, turbulent, and even violent in the 1790's, making Wilson's life difficult. Scholarly and reliable on the sharply divided political scene.

Wilson, James. *The Works of James Wilson*. 2 vols. Philadelphia: Lorenzo Press, 1804. Reprint. Edited by Robert G. McCloskey. Cambridge, Mass.: Harvard University Press, 1967. A reprinting of material published in 1804 by Wilson's son, with valuable additions. The editor's extensive, learned introductory essay is especially good, and the "bibliographical glossary" is most useful in identifying Wilson's vast scholarly resources. Mostly lectures on law, though nine miscellaneous writings include four important speeches.

Richard D. Miles

WOODROW WILSON

Born: December 28, 1856; Staunton, Virginia
Died: February 3, 1924; Washington, D.C.

As twenty-eighth president of the United States (1913-1921), Wilson was responsible for American entry into World War I, was one of the formulators of the Paris peace settlement, and was the principal architect of the League of Nations.

Early Life

Thomas Woodrow Wilson's passion for constitution-making came from his childhood experience in drafting a set of rules for a neighborhood club that met in a hayloft. From then on, he tried to reform any organization he joined, crafting new sets of procedures and aims and then going on to repeat the procedure somewhere else. He rarely let himself get involved with practical application; he was essentially a policymaker. Also from his early days, or more specifically from his stern father, Joseph Ruggles Wilson, a Presbyterian minister and theologian, came his highly developed sense of moral righteousness. This was reinforced by his mother, the daughter of a minister, Thomas Woodrow, pastor of a church in Carlisle, England, before he migrated to the United States in 1836. As President of the United States, Wilson would have the privilege of preaching a sermon from his grandfather's old pulpit in 1919. It was one of the high points of his life.

When Wilson was a year old, his family moved to Augusta, Georgia, where he lived during the Civil War, a conflict which influenced his later determination to create an organization to guarantee international peace and cooperation. When he was fourteen, his father was appointed professor at the theological seminary in Columbia, South Carolina, and several years later became pastor of a church in Wilmington, North Carolina. In 1874, Wilson entered college, first at nearby Davidson College, then, the following year, at the College of New Jersey (later Princeton University), where he participated in literary activities and in debate. Upon graduation in 1879, he enrolled in the University of Virginia law school, which led him to a brief and unsuccessful legal practice in Atlanta, Georgia. In 1883, he entered The Johns

Woodrow Wilson *(White House Historical Society)*

Hopkins University, receiving his Ph.D. in government and history three years later.

Over the next decade and a half, Wilson held a variety of academic positions, at Bryn Mawr College, Wesleyan University in Connecticut, and Princeton University, of which, in 1902, he became president. He devoted himself to reshaping undergraduate education, working to institute a preceptorial system whereby students and professors would live together in quadrangles to follow common scholarly pursuits; the plan, however, was opposed by the trustees and never adopted. Wilson also failed to gain control of the graduate school, a loss to his self-esteem that made him turn to politics as compensation.

In 1910, Wilson accepted the Democratic nomination for the governorship of New Jersey and ran on a Progressive platform, promising to reform the election system with direct primaries, to introduce anti-trust legislation, and to wipe out corruption. He was elected by a plurality of forty-nine thousand votes and immediately proceeded to enact his program despite the fact that the Republicans enjoyed a majority in both houses of the New Jersey congress. His success brought him wider attention, and in 1912, he was persuaded to become a contender for the Democratic nomination for President of the United States, winning on the forty-sixth ballot against the party favorite, Speaker of the House Champ Clark.

Wilson brought his Progressivism into national politics as the New Freedom. He ran against a badly divided Republican Party—split between the candidacies of William Howard Taft and Theodore Roosevelt—and won forty-two percent of the national vote, one million votes less than the combined tally of his opponents. In the electoral college, however, he got 435 votes to their ninety-six. With both houses of Congress now under Democratic control, Wilson looked forward to carrying out the major reforms for which he had fought during his campaign.

Life's Work

Wilson's entire political experience had been with domestic politics, and once in the White House, he took a direct role in the presentation of his legislative program to Congress. In short order, he saw adopted a federal income tax, the Federal Reserve Board to control the nation's currency, and the Clayton Anti-Trust Act, which strengthened labor's right to strike. It was Wilson's role in foreign affairs, however, for which he is best known.

His inauguration coincided with the outbreak of a revolt in Mexico against General Victoriano Huerta, who had become president with the connivance of the American ambassador Henry Lane Wilson. Woodrow Wilson considered the Mexican strongman a bloody usurper and denied him United States recognition. He decided to arrange Huerta's downfall. To this end, he authorized aid to Huerta's opponents. When this failed to do the job, he opted for direct military intervention. In April, 1914, after a bloody battle with the Mexicans, the marines occupied the port of Vera Cruz. The city remained under American control for the next half year, finally being handed over to Venustiano Carranza, one of the contenders for national power whom Wilson thought a more acceptable Mexican president. Wilson professed to be turning over a new leaf in American relations with the countries of Latin America, replacing the crass dollar diplomacy practiced by his predecessors with a policy of high moral purpose; intervention by any other name, however, still smelled the same. Wilson clearly did not shy away from meddling in the affairs of other countries if he found a suitable rationale for doing so. His confidence that he knew what was best for others led him to establish a virtual protectorate over Haiti in 1915 and to institute United States military government over Santo Domingo the following year. Wilson might have expressed a desire to prepare the Philippines for self-government, but this hardly prevented the United States from being seen as an imperialistic bully. Wilson's concern for the fate of Third World nations was minor, however, compared to his preoccupation with the major conflict now going on in Europe.

On August 4, 1914, the day Germany invaded Belgium, Wilson officially admonished the American people to remain neutral in both thought and deed. The declaration was willingly accepted as the magic formula for nonparticipation; yet American neutrality was a sham from the beginning. Wilson's one-sided enforcement of American neutrality rights showed that he was clearly committed to the victory of the Entente. Moreover, Wilson saw nothing wrong with putting the industrial capacity of the United States at the service of the British and the French, something the Germans could not tolerate for long. Yet when German submarines began sinking merchant ships in the war zone around the British Isles, Wilson was outraged. He even believed that Americans traveling on belligerent ships should be free from attack. He was not yet willing, however, to let his indignation develop into a declaration of war.

Wilson won the election campaign of 1916 with the slogan "He kept us out of the war." He continued to talk peace but now emphasized preparedness and, in a speech given on January 22, 1917, started to enumerate war aims. He emphasized the necessity of establishing "a peace that will win the approval of mankind," a peace based on "an equality of rights" and on the "principle that governments derive all their just powers from the consent of the governed." He also endorsed freedom of the seas, disarmament, and collective security. By these vague and impressionistic "principles of mankind," Wilson committed the United States to a role in peacemaking that could only be achieved if the nation participated directly in the war. Thus, he clearly separated himself from his previously alleged policy, and indeed from a majority of his own people. He already had an excuse for entry as the Germans had committed themselves to unrestricted submarine warfare.

On April 2, 1917, Wilson delivered his war message to Congress, claiming that "the world must be made safe for democracy." American participation proved crucial to Allied victory and gave Wilson his great opportunity to write a constitution for the world. The establishment of the League of Nations was the fulfillment of a boyhood dream. The most important part of the League of Nations Covenant lay in Article 10, in which the members undertook to preserve against aggression the integrity and political independence of the others. To assure acceptance, the league was made an integral part of the Treaty of Versailles with Germany.

Article 10 struck some United States senators, however, as a danger to American sovereign rights, and they insisted that before ratification certain modifications be made. Wilson, though, fought all change, believing that this would only weaken the moral authority of the United States to protect other states from aggression. In an effort to improve the treaty's chances, he made a direct appeal to the American people in a nationwide speaking tour. He collapsed in Pueblo, Colorado, and was rushed back to Washington paralyzed and without the power to speak. His wife Edith became his main link with the outside world.

The treaty, containing the reservations on the league, was offered for ratification twice, on November 19, 1919, and on March 19, 1920. It failed both times, mainly because Wilson urged his supporters to vote against it. Thus, it was killed on his orders. The United States never joined the League of Nations and later made a separate peace with Germany.

Wilson's administration ended on March 4, 1921. Wilson continued to live in Washington but took no further part in the city's political or social fife. When he died, on February 3, 1924, he was buried in the non-Presbyterian National Cathedral, his wife being Episcopalian.

Summary

Wilson had come to the Paris Peace Conference on a crusade, convinced that he alone of all Allied leaders represented the general will of the people. It made no difference that his own Democratic Party had lost both houses in the recent November elections, and he took no steps to make his peace delegation bipartisan. He had told the American people that the armistice had given them everything for which they had fought, but he believed that the defeat of Germany was not enough because it was now his duty to assist in the establishment of just democracy throughout the world. Such knight-errantry was not favored by his fellow countrymen, who believed that the defeat of the Kaiser meant that it was really over "over there."

Wilson was correct in assuming that the United States had a stake in the war, though he did not enter to preserve the balance of power. He defined his goals in terms of destroying the whole international system upon which that equilibrium had been based. The United States emerged from the war the strongest power in the world, but if the pursuit of a new world order involved, as Wilson maintained that it should, the destruction of the sovereignity of the nation-state, the Americans could lose what they had acquired. Wilson was convinced, however, that all problems and threats to national security could be solved through participation in the League of Nations.

The president believed that this organization would have a chemical effect on mankind, making people "drunk with the spirit of self-sacrifice." He saw its responsibilities to extend beyond peacekeeping, even obliging all states to guarantee equality to their racial and religious minorities and to require them to apply universal standards of work, including the eight-hour day.

Unfortunately, Wilson saw things in moral terms while the Europeans saw them in strategic. They looked upon the League of Nations as a device through which they could project their power, not as, in Georges Clemenceau's words, "a bridge leading to the new Jerusalem." Wilson was torn between two contradictory positions: He professed a belief in the sovereign equality of states, but he believed in the use of force for the good of civilization. Unfortunately, not everybody trusted the United States to act in any interest but its own. What appeared to Wilson as "unalterable lines of principle" frequently struck others as American realpolitik. Wilson was a persuasive orator, and his idealistic sloganeering had great appeal. The conduct of foreign affairs along lines of high morality had a lofty attraction, but often, too often, it could become the refuge of a scoundrel.

Bibliography

Bailey, Thomas A. *Woodrow Wilson and the Great Betrayal*. Chicago: Quadrangle Books, 1963. Concentrates on the attempts to get the Treaty of Versailles, containing the League of Nations, ratified by the Senate. Particularly good in describing the differing points of view of Wilson's opponents as well as the president's own stubbornness. In his conclusions, though, Bailey is a bit simplistic in assuming that the United States, as a member of the League of Nations, would have played a great role in European politics.

Baker, Ray Stannard. *Woodrow Wilson and World Settlement*. Garden City, N.Y.: Doubleday, Page and Co., 1922. The author draws heavily on his own experiences as Wilson's press secretary at the Paris conference. Although he holds Wilson in high esteem and his account lacks analysis, Baker deserves credit for being one of Wilson's first biographers, his presentation furnishing a basis on which other more thoughtful accounts were written.

Bragdon, Henry W. *Woodrow Wilson: The Academic Years*. Cambridge, Mass.: The Belknap Press of Harvard University Press, 1967. Shows how Wilson's style of leadership in academe presaged his later career as president. Traces Wilson's transition from conservatism to Progressivism through an analysis of his published writings, speeches, and lecture notes. Maintains that earlier mild attacks of arteriosclerosis accounted for his aggressiveness and refusal to compromise.

Buehrig, Edward H. *Woodrow Wilson and the Balance of Power*. Bloomington: Indiana University Press, 1955. One of the few studies that gets at this subject and with good reason, since balance-of-power considerations were never essential elements in Wilson's thinking, his concept being the projection of world power by the English-speaking nations.

Daniels, Josephus. *The Life of Woodrow Wilson: 1856-1924*. Philadelphia: John C. Winston, 1924. Essentially a panegyric written by a member of Wilson's cabinet who was one of the most dubious of political creatures: a Southern liberal.

Devlin, Patrick. *Too Proud to Fight: Woodrow Wilson's Neutrality*. New York: Oxford University Press, 1974. Shows how American entry into the war related to Wilson's sense of morality and his desire to gain representation at the peace conference as a ticket to remaking the world order. Devlin, a British jurist, has largely relied on the primary research of others, but he mastered the intricacies of Wilson's day-to-day diplomacy, which he presents in great detail.

Esposito, David M. *The Legacy of Woodrow Wilson: American War Aims in World War I*. Westport, Conn.: Praeger, 1996.

Heckscher, August. *Woodrow Wilson*. New York: Maxwell Macmillan International, 1991.

Knock, Thomas J. *To End All Wars: Woodrow Wilson and the Quest for a New World Order*. New York: Oxford University Press, 1992.

Link, Arthur Stanley. *Wilson*. 5 vols. Princeton, N.J.: Princeton University Press, 1947-1965. A painstakingly researched and meticulously documented study, letter by letter, memoir by memoir, document by document. Seldom is heard a discouraging word, however, on Wilson himself. For example, Link gushingly calls Wilson's preposterous note to the Germans following the sinking of the *Lusitania* (the one upholding the rights of Americans to travel anywhere they want on the high seas) so "bold as to be almost breathtaking."

Schulte Nordholt, J. W. *Woodrow Wilson: A Life for World Peace*. Translated by Herbert H. Rowen. Berkeley: University of California Press, 1991.

Smith, Gene. *When the Cheering Stopped: The Last Years of Woodrow Wilson*. New York: William Morrow and Co., 1964. A journalistic account of the year and a half following Wilson's stroke. Smith, a reporter for the *New York Post*, describes the "petticoat presidency" presided over by Wilson's dedicated but often spiteful wife in colorful detail and with great sympathy. Wilson's stature was enhanced through suffering, and, despite incapacitation, his popularity with the American people remained strong.

Weinstein, Edwin A. *Woodrow Wilson: A Medical and Psychological Biography*. Princeton, N.J.: Princeton University Press, 1981. Despite the obvious handicap of not having had direct contact with the subject, nor access to a professional case history, this provocative study by a former professor of neurology at Mount Sinai Medical School in New York is the best attempt to explain Wilson's behavior clinically.

Wm. Laird Kleine-Ahlbrandt

John Winthrop

Born: January 12, 1588; Edwardstone, Suffolk, England
Died: March 26, 1649; Boston, Massachusetts

Winthrop was committed to the ideal of creating a Christian commonwealth, and his determined leadership was crucial to the establishment of the Massachusetts Bay Colony.

Early Life

John Winthrop was born January 12, 1588, in the small English village of Edwardstone in Suffolk. His mother, née Anne Browne, and his father, Adam Winthrop, lived at Groton Manor in Suffolk. Winthrop's grandfather, also named Adam, a successful London cloth merchant, had purchased the manor from Henry VIII in 1544. It had been part of a monastery confiscated by the monarch. Winthrop received an extensive education beginning at age seven with instruction from a local vicar. At fifteen, he entered Trinity College, Cambridge. Winthrop remained there less than two years, but later studied law at Gray's Inn, one of the London Inns of Court. He started a family at a tender age; his father arranged a marriage to Mary Forth when he was only seventeen, and he became a father at eighteen. Over the next twelve years, Winthrop moved from his dowry lands at Great Stambridge back to Groton, presided over the manorial court, served as a justice of the peace, and assumed control of the family lands on the manor. In the 1620's, he widened his horizons by developing a lucrative London law practice. It enabled Winthrop to make contacts in the government and led to his selection in 1627 as an attorney in the King's Court of Wards and Liveries, a court which administered the estates of minor heirs to lands held from the king.

As he matured, Winthrop became ever more committed to the faith of the Puritan reformers in the Church of England. Advocates of the teaching of John Calvin, Puritans believed that God had predestined salvation for only a few. From his early teens, Winthrop had followed a rigorous regimen of prayer and study in search of signs that God had selected him. While he struggled for assurance of that elect status, Winthrop also sought to place his relationship with God ahead of all else—his family, his work, and his love of hunting, food, and drink. He never became an ascetic; he believed God's creations should be enjoyed but always with proper moderation. His faith made Winthrop a stern and determined man; this was clearly evident in a painting of the mature Winthrop. His serious countenance, graced by a Vandyke beard and ruffled collar, befits a man with a sense of purpose.

Life's Work

Winthrop probably would have been known only as one of the lesser English gentry had not a series of economic, religious, and personal crises in the late 1620's caused him to leave England. Inflation, smaller returns from the fixed rents he could charge the tenants on his land, and a depression in the Suffolk textile trade all dearly cost the squire of Groton. His disappointing financial situation worsened in 1629 when Winthrop lost his attorneyship in the Court of Wards and Liveries. He was only one of numerous casualties in the campaign of Charles I to remove Puritans from secular and religious positions. The king's Catholic wife, the appointment of William Laud (a resolute anti-Puritan) as Bishop of London, and the dissolution in 1629 of a Parliament heavily influenced by Puritans all caused dissenters to despair about their future in England. They did not see much hope for their faith under a monarch who opposed their advocacy of simpler services and a Calvinist theology in the Church of England. Winthrop had a more immediate reason for feeling that he was living in an evil and declining nation. Long concerned by what he considered a lax moral climate in the nation, Winthrop was appalled by the behavior of his son Henry. The nineteen-year-old had gone to the West Indian island of Barbados in 1627. Upon his return two years later, Henry did little more than carouse with boisterous friends in London. Winthrop believed that it was imperative that he act to save his family and preserve his faith. He worried that migration meant abandoning his homeland, but he hoped that the creation of a model Christian community in North America would show England the way to reform.

Winthrop worked with the members of the Massachusetts Bay Company to achieve his goal. Made up of substantial landowners, merchants, and clergymen, the company selected Winthrop as its governor. He organized the ships, settlers, and provisions for the expedition and then led more than one thousand people to Massachusetts in

1630. In the next nineteen years, Winthrop retained an important role in the colony's government; twelve times he was elected governor. Throughout those years, he struggled to keep the settlers committed to building a cooperative, godly commonwealth.

Challenges to Winthrop's vision emerged quickly. Few were willing to settle in a single, compact town as Winthrop had hoped; in addition to Boston, six towns were formed in the first year alone. The cheap land, the high wages paid to scarce skilled workers, and the profits to be made in commerce led many to a greater concern over the material benefits of Winthrop's colony than its spiritual. Price and wage controls mitigated the impact of the more acquisitive settlers but could not completely suppress the growing economic individualism. More troubling to Winthrop than the greed of some colonists and the dispersal of settlement, however, was religious dissent. Winthrop and his supporters did not migrate to Massachusetts to create a utopia of toleration; rather they moved to worship in a singular fashion—in self-governing congregations of God's elect. Consequently, Winthrop fought all attempts to undermine that effort.

The first significant trouble came from Roger Williams, a minister who arrived in the colony in 1631. Among other things, Williams demanded that the colonists repudiate all ties to the Church of England, a position contrary to Winthrop's resolve to reform, not break from, the established church. Williams also argued that the elect should not worship with the unregenerate, an idea repugnant to Winthrop, whose hope for a unified colony dictated that persons of all conditions worship together. A brilliant woman, Anne Hutchinson, presented an even greater threat. Not long after her arrival in 1634, she began to hold mid-week meetings in her home. Hutchinson used these popular gatherings to criticize ministers whom she believed erred in their sermons. All but two, she charged, taught a Covenant of Works—that good conduct could lead to salvation—rather than a Covenant of Grace—that salvation was obtained only through God's grace. Her attacks on the clergy made Hutchinson a danger to the established order. When she later claimed that she received divine revelation, Hutchinson became a pariah to Winthrop. When persuasion failed to convince the two dissenters to retreat from their positions, Winthrop supported the decision to banish them, Williams in 1636 and Hutchinson two years later. Other dissenters also suffered banishment or were forced to migrate to other regions. The departure of these people ensured a religious orthodoxy that prevailed throughout the colony's first two decades.

In addition to these religious conflicts, Massachusetts faced other vexing problems. Disputes over who could participate in the government were resolved by permitting male church members to vote. Complaints from outlying settlements that their interests were not being served by Boston lawmakers were handled by allowing each town representation in the colony's General Court. The outbreak of civil war in England in the early 1640's dramatically reduced the immigration to Massachusetts. Immigrants had been the chief consumers of the colony's produce, and with the decline in their numbers, the economy slumped badly. Prices fell until the Puritans found new markets in the Canaries and the Caribbean Islands. Winthrop figured prominently in the resolution of these difficulties; he helped work out the political problems, and he maintained contacts and promoted trade in the West Indies.

Winthrop usually avoided the extremes in both secular and religious matters. He deplored the ideas of separatist dissenters such as Williams, for example, because he believed that they would lead to the chaos of dozens of little utopias. Yet other leaders in the colony, notably Thomas Dudley, criticized Winthrop for being too lenient with dissenters. His general commitment to moderate positions offended many, but it helped preserve the Puritan experiment in the New World, one with more than fifteen thousand inhabitants at his death in 1649. Besides a grateful colony, Winthrop was survived by six of his sixteen children and his fourth wife.

Summary

As he led the Puritan expedition across the Atlantic in early 1630, Winthrop had time to think about the meaning of their collective effort. He drafted a lay sermon containing those reflections, and he delivered it to the passengers prior to their arrival in Massachusetts. Entitled "A Modell of Christian Charity," it remains one of the most eloquent statements of Christian brotherhood. He explained to his followers

> wee must be knitt together in this worke as one man, wee must entertaine each other in brotherly Affeccion . . . wee must delight in eache other, make others Condicions our owne rejoyce together, mourne to-

> gether, labour, and suffer together, allwayes haveing before our eyes . . . our Community as members of the same body. . . .

His effort to convince settlers to subordinate their self-interest to the good of the community was far from successful. Yet through his example and his support of laws governing economic behavior, Winthrop helped keep in check the individualism he believed would destroy the colony.

Perhaps Winthrop's greatest impact on American life was his evocation of a sense of mission. He thought that the tired generations of the Old World were eagerly observing the Puritan effort to build a model religious society. "For wee must Consider," he claimed, "that wee shall be as a Citty upon a Hill, the eies of all people are uppon us." Winthrop and fellow Puritans believed that they were God's new chosen people, a new Israel. Succeeding generations have shared this sense that America had a special destiny to be a light to other nations. They have revealed their debt to the great Puritan leader each time they borrowed his metaphor and claimed that America must be as a city upon a hill.

Bibliography

Bremer, Francis J. *The Puritan Experiment: New England Society from Bradford to Edwards*. New York: St. Martin's Press, 1976. Bremer provides a comprehensive account of the Puritans through the mid-eighteenth century. In addition, he includes a helpful discussion of secondary works and a guide to the most important primary sources on the Puritans.

Miller, Perry. "Errand into the Wilderness." In *Errand into the Wilderness*. Cambridge, Mass.: Harvard University Press, 1956. This is an essay by the leading historian on the Puritan mind. He describes both the exhilarating sense of mission Winthrop shared with other leaders in the 1630's and the disappointment of a later generation when it realized that England had paid scant attention to the errand of reform they had run for God.

Morgan, Edmund S. *The Puritan Dilemma: The Story of John Winthrop*. Boston: Little, Brown and Co., 1958. Morgan's book is not only the best available biography of Winthrop, but also one of the clearest presentations of Puritan thought. He discusses Winthrop's life in

England and America and in the process details the struggle faced by a pious man in a corrupt world.

__________, ed. *The Founding of Massachusetts: Historians and the Sources*. Indianapolis: Bobbs-Merrill Co., 1964. This is a helpful collection of primary sources from the first five years of the Massachusetts Bay Colony. Notably, Morgan includes more than one hundred pages from Winthrop's letters, journal, and miscellaneous other papers. There are also excerpts from the works of four historians' accounts of the colony.

Morison, Samuel Eliot. *Builders of the Bay Colony*. Boston: Houghton Mifflin, 1930. Reprint, 1958. Morison profiles more than a dozen individuals in these lively essays originally published in 1930. The profiles attempt to rehabilitate the long-tarnished image of Puritans, they serve as an excellent introduction to the leading personalities in seventeenth century Massachusetts. The longest is on Winthrop, and in it Morison portrays him as a pious yet practical leader.

Moseley, James G. *John Winthrop's World: History as a Story, The Story as History*. Madison: University of Wisconsin Press, 1992.

Rutman, Darrett B. *Winthrop's Boston: A Portrait of a Puritan Town, 1630-1649*. Chapel Hill: University of North Carolina Press, 1965. A well-researched and well-written work on the Puritan capital during Winthrop's life. A study of the town's government, church policies, population trends, and economic development, it reveals how far Bostonians strayed from Winthrop's goal of a cooperative godly community.

Schweninger, Lee. *John Winthrop*. Boston: Twayne, 1990.

Vaughan, Alden T., and Francis J. Bremer, eds. *Puritan New England: Essays on Religion, Society and Culture*. New York: St. Martin's Press, 1977. This collection of essays, written by leading scholars, covers many areas of Puritan life—religion, witchcraft, government, economics, family, and race relations. Several include references to Winthrop.

Wall, Robert E. *Massachusetts Bay: The Crucial Decade, 1640-1650*. New Haven, Conn.: Yale University Press, 1972. A detailed account of the political events of the 1640's. Wall describes the growing conflict between leaders from Boston and those in other towns jealous of their power.

Larry Gragg

U.S. Government Leaders

TIME LINE

Name	Date
JOHN WINTHROP, 919	January 12, 1588–March 26, 1649
WILLIAM BRADFORD, 85	March, 1590–May 19, 1657
INCREASE MATHER, 609	June 21, 1639–August 23, 1723
WILLIAM PENN, 637	October 14, 1644–July 30, 1718
BENJAMIN FRANKLIN, 263	January 17, 1706–April 17, 1790
THOMAS HUTCHINSON, 453	September 9, 1711–June 3, 1780
ROGER SHERMAN, 744	April 19, 1721–July 23, 1793
SAMUEL ADAMS, 29	September 27, 1722–October 2, 1803
GEORGE MASON, 603	1725–October 7, 1792
GEORGE WASHINGTON, 880	February 11, 1732–December 14, 1799
JOHN ADAMS, 9	October 30, 1735–July 4, 1826
PATRICK HENRY, 389	May 29, 1736–June 6, 1799
JOHN HANCOCK, 325	January 12, 1737–October 8, 1793
JAMES WILSON, 901	September 14, 1742–August 21, 1798
THOMAS JEFFERSON, 482	April 13, 1743–July 4, 1826
JOHN JAY, 475	December 12, 1745–May 17, 1829
JAMES MADISON, 591	March 16, 1751–June 28, 1836
ALEXANDER HAMILTON, 316	January 11, 1755–July 12, 1804
JAMES MONROE, 616	April 28, 1758
ALBERT GALLATIN, 287	January 29, 1761–August 12, 1849
ANDREW JACKSON, 460	March 15, 1767–June 8, 1845
JOHN QUINCY ADAMS, 17	July 11, 1767–February 23, 1848
DEWITT CLINTON, 175	March 2, 1769–February 11, 1828
WILLIAM HENRY HARRISON, 368	February 9, 1773–April 4, 1841
HENRY CLAY, 150	April 12, 1777–June 29, 1852
DANIEL WEBSTER, 888	January 18, 1782–October 24, 1852
THOMAS HART BENTON, 65	March 14, 1782–April 10, 1858
JOHN C. CALHOUN, 125	March 18, 1782–March 31, 1850
MARTIN VAN BUREN, 856	December 5, 1782–July 24, 1862

Name	Date
ZACHARY TAYLOR, 817	November 24, 1784–July 9, 1850
JOHN TYLER, 848	March 29, 1790–January 18, 1862
JAMES BUCHANAN, 98	April 23, 1791
THADDEUS STEVENS, 771	April 4, 1792–August 11, 1868
SAM HOUSTON, 424	March 2, 1793–July 26, 1863
STEPHEN FULLER AUSTIN, 58	November 3, 1793–December 27, 1836
JAMES K. POLK, 665	November 2, 1795–June 15, 1849
MILLARD FILLMORE, 250	January 7, 1800–March 8, 1874
WILLIAM H. SEWARD, 738	May 16, 1801–October 10, 1872
FRANKLIN PIERCE, 657	November 23, 1804–October 8, 1869
SALMON P. CHASE, 141	January 13, 1808–May 7, 1873
JEFFERSON DAVIS, 192	June 3, 1808–December 6, 1889
ANDREW JOHNSON, 491	December 29, 1808–July 31, 1875
ABRAHAM LINCOLN, 554	February 12, 1809–April 15, 1865
CHARLES SUMNER, 791	January 6, 1811–March 11, 1874
JOHN C. FRÉMONT, 278	January 21, 1813–July 13, 1890
STEPHEN A. DOUGLAS, 216	April 23, 1813–June 3, 1861
EDWIN M. STANTON, 764	December 19, 1814–December 24, 1869
FREDERICK DOUGLASS, 221	February, 1817?–February 20, 1895
ULYSSES S. GRANT, 301	April 27, 1822–July 23, 1885
RUTHERFORD B. HAYES, 380	October 4, 1822–January 17, 1893
WILLIAM MARCY TWEED, 841	April 3, 1823–April 12, 1878
JESSIE BENTON FRÉMONT, 272	May 31, 1824–December 27, 1902
CARL SCHURZ, 732	March 2, 1829–May 14, 1906
CHESTER A. ARTHUR, 49	October 5, 1829–November 18, 1886
JAMES G. BLAINE, 72	January 31, 1830–January 27, 1893
JAMES A. GARFIELD, 293	November 19, 1831–September 19, 1881
BENJAMIN HARRISON, 360	August 20, 1833–March 13, 1901
GROVER CLEVELAND, 158	March 18, 1837–June 24, 1908
MARCUS A. HANNA, 335	September 24, 1837–February 15, 1904
JOHN HAY, 374	October 8, 1838–July 1, 1905
WILLIAM MCKINLEY, 583	January 29, 1843–September 14, 1901

Name	Date
ELIHU ROOT, 720	February 15, 1845–February 7, 1937
JOHN PETER ALTGELD, 43	December 30, 1847–March 12, 1902
GEORGE WASHINGTON WILLIAMS, 894	October 16, 1849–August 2, 1891
HENRY CABOT LODGE, 562	May 12, 1850–November 9, 1924
ROBERT M. LA FOLLETTE, 548	June 14, 1855–June 18, 1925
WOODROW WILSON, 910	December 28, 1856–February 3, 1924
WILLIAM HOWARD TAFT, 808	September 15, 1857–March 8, 1930
THEODORE ROOSEVELT, 713	October 27, 1858–January 6, 1919
WILLIAM JENNINGS BRYAN, 91	March 19, 1860–July 26, 1925
CHARLES EVANS HUGHES, 430	April 11, 1862–August 27, 1948
WILLIAM E. BORAH, 78	June 29, 1865–January 19, 1940
WARREN G. HARDING, 342	November 2, 1865–August 2, 1923
HENRY L. STIMSON, 784	September 21, 1867–October 20, 1950
CORDELL HULL, 439	October 2, 1871–July 23, 1955
CALVIN COOLIDGE, 184	July 4, 1872–January 5, 1933
ALFRED E. SMITH, 751	December 30, 1873–October 4, 1944
HERBERT HOOVER, 401	August 10, 1874–October 20, 1964
NELLIE TAYLOE ROSS, 726	November 29, 1876–December 19, 1977
FRANCES PERKINS, 644	April 10, 1880–May 14, 1965
JEANNETTE RANKIN, 681	June 11, 1880–May 18, 1973
GEORGE C. MARSHALL, 598	December 31, 1880–October 16, 1959
FRANKLIN D. ROOSEVELT, 703	January 30, 1882–April 12, 1945
HARRY S TRUMAN, 833	May 8, 1884–December 26, 1972
NORMAN THOMAS, 824	November 20, 1884–December 19, 1968
JOHN FOSTER DULLES, 228	February 25, 1888–May 24, 1959
HENRY A. WALLACE, 871	October 7, 1888–November 18, 1965
ROBERT A. TAFT, 800	September 8, 1889–July 31, 1953
HARRY HOPKINS, 416	August 17, 1890–January 29, 1946
DWIGHT D. EISENHOWER, 236	October 14, 1890–March 28, 1969
WILLIAM AVERELL HARRIMAN, 350	November 15, 1891–July 26, 1986
DEAN ACHESON, 1	April 11, 1893–October 12, 1971

Name	Date
HUEY LONG, 569	August 30, 1893–September 10, 1935
J. EDGAR HOOVER, 409	January 1, 1895–May 2, 1972
MARGARET CHASE SMITH, 757	December 14, 1897–May 29, 1995
ADLAI E. STEVENSON, 776	February 5, 1900–July 14, 1965
HELEN GAHAGAN DOUGLAS, 210	November 25, 1900–June 28, 1980
CLARE BOOTHE LUCE, 577	April 10, 1903–October 9, 1987
RALPH BUNCHE, 104	August 7, 1904–December 9, 1971
OVETA CULP HOBBY, 395	January 19, 1905–August 16, 1995
LYNDON B. JOHNSON, 502	August 27, 1908–January 22, 1973
RONALD REAGAN, 688	February 6, 1911
HUBERT H. HUMPHREY, 446	May 27, 1911–January 13, 1978
THOMAS PHILIP O'NEILL, JR., 630	December 9, 1912–January 5, 1994
RICHARD M. NIXON, 623	January 9, 1913–April 22, 1994
GERALD R. FORD, 257	July 14, 1913
JOHN F. KENNEDY, 517	May 29, 1917–November 22, 1963
GEORGE C. WALLACE, 864	August 25, 1919
HENRY A. KISSINGER, 540	May 27, 1923
ROBERT J. DOLE, 203	July 22, 1923
GEORGE BUSH, 111	June 12, 1924
JIMMY CARTER, 133	October 1, 1924
ROBERT F. KENNEDY, 524	November 20, 1925–June 6, 1968
ALAN GREENSPAN, 309	March 6, 1926
MARTIN LUTHER KING, JR., 531	January 15, 1929–April 4, 1968
H. ROSS PEROT, 650	June 27, 1930
DIANNE FEINSTEIN, 244	June 22, 1933
JANE BYRNE, 118	May 24, 1934
BARBARA JORDAN, 510	February 21, 1936–January 17, 1996
COLIN L. POWELL, 674	April 5, 1937
MADELEINE ALBRIGHT, 37	May 15, 1937
JANET RENO, 697	July 21, 1938
JESSE L. JACKSON, 468	October 8, 1941
BILL CLINTON, 166	August 19, 1946

INDEX OF PRESIDENTS

No.	Term	President	Page
30	1923-1929	Calvin Coolidge	184
31	1929-1933	Herbert Hoover	401
32	1933-1945	Franklin D. Roosevelt	703
33	1945-1953	Harry S Truman	833
34	1953-1961	Dwight D. Eisenhower	236
35	1961-1963	John F. Kennedy	517
36	1963-1969	Lyndon B. Johnson	502
37	1969-1974	Richard M. Nixon	623
38	1974-1977	Gerald R. Ford	257
39	1977-1981	Jimmy Carter	133
40	1981-1989	Ronald Reagan	688
41	1989-1993	George Bush	111
42	1993-	Bill Clinton	166

Name Index

J

K

L

M

N

O

P

R

S

T

V

W